Photograph by Maisie Harrod Marsden, aged 6 years

The author is a 74-year-old retired general medical practitioner, originally from Hull; but he has lived in Cheltenham for the last 49 years, working at a local surgery for 34 of them.

He has been researching the Harrod family history for a long time. His interest was partially prompted by the fact that his father was an orphan who grew up in difficult circumstances, and he knew nothing of his family until he began his research after his parents' death over 30 years ago.

Having collected an enormous amount of information about the family, and the family grocery, Harrods, he decided he wanted to write down the story to share with others.

His first published book was a story of the early years of the Harrods store, entitled *The Jewel of Knightsbridge*. This covered the time when the Harrod family was in charge.

He has always wanted to publish the story of his paternal grandmother and here it is.

These days, he is researching for a book about Harrods after the Harrod family.

When he is not sitting in front of a computer, he plays a lot of tennis, he is a dedicated follower of Gloucester Rugby and spends time with his wife in their second home in the south of France – sometimes in front of a computer. The trips to France involve a detailed examination of the local food and wine.

To John Stanley Harrod, my father. (1906–1971). I may have inherited his doggedness and attention to detail.

Robin Harrod

The Misconceptions of Miss Harrod

AUSTIN MACAULEY PUBLISHERS™

LONDON • CAMBRIDGE • NEW YORK • SHARJAH

A CIP catalogue record for this title is available from the British Library.

ISBN 9781528997942 (Paperback)
ISBN 9781528997959 (ePub e-book)

www.austinmacauley.com

First Published (2021)
Austin Macauley Publishers Ltd
25 Canada Square
Canary Wharf
London
E14 5LQ

Apart from my long-suffering wife, and all the family, the names of those who have given me help and support has become too long to list. They know who they are already.

Table of Contents

List of Photographs

List of Charts

Part 1

A Prologue

How it all began.

It was all Alex's fault. "Can we do our family tree, Daddy?"

Alex is my youngest daughter. It was 1986 and she was 11 years old, and had just got home from school. They had been learning how to make a family tree, and what it meant. She had brought home the blank tree for my wife and I to complete with her.

This was a problem. There was very little I could tell her, much of my family's history was a blank.

My two older brothers and I were very short of family history, in fact, we were very short of relatives. By 1986, we had lost both our parents and had already, some many years before, lost the only grandparents we had known, those on my mother's side. To compound the lack of relations, we had never been close to or in regular contact with the known uncles, aunts and cousins on my mother's side of our family.

It seems rather odd to me now that during my childhood it had never struck me as strange that we had few relatives and no known ancestors. As a growing teenager, I began to realise that friends and girlfriends often had large extended families and I was a little jealous of their numbers and their often-chaotic relationships.

Nevertheless, we were a happy family with lots of friends. We knew nothing at all about the family on my father's side and precious little about my mother's.

My wife's family was relatively intact when I first met her, and she had numerous more distant relatives but knew little about many of them.

So, the tree constructed for my daughter was rather lop-sided and limited.

On my side, Mum's mother, Grandma Stanley had lived in a street off the Hessle Road in Hull, with her unmarried son, my Uncle Raymond. This area was the heart of the local fishing industry; streets of back-to-back terraces within easy walking distance of the Fish Docks. The fishing industry was huge and almost everyone in this part of Hull was employed in it.

It was a pretty rough area compared to Hessle, the suburb to the west of Hull, where my family and I lived when I was a child.

My older brothers had seen a lot more of Grandma before she died than I, although I had stayed with her on a few occasions when my parents were on holiday or when Dad had been ill.

She had always seemed a distant and rather strict figure. I did not understand as a child that she had led a very hard life, bringing up her family of five on her own in the days before any financial help was available from the state.

Mum's dad, Grandpa Stanley, had been a trawler skipper. This was the age of small steam-driven trawlers that spent several days in the North Sea and Icelandic waters on each trip. No health and safety, no comforts, no sophisticated navigation aids, and no refrigeration for the catch. It was tough.

On the only occasion when I remember meeting him, late in his life, he had a wooden leg just like Long John Silver! He had lost his leg in an accident at work. He died in 1952, aged 66, when I was seven years old.

I was told that he had left Grandma some years before and lived much of his time with relatives, and perhaps even a 'fancy woman', in Fleetwood, across the Pennines. When I was able to find out more, much of that story proved not to be true. We knew nothing about, nor had we ever enquired about, our more distant Stanley relatives. There were photographs from between the wars, but no labels on most.

Dad's family history was almost a complete blank. He had been an orphan and he had had made it plain to us all that he did not wish to investigate his origins any further. His view was that, 'if they didn't want me, I do not want them'.

There had always been a family myth that perhaps we were related to the founders of the famous store, 'Harrods of Knightsbridge', but nothing was known to suggest this was possible.

Dad died in 1971, and I continued to respect his wishes regarding any research of his background until Mum died in 1986, the same year that Alex was hoping to complete her family tree.

Going through their paperwork as we cleared her flat, I discovered some documents about Dad which I think had been shown to my brothers a few years earlier, but which I had never seen before.

There was a small notebook containing Dad's own story of his early years, written by hand in 1964, the year after I, the last of 3 boys to leave home, had gone to college. There was a copy of his birth certificate and several letters about his 'adoption'. His story started with 'Chapter 1', then 'Chapter 2', as though the story would continue, but it ended abruptly at the end of Chapter 2.

The stimulus of these finds, together with Alex's questioning, was enough to get me going.

So began a journey that I never envisaged I would still be on 30+ years later, with as many questions unanswered as answered.

When I started the research, it involved trawling though reams of lists, books, papers and microfiches, and travelling round the country searching local libraries and records offices. I never imagined then that in retirement I would spend most of my time in front of a computer.

Many of the discoveries have emerged by chance when following a seemingly hopeless lead, but the majority just required dogged hard work and persistence.

As most family history researchers will have discovered, it is a major regret that I did not ask more questions whilst my parents were alive. Tracing history retrospectively is much more difficult and time-consuming, and inevitably produces rather sterile facts, lacking the detail and warmth of personal anecdotes and communications. It made me determined to find as much verbal history as remained available.

The early stages of the investigation were very exciting. During those first few years, I spent a great deal of time travelling across the country, mostly chasing shadows. I wrote dozens of letters for information and help. However, I did make some startling discoveries.

What follows is the story of my discoveries about the life of my grandmother Beatrice Martha Harrod who very naturally became the epicentre of my story. Part 1 tells her story, and Part 2 gives more detail and background of the family and can be read if desired.

I have dedicated the book to my father. He had a very rough deal in his early life, but fought his way out of the mire and found peace and a successful family.

I wonder sometimes if, despite his protestations, he would have wanted to know more about his background. Perhaps he was frightened of being disappointed or ashamed.

I would like to think that that he would have wanted to read this story.

The information contained in this story has been sourced from many places, some from official websites, some unofficial, some from individuals who have done their own research and as much as possible from living relatives. Accuracy cannot be guaranteed, but has been strived for.

When I first started writing this story, I was determined to stick strictly to facts that could be verified and memories personally passed to me. Having tried to offer the story to publishers large and small, I was told that though the story was interesting, and the research effort evident, it was just not commercially viable. After a period of sulking, I decided to follow some advice given to me some years ago by Dominic Lawson, who suggested the story would be more marketable if it was 'lightly fictionalised'.

I spent some time trying to do this and failed. I found I could not alter and add to the research and factual findings I had made. I could not add words and thoughts to those characters who were mostly unknown to me. I was not a fiction writer.

I decided to go back to my factual story, extend the research about some of the characters already involved, and make more educated guesses to fill in some of the gaps. Wherever I have done this I will say so.

Chapter 1
Beatrice Martha

10 February 1958

In 1958, my father was 51 years old and he was living in complete ignorance of the continued existence of his mother, Beatrice Martha Harrod, and of all her exciting relatives who would later be uncovered.

On the 10 February of that year, she signed her last Will and Testament. It would have been a time for reflection.

I suppose she might have been living, not in ignorance, but certainly consciously unaware of the continued existence of my father.

My experience as a family doctor tells me that, in common with most mothers who have given away a child, it is more than likely that he intruded into her thoughts frequently. Invading the course of everyday tasks and events she would have speculated about his whereabouts and his circumstances, and all the 'ifs' and 'buts' and 'might have beens'.

She was 80 years old in 1958 and was living at the Murrayfield Guest House in Tunbridge Wells. Her son, Michael, and his family lived close by, her two daughters a few miles away.

Beatrice Martha had had a most remarkable life.

She must have looked back over the years with some sadness and regret. Most of us will do this to a certain extent as we get older, but I now know she had reason for more sadness and regrets than most.

It was a straightforward Will, appointing one daughter and her son as the Executors and Trustees, and leaving her estate to her two daughters and her son. Two other elderly residents of the Guest House witnessed the Will.

Only a mention in the Will of a Settlement between herself, her mother-in-law and her brother-in-law, dated the 10 October, 1931, hinted at something more complicated in her life and relationships.

Three months later, Beatrice Martha was dead. She died a confused old lady in the Priory Hospital, Roehampton on the 21 May, 1958.

Though her death certificate looks on first reading rather complex, with several diagnoses listed, basically she had died of old age and decreasing mental functions.

In 1958 the Priory Hospital was a modest nursing home establishment dealing mostly with patients with mental problems, including dementia. The Priory Hospital remains London's longest established independent psychiatric hospital and has been in continuous operation since its launch in 1872, when Dr William Wood moved his patients from Kensington to Roehampton, South West of London, where he felt the then country atmosphere was conducive to healing.

Today, often referred to by the media just as 'The Priory', it has had an international reputation and is best known for the treatment of celebrities with various addictions. It has been described as the British equivalent of the Betty Ford Clinic. In more recent years, its reputation took a knock following a series of problems involving patients who were being treated there and poor CQC reports of visits in 2016 and 2017. The latest report from March 2019 shows considerable improvement and a better rating.

Before moving to the Guest House in Tunbridge Wells, Beatrice Martha had for some years, probably since the end of the Second World War, lived with her single daughter Bridget in a number of Private Hotels in the Gloucester Road and Cromwell Road area of West London.

Bridget worked with what was then called British European Airways, B.E.A., acting as a 'General Facilities Officer' at Heathrow. She was in charge of the meeting and greeting of V.I.Ps.

By 1958, Beatrice Martha had been widowed for over 30 years, and apart from one widowed sister, was the last remaining of her seven siblings, a brother, six sisters, and their husbands.

Despite having lived with her daughter, and then at the end near her son, she must have felt very much alone as she faced increasing frailty and a fading memory. What had she done to deserve this? Throughout her earlier life, she had managed to alienate most of her family and friends and was generally disliked. She became a dominating mother and a snob.

Since those times, she had had plenty of time for reflection on her mistakes in life, though these were not totally of her own making. Her guilt and anger had made her a bitter woman who was then unpleasant to many of those who had tried to help her.

Her biggest mistakes were her illegitimate children. In addition to her family of three children resulting from her marriage to her husband, Bertie, she had given birth to two children before her marriage, and carried the guilt of those births pretty much on her own for the next 50 years. By 1958, there was no one else left in the world who knew anything about these events, apart from the children themselves.

To complicate her life, her husband had been killed when their own children were young and he had left behind an almighty financial disaster for her to cope with on her own.

Her two mistakes were of course not her errors alone. The fathers of these illegitimate children were equally responsible, but as was common in those times, they did not share any of the burden with her.

On the credit side, she thought she had made suitable arrangements for the future of these children, but as Robert Burns wrote and we shall see, *'The best-laid schemes o' mice an' men, Gang aft agley.'*

So what went wrong?

Beatrice Martha was born in 1877 in what was then a leafy semi-rural Sydenham, south of London. Her family was comfortably off, verging on wealthy, and she would not have wanted for much during her childhood and early life. Her father was from a family of non-conformists and worked in 'trade' in London, so she would never have gained access to the upper echelons of society, however much money he made. Later in life though, she would certainly aspire to be part of that level of society.

These limitations had not stopped her father from accumulating enough assets to retire from business in 1891 at the age of 50, when Beatrice would have been 14 years of age. It meant that he was able to move to a country mansion in Devon, away from the smell and smoke of London, and become a country squire and benefactor. He loved it.

In consequence, until the family moved back to the Home Counties in 1902, Beatrice spent all her teenage years and beyond, between the age of 14 and 25, in what must have seemed a rural backwater. She had limited exposure to fashionable London, and more importantly for her, eligible bachelors. This exclusion from 'society' was not total, her father still kept a 'town' house in Kensington.

Her years in Devon and Sussex were broken in 1901 by a family trip abroad, taken whilst their new house in Sussex was being altered and prepared. This seemingly took the form of a classic 'European Tour', much as earlier generations had taken, though there is only circumstantial evidence to confirm the dates and itinerary.

The trip helped to open the 24-year-old Beatrice's eyes to what was out there, and probably encouraged her to spend some more time on the Continent in the years to follow.

Despite these opportunities, by 1905, when she would have been 28 years old, she was still a spinster, and things began to go wrong for her.

Chapter 2
Stanley Taylor

Early 1910

In early 1910, my father, Stanley Taylor was living with his 'Mam and Dad' in the south of Manchester. He was a happy little chap, an only child, and much loved by his parents.

In this secure and warm household, he had no idea of the dramatic events that were to change his life over the following few years.

Over 50 years later, in the spring of 1964, when life had been settled again for some time, Stanley and my mother, Nalda, were living alone for the first time in 25 years. They lived in North Ferriby, a village a few miles west of Hull. They were 57 and 51 years old respectively.

Dad was an ophthalmic optician with a thriving business in Hull.

They were alone because I, the youngest of their three sons, had been the last to leave home the previous autumn to start my training at Medical College in London.

My eldest brother and his wife had just had their first child, a daughter, who was my parents' first granddaughter. They lived in Surrey, where my brother also worked as an optician.

My middle brother had recently got married. He was another optician and was working with Dad.

Now with more time on his hands, after many years of bottling up the memories of his early life, my father decided to start writing the story of his early life. I am not absolutely sure why he wanted to write it down, or why he had decided to start at this precise moment in time, but some reasons are probably easy to guess.

The act of writing was almost certainly a way to unburden himself. His life had reached a watershed and it was perhaps just the right time to begin. He had more time and a quiet house. Perhaps he intended to tell his story as a legacy for his descendants?

He was not in the best of health. He had a variety of medical problems including a large lump in his neck. This had been there for some years and was growing steadily. He had not been given a definite diagnosis despite several biopsies and investigations, and had been told 'not to worry about it'.

Not untypical advice by doctors of the day when faced with disclosing an unwelcome diagnosis.

I suspect it was unlikely he would have been able to follow this advice. He was an intelligent man and could work it out for himself. The 1960s were just at the tail end of an era when surgeons often deemed it was their decision to make whether a patient should be given the facts or not.

My mother told me later that the doctor told her the diagnosis, a carcinoma of the parotid salivary gland, but also said to her that Dad should never be told.

Now that the children had all left home and looked set for successful careers, Dad was considering a move to nearby Scarborough, with the intention of continuing to work part-time in Hull, barely an hour away by train.

So he started.

He wrote Chapter 1 and Chapter 2 of his story, beginning with his first memories from about the age of four, in 1910, and covering a period of about two years.

His story stops abruptly at the end of Chapter 2, at a particularly painful time in his young life, when he was abandoned for the second time. Chapter 3 was never written.

What follows is the first part of his story as he wrote it, followed by some explanation by me and the results of my research into the substance of the story.

'Chapter 1. Enter – Stanley Taylor.

In approximately the years 1910-1911, I found myself in the large city of Manchester, living in the home of Mr and Mrs Taylor and completing the three of the family.

As I write in the year 1964, I rely on the deep memory folio of 53 years – and whilst those incidents which are to be recorded are vivid and clear, besides being truthful, they are of necessity fragmentary, and concern isolated high spots of a child's early experiences.

I am in a happy home – possessed of all that a child chiefly needs at the age of 4 or 5 years, love, protection, food and clothing.

I am attached to Mr and Mrs Taylor, as any child would be, as my Mam and Dad – and although I have no recollection of their Christian names, or even manner of speech, I am sure they are a very happy couple and for some reason, devoted to me, at least over the period I was in their care.

Whatever the true reason that had resulted in my awakening to my own existence in their home, it seems at least sound evidence for their love toward me that they had chosen to allow me to be known by their own surname, so I was Stanley Taylor, and stayed pending further developments.

How long I had been in the Manchester home is beyond my memory. And not until some years later did I learn any facts of my earlier history.

When opportunity finally occurred for me to read the only three small documentary evidences that have been retained throughout my various fortunes, I discovered that Stanley Taylor was not my beginning, nor was Manchester my first home.

According to my birth certificate, perhaps the most important document I possess – I was born at 22, Cheniston Gardens, Kensington, London, on September 21, 1906.

My mother's name is given as Beatrice Martha Harrod, and my father's name space is conspicuous by its blankness.

Therefore, at whatever stage I became first named Stanley Taylor, I was certainly born and christened (Church of England) John Stanley Taylor. The existence of the prefixed Christian name John and the surname Harrod was not known to me until I was in my teens.

Who was Beatrice Martha Harrod, and from where did she hail?

Alas, apart from the certainty that she gave me birth, no further questions can be answered, apart from the evidence I later unearthed, that she came specially to 22 Cheniston Gardens for her childbirth, this address at that time being a private nursing home.

Did we part company at 22 Cheniston Gardens or by chance, was the loving Mrs Taylor in reality Beatrice Martha Harrod? I shall never know!

I return my story therefore to the Manchester home, and delve into my memory for the clear picture of incidents that are even now clearly impinged in my storehouse.

I can list them briefly and concisely

1. *The family home.*
2. *The gramophone shop.*
3. *The Manchester district Fever Hospital.*
4. *The street accident.*
5. *The London Road Railway Station.*

A strange mixture it must seem, when I know it is the sum total of my brief Manchester experience, and that I cannot name or identify any more closely the addresses concerned.

The family home was a house amongst others, in a long street of identical properties off one of the main shopping roads. I believe it was fairly spacious, of middle-class status. The only room I remember was my own bedroom, (it seemed large) and when I was in bed, I can state the entrance door was opposite my view, as I lay on my right side and looked ahead. And if this room is my only memory, so is this exactness of my posture, and positioning of the door – my only memories of incident within the room.

One morning, in daylight, the noise of the door opening awakened me, and there to my horror stood in the doorway, a woman dressed in some form of cloak with a mask on her face!! I screamed with terror, as the figure advanced towards me, almost to my side, before realising my distress, the mask was lowered, and there stood my 'Mam' Mrs Taylor!!

The emotions of the moment live with me still. She was all remorse and tried to comfort and express her regret at causing me so much distress, and for myself, although I was glad to feel her arm around me, I hated her for her foolish prank, which had been intended to be for my amusement.

I cannot say I have forgiven her – or the memory would surely have faded.

The face mask leads me to remember the gramophone shop, as afterwards it was there, I had first seen it. The gramophone shop was situated in the busy shopping road already described, and was on the opposite side of the road to the street entrance, and perhaps some ten minutes' walk from home.

The shop belonged, or at least managed by my 'Dad' Mr Taylor.

It was the hey-day of the horn-gramophone, and I got the impression that it was a busy shop dealing exclusively in these newly marketed music boxes.

I was taken on frequent visits to the shop – but only one clear picture remains – and that fits in with the mask.

A special window display impressed me greatly. The whole window area was arranged as if looking from the outside, to within a cosy old folks living room. On a table stood a gramophone – horn in position, and record on the revolving table. Sat in a chair, was an old lady, cap on head, shawl on shoulders – leaning forward and listening to the "music", and stood by her side was her "husband" sharing her pleasure. The "old lady" wore the mask – that later frightened me so much!

At some interlude of time, I found myself in a Fever Hospital on the Manchester outskirts, and in isolation. I knew nothing of why then, but later I learned I had scarlet fever and diphtheria – and was probably very ill. I carry with me to this day the evidence of that calamity, in a scar of trachiopia in my neck.

Two incidents only remain to me of my hospital sojourn. One summer's day, in high hot sunshine, my "Mam" came to see me. She was in some form of summer dress – but whilst I remember how wonderful it felt to see her, my joy was first spoilt when she was only allowed to see and try to speak to me from outside the window of the ward. She brought chocolate with her – and probably some fruit and flowers besides, but chocolate I certainly do remember. She talked for some time, but I had a peculiar feeling that I may not ever see her again– and to me, her visit was a sad one, as it came to the time for her to say goodbye. I remember her leaving the window – and walking along the path leading outside the grounds, with an occasional turn around to wave until she was out of sight. I sobbed – not at all because her visit was over – but because deep down I felt this was for some strange reason a final goodbye.

As events unfolded, it was not itself the final goodbye – but very certainly the prelude to it. Only one other incident at the hospital comes to mind – and one that is vividly amusing.

The day arrived for my leaving the hospital. I was deposited sitting on a shelf within some sort of out-kitchen, outside the main hospital building. The shelf stood perhaps four feet from the ground, so that I dangled my legs loosely clear of the ground. I was in bed clothes, and apparently some form of motor truck which brought hospital supplies – was to take me to another building for my clothes before going home. The truck arrived outside – and in walked the driver with a very large oval shaped tin bath – handles both ends – full of steaming hot rice pudding with rich, brown milk skin overall! He laid this down at my feet, with little regard that I might easily have fallen plumb in the middle. This I did not do – but to me it was a fascinating sight – especially as rice pudding was and remains a favourite.

The rice pudding and I remained alone for quite a while, until he came to take me.

I returned home – and stayed without incident – until one day – going to the shop, I seemed to get detached from my "Mam" and began to cross the road to approach the shop – and came into collision with a cyclist. I was knocked to the ground and was bleeding with some head injury, and taken to hospital. My stay was brief, and I did not suffer any ill-effects as far as I know.

I come to my last picture image of those Manchester days, and a strange and seemingly unimportant one at that. For some reason of a journey or more than one, I became familiar with the name, London Road Railway Station. I can remember it in some detail, as on approach the road and foot traffic moved downhill through a subway, the rail lines running across the bridge above. The walls of the subway were of white glazed bricks, and midway within the subway was an entrance up some steps to the railway level and on to the station itself. This vision of the approach, station, and even its name, remained as clear a memory to me that some thirty years later when a visit to Manchester was an opportunity, I was able to confirm the accuracy of my childhood fascination.

I have no more incidents of Manchester – and the detail of the railway has its significance, for I was told I was going to stay for a time with some friends – (they may have been relatives of the Taylors) at Macclesfield.

I do not remember anything of the journey – and little enough of Macclesfield itself, and my stay there must have been brief. But it had small incident of great future importance to my life.

I cannot remember the name or nature of my new home or its residents. I know I was not the only child, and I also know these people also had a shop – but this time, it was fried fish, chips, and peas!

The house was immediately attached and next door to the shop – and the whole road was on a hilly slope, with the shop floor level a little below ground level, so that there were one or two steps down to the shop from the street entrance. I used to go into the shop before bed-time, with a small plate – for my supper of peas and chips.

I went to my first primary school in Macclesfield – I think daily but I am not sure, though I do remember a classroom with a lot of pictures on the wall – and I clearly remember this is where I learnt and remembered ever after my first hymn:-"Sun of my soul, Thou Saviour dear".

I had many sad and distressing occasions later to recall this hymn, (not for its words particularly) but to afford some consoling memories.

The incident of importance now arrived. I had not seen the Taylors since I left Manchester – and one morning whilst I was still in bed – the woman of the house came and showed me a picture card which had arrived for me.

On the picture side was the photo-print of a large ocean passenger liner – and from the other side was read to me a message from "Mam" to say she had sailed away on this ship to Australia – and that my "Dad" was coming to Macclesfield to collect me, and together we would follow in another ship and join her.

I think I was glad and excited to hear this – and whether it was intentionally true or false, certainly, I know the news was given to the school, and when the final day arrived a special class party was held to wish me goodbye.

My "Dad" arrived and we went on our long journey to Liverpool!!!'

I felt I had to find out what had happened to him following his birth and during those early years in Manchester, Macclesfield and Liverpool.

Manchester at the beginning of the 20th century was a busy city and an enormous manufacturing centre. It must have been an exciting place for a little boy.

Dad's first memories of the Taylors and Manchester were when he was about four years old and his journey from Macclesfield to Liverpool was at the end of the year in 1912, when he would have been six years old. Fortunately for me, almost all of Dad's memories recorded in his story have proved upon investigation to be astonishingly accurate, and because of that, they have been very helpful in finding more information.

Despite his hospital admissions, this must have been a very happy time in Dad's life. He was the only child in a secure, warm and loving family. The Taylors seem to have been in a sound financial position, and unless the shop proved a failure and prompted the plan to move abroad, money would not have been a problem in this little boy's life. When a decision was made to emigrate, it sounds as though the Taylors had not talked with John Stanley about what was going to happen, as the postcard from 'Mam' came as a real surprise.

I have researched the Taylor family. Most of the Taylor's relatives I have discovered lived in either Manchester or in the surrounding towns and cities, and no doubt young Stanley would have visited them and have been visited by them on occasions.

The plan to leave Dad in Macclesfield does not seem to have upset him. He almost certainly knew the people who were to look after him, and a rail journey and a stay in a new town would have been exciting. Living with a fish and chip shop next door would have been a bonus.

The only slight shadow over his time in Manchester was Dad's feeling when he saw his mother in hospital that she was going to leave him. Was this a product of some uncertainty already hanging over the family, or the benefit of hindsight when Dad wrote his story?

My search to find the correct Mr and Mrs Taylor in a city the size of Manchester was like finding the proverbial needle in a haystack. There proved to be over 8,000 Taylors living there in 1911. I did not know the Taylors' Christian names or their address.

Despite writing many letters for help to local historians and the Local History Society, no really positive results were produced, and I realised that more information would be needed to identify the family. His admission to a fever hospital, as recorded in his story, was the most likely source of further information.

In 1988 I paid a visit to the Greater Manchester Records Office and Archives Department and found that the likely hospital was Monsall Fever Hospital, on Monsall Road. This was a hospital typical of the times, of an enormous size and almost self-contained on its 33-acre site. They would have admitted all infectious diseases, including smallpox and typhoid, and most of the patients were children.

The hospital changed in use several times in the ensuing years and by the time of my visit had long since been demolished.

The hospital was closed in 1994 and demolished soon afterwards to make way for an industrial estate. Two years before its closure it made its lasting claim to fame – it was used to film the hospital scenes for Emily Bishop's breakdown in Coronation Street.

As Dad correctly suggested, at the time of his admission it would have been closer to the then outskirts of Manchester. The Hospital was in a district north of the city centre, whereas the Taylors lived to the south east of the city centre, off the Stockport Road.

Surprisingly, despite the loss of many Manchester records during the bombing in World War II, I discovered that his hospital records were intact and in the custody of the Register General, but were at that time closed to inspection under the 100 years rule. This rule is intended to prevent disclosure of any living person's details. The index to the records, which was available for view, tantalisingly listed some basic information – 'Stanley Taylor, aged 5, Ward 11, Doctor Pritchard. Admitted 1 May 1912. Church of England'. Still no names or address for the Taylors.

I felt an approach for release of the records might be successful as all of those involved were no longer alive, and I was a medic.

In order to obtain early access to the records, permission would be needed from the Health Authority, to whom I then wrote. The archivist in Manchester was not at all hopeful that permission would be granted and seemed very pleased with her opinion. The request to the Health Authority was passed on for a decision, rather surprisingly, to the local Hospital Manager and a local Consultant. I wrote to both of them and they readily agreed to the request after my 'I'm a doctor' card was played. This decision was confirmed by the Public Record Office, and I was off.

The booked visit to view the records in Manchester Library proved interesting, and very enlightening. The archivist charged with producing the records that day was the same one who had been very negative when the initial enquiry had been made about obtaining permission. She obviously resented the fact that my request had succeeded, and was intent on making my stay as uncomfortable as possible. Numerous instructions were given to me about the rules and regulations. There was a great deal of 'tutting' and 'shushing' when, by chance, I met at my table in the reading room one of the local historians with whom I had previously corresponded. The fellow researcher had overheard the archivist using my name and had approached me!

As the permission to view the records was granted solely to me, the archivist would not let the historian talk to me or come within several feet of the records book whilst it was open. We had to talk outside.

The information gleaned from the visit was extremely useful.

The records showed that Stanley Taylor's Hospital Number was 691, and that he had been admitted to Ward 11 on the 1 May 1912, and discharged 21 days later on the 22 May 1912.

The diagnosis was given as scarlatina (scarlet fever), adenitis (glands) and abscess. I remember Dad had a deep scar on the side of his neck typical of an abscess. I knew somehow that Dad had also had a 'trachiopia', as he called it, at some stage in his childhood. Now better known as tracheotomy, this was a hole made into the windpipe in the front of the neck. In those days this was usually needed as a result of breathing problems during an attack of diphtheria.

There was no record of diphtheria during this admission, though Dad was always certain he had suffered from this condition. This must have been during a separate hospital admission at an earlier age, which is more common.

He failed his medical for the army at the start of the second war because of a heart weakness; he was told this was due to pericarditis and had been caused by the diphtheria. That is a recognised but rare complication of this disease.

One of the commonest causes of adenitis in the neck at that time would be tuberculosis, or T.B.

It might account for the fact that in later life when he suffered a recurrence of T.B., Dad was told he had a scar on the lung from previous T.B., and that his tests confirmed an infection in earlier life.

Importantly, the Manchester records stated he made a full recovery after his hospital admission.

Those of you who watched the factional 'Casualty 1900s' series on television in 2008 will remember that scarlatina was a very serious disease indeed in those days and often proved fatal. In that series, which was based on my own teaching hospital, the (now Royal) London Hospital, a young woman patient died, and a nurse who had been in contact with her only just survived.

Just as in the TV series, Dad would have been very ill and would have been nursed in strict isolation in a darkened cubicle with only supportive measures to help. There was no other treatment in those days. There would be no antibiotics for some years; penicillin was not 'rediscovered' by Fleming until 1928.

My research has unearthed some photographs of Monsall Fever Hospital. There were separate dedicated wards for Scarlet Fever and Diphtheria, and which ward was Ward 11 is not known.

His memory about rice pudding was interesting. Throughout his life I remember that this was his favourite pudding, and often appeared on our dining table. It was fortunate that Mum turned out to have the required skills to produce a mean rice pudding – a miniature of the one in the tin bath.

His memory of the hot summer day and his mother in a summer dress was difficult to square with the weather in May 1910. The first three weeks of the month were cold, stormy and wet, with occasional hail storms. There was a dramatic change between the 20th and 24th when the weather was sunny and warm. It would suggest that this visit was just before his discharge. The day of his discharge, the 22nd was also warm, hence him being left on a bench outside in his pyjamas.

Dad mentioned in his story a further shorter admission to hospital, sometime later, after being knocked over by a cyclist. On that occasion, he made a rapid recovery after a short stay. No attempt has been made to trace this admission in the records as the hospital involved is not known. The busy Stockport Road would certainly have been a danger for a small child crossing the road.

According to Dad's story, his mother was present at the time of both admissions, so this confirms she certainly did not leave for Australia until at least sometime after the 21 May 1912.

Most helpfully for my research, the hospital records gave more information, the name of his father and an address for Dad and his family – 27, Legh Place, Ardwick, Manchester. With this information, and with the help of the local directories and rating records, the position of both their house and the shop were found.

Those directories also gave me some dates; so that I could work out for how long the Taylors had lived in the area.

During that early visit, and a subsequent visit to Manchester, the geography of Dad's story was confirmed. His memories really were remarkably accurate.

The house and the shop have long ago been knocked down. There was major bomb damage in the war, and most of area has been rebuilt, but an old map and the visit revealed the layout that Dad had described. The house was in a terrace of houses on the north side of Legh Place, which was a small street off the busy main Stockport Road leading out of Manchester, in the district of Ardwick.

Legh Place has since been renamed Lauderdale Crescent and the even-numbered houses on the south side of the street remained intact at the time of the visit as a row of small Victorian terraced houses. Since then, extensive rebuilding has replaced these with 3 storey townhouses. The area is very close to Manchester Royal Infirmary and Manchester University.

To get to the shop from the house would have involved a short walk down Legh Place, crossing the Stockport Road and walking a few yards south-east down that road away from Manchester. The shop was on the opposite side of the road to Legh Place, and about 10 minutes away on foot.

This part of Stockport Road is about a half to one mile from the city centre, and was a busy thoroughfare with many shops. Ardwick was a suburb which has since been gradually absorbed into Manchester.

The Electoral Roll lists a 'Percy Joseph Taylor' at 27, Legh Place in 1910/11, and 1912/13. The house was empty the following year. In Kelly's and Slater's Directories, a Joseph Taylor, a Printer's Traveller, was listed at 27, Legh Place in 1911, 1912 and 1913 but had gone by 1914. He was also listed at the shop address, 95, Stockport Road, as a Gramophone Dealer, with the same dates. There can be no doubt that all these listings were the same man. Either he must have left his job as a Traveller or kept it going whilst the shop was up and running.

Attempts to find out more about the shop were unsuccessful. The Local History Society had no records of it, nor had the Trade Directories. There was nothing to be found on an internet search of the local newspapers. Gramophones were still a novelty in 1910, so starting a new business like this must have been a risky venture.

The site of the shop is now occupied by a Bookers Wholesale building.

It seems unlikely that the Taylors would have set up this business if they had already made a decision to emigrate, or would then choose to emigrate if it was going well. So failure of the business may have prompted the idea of emigration to Australia.

The London Road Railway Station, now called Piccadilly Station, was not far from Legh Place, and the topography is again as described by Dad.

At this point therefore, I had discovered where Dad had lived in Manchester and the name of his 'father', but this information did not take me much further. I wanted to find out what had happened to Dad after his stay in Macclesfield and really needed to find a living descendant of the Taylors or their extended family to tell me more.

Trying to trace the Taylors using births, marriages and deaths was hopeless, there were far too many in the area and I had no idea of their origins or family connections.

It became obvious to me that what I needed was access to the 1911 census in order to get more details of those living at 27, Legh Place. Access was not available at the time of this research, the 1990s, as the 100-year rule applied to censuses as well as medical records, so for the moment, that was that.

I continued my research in a different direction.

By chance several years later, in 2007, whilst reading our daily newspaper, I noticed a short article stating that Naomi Campbell, the model, had obtained access to the 1911 census using the 'Freedom of Information Act'. The paper's genealogy website gave the details. In essence, henceforth, any named address could be searched on request, with a good reason, and for a £60 fee!

I had a good reason and it was worth £60.

Spurred on by this news, I wrote to the National Archives stating my case, and was granted access.

The census proved to reveal more than I had envisaged about the inhabitants of 27, Legh Place on the night of Sunday, 2 April 1911.

The house was listed as having five rooms, (for census purposes, a kitchen counted as a room, but a scullery, a lobby, a bathroom or closet did not). So with Dad recalling a separate bedroom of his own, at least two of the four remaining rooms must have been bedrooms, a typical two up, two down. With a kitchen/scullery at the back. He was a very lucky boy to have his own room in those days.

Six people were resident on the night of the census; so the sleeping arrangements would have had to change to accommodate them all.

The residents listed that night were:

-Joseph Taylor. Age 43. Head of House. Married 8 years. A Letterpress Printer. Born in Manchester.

-Emily Ann Taylor. Age 40. Wife. Born in Congleton, Cheshire.

-Thomas Moss Taylor. Age 76. Father of Head. Widower. Born in Newark, Notts.

-Robert Stonehewer. Age 50. Cousin of Head. Widower. An Iron Turner. Born in Congleton, Cheshire.

-Dinah Stewart. Age 11. Niece of Head. Born in Campbeltown, Scotland.

-John Stanley Harrod. Age 4. Adopted. Born in Kensington, London. The census listed Dad's birth name, and the fact that he was adopted. His birth name and birth place were therefore known to the Taylors who completed the census. They probably had in their possession the various letters and papers that Dad retained during his life.

The census gave me a good idea of the area at that time. The neighbours of the house were a labourer, a warehouseman, an upholsterer, a plumber and a joiner. It was very much an ordinary working-class area. There was a family next door with four daughters, aged eight, six, three and two. Dad would have been unusual at that time being an only child but would have had other children to play with.

It is odd that these potential playmates were not mentioned by Dad in his story.

The neighbours of the shop at 95 Stockport Road were a Physician and Surgeon at 91, a Dental Surgeon at 93, a China Dealer at 97 and a Grocer at 99.

By the time this census became available, other paths had emerged to help trace names on the internet, and Mrs Taylor's names and age had already been found. The names of the other relatives present then spawned a rush of research to try and find any living relatives of the Taylors who might know what had happened to them all.

The records revealed many of the Taylors' family and relatives at the turn of the nineteenth Century, and I was able to produce a large family tree for the Taylors. I came to know more about the Taylors' extended family than Joseph himself would have known.

Despite having found out so much, including the discovery of some rather distant living relatives, there was no one living in England with any knowledge of their fate. That was to change, more of that later.

Macclesfield

Macclesfield was a much smaller place than Manchester, with a population in 1910 of just over 80,000. It has always seemed odd to me that Dad was taken there, whether to friends or family, when the Taylors had both friends and family in Manchester.

However, Dad was probably happy to be parked in Macclesfield for a while when he became aware of his promised future adventure. He certainly seems to have had happy memories of the fish and chips. The postcard from his mother must have been both exciting and reassuring as well as giving him some status amongst his fellow pupils.

Macclesfield, from a family history perspective, was tackled in a similar fashion to Manchester, a spray of letter writing and appeals for information, together with visits to verify the story.

Dad was told he was going to stay with friends or relatives in Macclesfield. At what stage his mother left the family to travel abroad was not remembered by Dad. It seems reasonable to suppose that he was taken off to Macclesfield after Mrs Taylor left and whilst Mr Taylor was winding up the shop or trying to sell the business in Manchester, prior to following his wife abroad. There may also have been paperwork to chase up ready for the move. This must have been sometime after May 1912.

I have assumed that his stay would more likely have been with relatives rather than friends.

In that era, unlike today, the idea of 'friends' in another town would have been limited by any opportunity to meet them because of the lack of personal transport. Relatives would be more trustworthy.

His stay in Macclesfield was probably very short; at the most it could have been only a few months, and was probably much less.

His memories of Macclesfield are sketchy. He cannot remember the people involved apart from the presence of other children in the house. He remembered the geography, which was confirmed by a visit to the town.

During that visit it was possible to track down and visit the site of every Fish and Chip shop that had existed in 1911 and 1912. There were 35 of them in the Macclesfield Trade Directories, but there were only 15 still in existence by the time of my visit in 1989.

Of the 35 possibilities, only eight fulfilled the criteria of being situated on the slope of a hill, as Dad had described. Most had disappeared without trace, but at three of the eight sites the original buildings still stood. I took photographs of them, including one that might have fitted the bill. However, none of the remaining shops had a step down from the road into the shop as described.

A search of other local records, the Electoral Rolls and Directories, revealed the names of the occupants of these shops. At one of the eight sloping sites, a shop at 26, Paradise Street, Macclesfield, now no longer in existence, the occupant in 1914 was a Joseph Taylor. There were no other Taylors or relatives of the Taylors in residence before that date, so unless Joseph Taylor started another shop independently after disappearing from Liverpool, this was unlikely to be the correct shop. I now know after further research that this scenario would have been impossible.

None of the other shops contained particularly likely named candidates at this stage of the research.

However, when full access to the 1911 census became available in 2009, and the names of other relatives of the Taylors were known, several more candidates were found. There were two shops run by people with the surnames of Taylor-related families; one a Mrs Moss, and another Mr Smith. Neither however, was on a steep slope and neither of the families could be linked to our Taylor family.

Mrs Hannah Moss, a 'fried chip seller', at 142 Newton Road was the most likely, but she had a 20-year-old daughter in the house and no small children. The house was on a slight slope. Despite several attempts, I have been unable to link this Moss family to those connected to the Taylor family.

So, despite all the work, I could not positively identify Dad's fish and chip shop in Macclesfield.

Dad remembered going to Primary School in Macclesfield and says that this was his first time.

In 1912, almost all children were starting school at the age of five and staying there until they were 10 or 12. Progress had been slow. During the 1860s, one third of children in England and Wales did not go to school at all and right up until 1881 children there was no requirement to attend. From 1881 onwards, school became compulsory from the age of five to ten. Only in the twentieth century were young children no longer regularly expected to go to work alongside adults. By 1918 school attendance was not only compulsory, but the school leaving age was raised from 12 to 14 years old.

So it might have been expected that Dad would have been at school in Manchester from about September 1911 when he would have become five years old, but he had no memories of this. Perhaps with a birthday at the end of September, he may have missed the school entry in 1911 and so had to wait until 1912. It might also suggest that he was in Macclesfield at the beginning of the school term in early September 1912.

Many of the School Registers for his age group in Macclesfield for 1912 were available at the local Library, and some time was spent going through them. Some of the Registers had apparently been lost during bombing in W.W.II., so sadly the search was always going to be incomplete. Dad was not listed by name in any available register, so his school may have been amongst those lost. It is possible that Dad's stay was so short that he may not have been registered at all.

Appeals for information about Dad using the local Macclesfield newspapers were published, in the unlikely hope that there might be someone alive in 1989 who had known Dad in 1912, and remembered him, but there was no response.

My brother Peter, who has had a lifelong interest in steam railways, was able to confirm the probable journeys that Dad might have made, firstly from Manchester to Macclesfield; and later, in the company of Mr Taylor, the journey from Macclesfield to Liverpool. This journey was meant to be the start of a trip to board an ocean liner, in order to join his Mum at the other side of the world.

Dad would have been excited and could not have imagined what fate actually had in store for him.

It is almost certain that Dad's journeys in 1912 would have been by steam train. That was the main means of travel for most classes of folk in the early twentieth Century. Railways were enjoying their heyday. The roads, at least for travel of any great distance, were not in great shape and still a problem. Many people would walk long distances, a slow method, but cheap. Horses, carts and carriages were still in use so might have been the form of travel used to travel to Macclesfield. Motor cars were scarce and were mostly the prerogative of rich folk. It was in the following year, 1913, that British Automobile Traction, later to form part of the North Western Road Car Company, commenced a motor bus operation in Macclesfield. It would be another decade before the use of the charabanc for organised trips became commonplace. The canals were still thriving, despite the challenge from the railways, but unless you were part of a canal family, almost all canal travel was commercial.

How thrilling it must have been for a six-year-old boy, who would have seen and heard the trains at the London Road Station in Manchester, quite close to where he lived, to travel in one. I can remember, as a small boy of the same age in the early 1950s, the excitement of travelling by steam train to the seaside. How much more intoxicating would the smells and sounds of the train have been for young Stanley, unused to the mechanisation of my world.

The trains travelled at up to 30 m.p.h., an unprecedented speed for a youngster to experience in those days. He may of course have travelled in a train before. The Taylors might have made trips to the seaside, or elsewhere to see relatives. I think it is likely Dad would have remembered these in his story, as his time with the Taylors was such an enjoyable part of his young life and he remembered several other more minor incidents.

Dad's first journey from Manchester to Macclesfield, via Stockport, would have taken well under an hour and would have cost an adult, travelling Third Class, about a shilling, 1/ – as we wrote it. That is the equivalent of 5p in decimalised currency, and worth today about £1.50p. Children travelled at half price. The timetable for October 1911 shows that the fast trains took half an hour, and the slower trains, stopping at every station, took 45 minutes or so. Amazingly, there were 28 trains on that line every weekday! What a comparison with today.

The journey from Macclesfield to Liverpool would also probably have been via Stockport, changing at Manchester London Road Station for Liverpool. Depending on the time spent in Manchester, this would have taken much longer, perhaps 3 or 4 hours; and would have been more expensive at about 1 shilling and 7 pence for an adult, that is 1/7d. Again, there were plenty of trains to choose from each day. Dad does not mention a change of station in his description of the journey to Liverpool, but he remembers it was a long journey.

There is no hint in the story of the date when Mr Taylor and Dad travelled from Macclesfield to Liverpool. As the journey was via Manchester, it is possible, though unlikely, that they might have broken their journey there. The journey was probably undertaken quite late in the year of 1912, as the next parts of Dad's story relate to early January 1913.

Young John Stanley was about to undergo another change in his fortunes and all his childish optimism would evaporate.

Chapter 3
The Count

1892

In 1892, Eduard, Count Grotta zu Grottenegg was contemplating a second marriage. His intended, Marie, had been nursing him during his illness and she had been very attentive. She deserved a thank you in the form of a title for the rest of her life. She really had been attentive.

Eduard's full title was Count Grotta zu Grottenegg, Baron Finkenstein, and Imperial Count Kreyg. He was part of an extensive, illustrious and historic aristocratic Catholic family in the Austro-Hungarian Empire, owning several estates.

The Grotta family were from Malborghet-Malborghetton now in the Italian Canel Valley.

It was variously in the hands of the Venetians, the French and the Austro-Hungarian Empire. It is 62 miles north-west of Trieste.

The records name several Counts and Countesses Grotta zu Grottenegg but the relationship of most of them to Eduard are not known.

Eduard was born in Klagenfurt on the 17 May 1828.

Klagenfurt is the capital of the federal state of Carinthia in southern Austria. It is at present the sixth-largest city in the country. Founded in the 12th century, in the 19th century the city was an important centre of Carinthian-Slovene culture.

His father was an administrator, Imperial Count Josef Reich Grotta zu Grottenegg, Landstand von Kärnten und Ständischer Accis. He was born in about 1783 and died in October 1853 at the age of 70.

Following a similar path to most of the aristocrats of his era, Eduard entered the Theresianische Military Academy on the 18 October, 1839, aged 11 years. It is south of Vienna and is one of the oldest military academies in the world. He completed his military education 11 years later, in 1850.

He followed his father's career as a finance administrator. The details of his various jobs can be found in the newspapers of the day and the official State records.

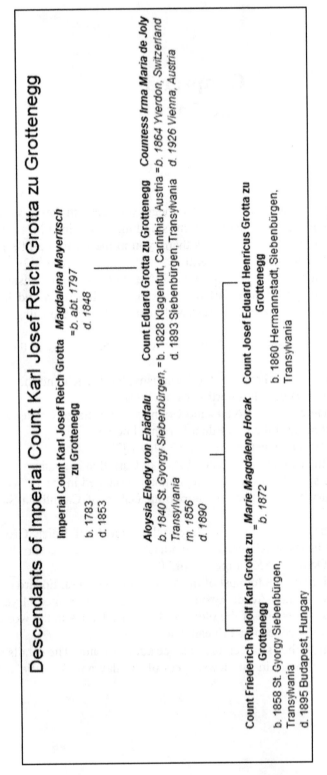

Descendants of Imperial Count Karl Josef Reich Grotta zu Grottenegg

Imperial Count Karl Josef Reich Grotta   *Magdalena Mayeritsch*
zu Grottenegg   = b. abt. 1797
                                           d. 1848

b. 1783
d. 1853

Aloysia Ehedy von Ehädfalu   Count Eduard Grotta zu Grottenegg   *Countess Irma Maria de Joly*
b. 1840 St. Gyorgy Siebenbürgen, = b. 1828 Klagenfurt, Carinthia, Austria = b. 1864 Yverdon, Switzerland
Transylvania   d. 1893 Siebenbürgen, Transylvania   d. 1926 Vienna, Austria
m. 1856
d. 1890

Count Friederich Rudolf Karl Grotta zu   *Marie Magdalene Horak*   Count Josef Eduard Henricus Grotta zu
Grottenegg   = b. 1872   Grottenegg

b. 1858 St. Gyorgy Siebenbürgen,   b. 1860 Hermannstadt, Siebenbürgen,
Transylvania   Transylvania
d. 1895 Budapest, Hungary

Chart 1: Descendants of Imperial Count Karl Josef Reich Grotta zu Grottenegg

He joined the Ministry of Finance working as an unpaid bookkeeper in the accounts department in 1851, then as the first tax assessor in Kronstadt, an island city 19 miles from St. Petersburg. It was an important trade centre, and during his time there was populated by many British merchants who became known as the 'English Factory'. Later, after the Crimean War, the Russians turned the island into a defensive centre and in the following decades it became the base for the Russian Baltic Fleet.

After two years he was moved to Siebenbürgen, better known as Transylvania, and now part of Rumania. Having been part of Hungary, in the mid-1800s it was absorbed into the Austro-Hungarian Empire under the Hapsburgs. He worked there for the Government in the capital, Hermannstadt (now Sibiu) for over 20 years, but was pensioned off in 1874 as he was a German speaker and the state now decided that the Hungarian language was necessary for government officials.

He was transferred back to Vienna to the Tax Department, where he lived from 1877 onwards and later worked there in the Imperial Royal Regional Financial Department.

His career C.V. does not make exciting reading, and so far, his name and the places where he worked have been the most interesting parts of it.

He seems to have led an exemplary and perhaps hum-drum life serving his master, the Empire.

More interesting are his marriages and children, which bring him into the story.

He married his first wife, Aloysia Ehedy von Ehädfalu in 1856, in Transylvania. She was from Sepsiszentgyörgy, a mostly Hungarian city in Transylvania.

They had two children, Friederich Rudolf Karl, born in St. Gyorgy Siebenbürgen in 1858, and Josef Eduard Henric, born in Hermannstadt in 1860.

They seem to have led unremarkable lives for many years.

Friederich, also an administrator, married Marie Horak, born in 1872, and they had a son, born in Budapest in 1895.

Josef joined the military as a cadet in 1875 in Vienna, and after graduation joined the Cavalry Brigade in Hermannstadt. He was especially praised for his swordsmanship and his riding skills. He became a Lieutenant in the 2nd. Hussars.

Things seemed to go a bit haywire in the Count's family after his return to Vienna in 1877, with various newspapers and records printing stories about the family.

Local newspapers report a court case in May 1877 which was brought by the Count against a young coachman who he alleged had run him over, whilst moving at a 'sharp trot'. He reported that it had caused injuries that took 20 days to heal. He demanded money for his medical expenses and damages but as the Count proved elusive, the hearing was cancelled and re-convened four times. The court lost patience with him and the man was acquitted.

In January 1883, Friederich became involved in a duel in Bratislava, acting as a second, and the courts sentenced him to two weeks in custody, 'in a dungeon'.

In August 1884, Josef was strongly reprimanded by his Regiment after getting into debt. He was put into house arrest for 30 days. He was obviously living a raucous life well beyond his means and had further trouble with the military in February and March 1887. He was pensioned off in 1890.

In 1888 Eduard himself faced a charge of fraud brought by a teacher's wife after non-repayment of a loan. He was found guilty.

On the 1 January 1890, Eduard's wife, Aloysia, died after a year-long battle against cancer. She was aged 54 and they had been married for 33 years. It was not long after this that Josef left the army.

It looks as though the Count himself became ill not long after this. No detail is available but he took on a nurse, Marie, to look after him, and in 1892 they married.

In 1893, Josef was in court following a suit brought by a confectioner in 1890, presumably for debt.

The records show the marriage of a Josef Grotta to Anna Orman in 1893, but there were several Josefs in the extended family so that this may not have been our Josef.

Also in 1893, there were more problems for Eduard. In April and May there were court cases involving him, with claims against him and others, including a Mrs Maria Missar, regarding financial irregularities involving a Civil Service Union charity of some sort. The hearing took place in his absence and the court did not know his whereabouts. The answer was that he was at his estate in Transylvania, where he died on June 14 after a four-month final illness. The cause of his death was given as apoplexy, (a stroke). He was aged 65.

The woes of the family did not stop there.

Friederich, now living and working in Budapest, took over the title as Count. He inherited the 'entailed' estate from his father, consisting of a large sum of money and several millions in land and property. Entailed is a word meaning a sort of trust arranged so that an estate passes within the ownership of the family through generations. Friederich's son was born in May 1895, when Friederich was already terminally ill, and he died three months later in August of that year. He was 38 years old.

Josef now became the Count, and despite the inheritance, seems to have got into further trouble with his extravagant ways. He had already been in court earlier in 1895, when whilst acting as an agent of a sewing machine factory, he was accused of various fraudulent transactions and embezzlement. The court criticised his 'foolish pranks' and luxurious lifestyle. He did not appear in court but was pursued by the Vienna prosecutor. He was probably in Budapest.

In 1897 Josef was again being sought for more debts, and though he did send some money he was not thought to have access to the family money to pay off all he owed.

The records go quiet after 1897 regarding Josef.

There was sighting of him on a guest list at a spa at Bad Ischl, a town in Upper Austria, and he was known to be living in Poland in 1917.

Though by no means certain, Josef may appear later in this story.

Marie, Eduard's second wife, definitely appears later in this story.

Chapter 4
Stanley Taylor

Late 1912

We left my father on the brink of his adventure, travelling by train to Liverpool with his father to catch the boat to Australia to join his mother. The last words we saw in his story were:

'My "Dad" arrived and we went on our long journey to Liverpool!!!'

But…not all was as it seemed. There was a twist in store for young John Stanley. He continued:

'However, it was not quite as far as Australia.
This was the last communication or contact I ever had with the Taylors, and I was left at a children's adoption home run by a spinster lady in Colebrook Road, Liverpool.
My stay in Liverpool was brief and without a single incident to recall. It was obviously a home in transit prior to possible adoption; and in recalling that I do possess my birth certificate, the only other documents I possess are:'

I now have possession of the documents Dad detailed, but in addition to that collection there is one further letter, dated earlier than the rest, which was for some reason omitted from Dad's story. I think this was purely an oversight, as it was kept with the rest of the correspondence. I include it here for completeness and because it does show more of the process involved.

1. A letter dated January 6, 1913, to a Mrs Sergeant of Hull, obviously in response to previous earlier correspondence. It came from:

"Miss Whishaw,
Children's' Branch of Hostel of Hope
47 Colebrook Road
Aigburgh Road
Liverpool"

It read:

"Dear Madam,

Thank you for your P.C. The little boy has already been offered and if not accepted will let you know.

We have a little boy 18 months old. Would you care to try him, he is quite healthy and strong, though not walking yet, and is a nice-looking child.

I suppose you want a Protestant boy."'

I think this letter refers to my father having already been offered elsewhere, and suggesting an alternative 'off the shelf'!! It makes the process sound like a test drive of a used car.

2. 'A letter to an applicant from Hull – who was asking for particulars of my history age etc. – with a view to adoption.

Dated February 13 1913 and addressed as from Miss Whishaw to Mr Seargent-

I quote; -

"Dear Sir,

Thank you for your letter.

I have received the reference from the Rev M. J. Poole and it is satisfactory.

The little boy Stanley is a very healthy boy, born Sept. 21, 1906, so is 6 years old.

His mother came of a very respectable family, and his father was a Merchant Captain.

He is a well-behaved child and obedient and clean in his habits.

If convenient to you, I will bring him to Hull next Tuesday Feb – 18th., arriving about 12.30 – but will let you know definitely when I hear if Tuesday is convenient."'

This letter obviously followed another intermediate letter from a Mr Sergeant, which was not retained, now offering to him either the original child mentioned earlier, or perhaps even a third child.

3. 'A second note asks that the adopter Mr L. Sergeant should meet the train arriving at Paragon Station, Hull at 12.28 from Central Station, Liverpool, on Feb 18th.' This note is missing.

4. 'A third and final printed note dated March 31st., states that the birth register is forwarded at the request of the Registrar General, for use in marriage, death, or any legal affairs.

To quote further: – "As it reveals the address where the child was born, we rely on the honour and good sense of the adoptive parents not to try and trace the mother. We are bound to keep her secret, as much as to keep their names and addresses private, and any communication would lead to disaster. This would spoil the adoption, and we would not hold ourselves responsible for consequences, seeing that the mother has absolutely renounced all claim to the child, and signed a legal document to that effect"

A further printed note of the same date points out:

'N.B. – No child can be registered in the name of the Adopters.
In case of marriage or death, only the registered name must be used.
If not baptised, additional Christian names may be put before the Child's registered Christian name, and the Adopter's surname added to the Child's surname in baptism…
… This child is baptised C. of E.
No Child's life may be insured by other than its own parents. It is illegal for Adopters to insure Children.'
So it was on this flimsy and unsatisfactory procedure – apparently wholly conducted by two people communicating in the post – without any supervision or legality worth the name – that I was launched into a new world at the age of 6½.
It is a cause of satisfaction that such a senseless arrangement could not be lawfully repeated today.' So ends the chapter "Enter Stanley Taylor".'

It is odd that each of the documents detailed above spell the name Sergeant differently.

When I first read his story, some years after his death, I was very moved by the sad tale. I had known he had been an orphan, but had never been told the circumstances. It helped me, over a period of time, to understand more fully my father's character and motivations. I found the detail of the story fascinating. It set me off on a journey of research that continues to this day.

Dad was back in another large city, the population of Liverpool being about 750,000 at that time.

Bedford Street South, the site of the Hostel of Hope in Liverpool as recorded in Dad's letters, is a short walk from the station and about ¾ mile from the dockside in Liverpool.

Dad's stay there did not merit any form of description in his story apart from the recognition of arrival at a children's home. He had obviously blanked out memories of what happened on his arrival.

So what transpired next remains one of many unanswered questions. My brothers and I have discussed long and hard the alternative explanations for his abandonment, and until very recently, despite extensive research, had found nothing to help understand why it had happened.

We had many theories.

Did an accident or illness befall Joseph Taylor, causing injury or death such that he could not continue with his plan to travel to Australia? A search of local newspapers and death records did not find any evidence for this explanation.

Did Dad fall ill and have to be left behind whilst Mr Taylor travelled to Australia? Dad made no mention of this.

Did Joseph Taylor never intend to follow his wife? Did he have perhaps another relationship and the child became an encumbrance? However, no evidence of Joseph Taylor could be found to suggest he remained in the U.K. after 1912.

Did Mrs Taylor write from Australia with some message to delay or postpone your journey?

Did Joseph and his wife fall out such that she did not want them to join her in Australia?

Was there some administrative hitch which prevented Joseph, or Dad, or both, from leaving England?

Did Joseph Taylor get on a boat by himself after leaving Dad?

Was it ever the Taylors intention to take Dad with them at all? Was the whole business a charade to keep this fact hidden? This last idea seemed very unlikely and far too complicated.

Had Mrs Taylor never travelled to Australia at all, and then perhaps they both moved elsewhere in Britain?

The possibilities were endless.

I had always been inclined to believe the story that his mother did indeed sent a postcard of the liner taking her to Australia whilst he was in school in Macclesfield, and that it was their intention that he and Mr Taylor would join Mrs Taylor in the future in Australia. The picture on the postcard and the message being read out in school was an enormous and memorable event for Dad. It seems too complex to be contrived, and would have been very cruel if it was a cover story prior to a planned abandonment. Why bother with this if it had all been planned before, why not just leave Dad somewhere else? The only possible explanation for this sort of conspiracy would have been that if the Taylors wanted a cover story to avoid anyone trying to trace them. But again, far too complex.

I was intrigued that Mrs Taylor left the country first, presumably to begin setting up their new life abroad. When most families emigrated, it was much commoner for the man of the family to go first, find a job and accommodation, ready for everyone else to follow. Perhaps Mr Taylor had to remain to sell the shop. Possibly there were already relatives in Australia and she went to join them to await the rest of the family.

It is difficult to be certain from Dad's story whether the postcard was sent by Mrs Taylor before her journey started, from the dockside for instance, or from an intermediate destination on the trip, or even upon reaching Australia.

How I would love to find this postcard!

Many of the ships travelling to Australia called at Marseilles, Suez, Cape Town and Rangoon or Singapore on the way to Australia, so the card could have been sent from any of these places. The whole journey by sea would have taken about six to eight weeks, and if the card had been sent from Australia, it would have taken a further six to eight weeks to get back to England, making a minimum total of three to four months from posting to delivery in Macclesfield.

It seems pretty certain from Dad's story that Mrs Taylor travelled to Australia at some time after his discharge from hospital on the 22 May 1912, and before the end of that same year when Dad had been taken to Liverpool. There would have been just enough time, if she had travelled in June or July 1912, and Dad had stayed in Macclesfield until the December of that year, for the postcard to have arrived in time all the way from Australia.

The postcard stated Mrs Taylor was already on her way to Australia, so the earliest time when it was likely to have been written was when she had at least boarded the boat, and assuming that post was taken off before the boat sailed, it would have got to Macclesfield almost immediately.

Once having sailed, there would have been little time for another message from her to reach England in time to delay or postpone her husband's journey if the situation had changed.

It was about 18 months after the start of Dad's story with the Taylors, when he was left behind in Liverpool, and by that time he was just over six years old. He may have been with the Taylors for some time before his story starts, possibly from soon after his birth. The story gives the impression of a secure home and family life and suggests he loved them both, and was loved by them. This makes it unlikely that the Taylors would have willingly abandoned him.

In the days before the records were digitalised, my brothers and I visited the Public Records Office in Kew, and trawled through the original passenger records of all the vessels which left Liverpool bound for Australia between 1910 and 1915, looking for a Mrs and then Mr Taylor, presumably travelling separately. No definite results were found. I have repeated this search since on several occasions, both at Kew and on line, and included searches for boats that left from different ports and to different destinations apart from Australia. Once again, there were no absolutely definite results.

There were some entries in the passenger records between June and December 1912 which could be possible sightings for Mrs Taylor's travel.

- A Miss E. Taylor left London on the 30 August 1912 on board the 'Orvieto', bound for Sydney, Australia. However, she was listed both as unmarried and that she was due to return to reside in England after her trip. An unlikely candidate.
- A Mrs Taylor left London on the 27 September 1912 on board the 'Otranto', bound for Sydney, Australia, but she was listed as being bound not for Australia but for the next stop in New Zealand. The 'Otranto', built in 1909, served as an armed cruiser during World War I and coincidentally in this role was part of the story of a distant relative of mine a few years later. It is possible that the Taylors had initially planned to go to New Zealand, but later findings would suggest that Australia was the intended destination.

- A Mrs Taylor, a 'housewife' aged 42, the correct age for Emily Ann Taylor, left London on the 4 October 1912 on board the 'Zealandic', which was bound for New Zealand. She was, however, due to disembark in Sydney, a port of call on the way. A possibility.
- In the incoming passenger records for Australia, a Miss P. Taylor, aged 42, a 'domestic', is listed as arriving in Sydney in November on board the 'Zealandia'. Was this the same person or the same boat as the 'Zealandic'? The timing is right. Other records show that the Zealandia, definitely a different boat to Zealandic did sail to Australia, but not in 1912 from England, so the first listing may have misspelt the name.
- A Miss Taylor also left London for Sydney, Australia, on 24 October 1912, on board the 'Orama'. She also was listed as due to return as a resident in England.

The Mrs Taylor on board the 'Zealandic' seemed the most likely candidate, being married and the right age, but she could not be traced with any certainty at the Sydney end to confirm identification. Why would she have chosen to leave from London?

As it seemed impossible to pick any of these women with any certainty as the correct Mrs Taylor, for time being I gave up that line of research and looked elsewhere. I thought I had got as far as I could go.

Turning to possible sailing dates for Mr Taylor, he would have intended to travel to Liverpool with Dad towards the end of 1912, or in very early 1913, as it had to be before the date of Dad's first records from the Hostel of Hope, which was the 6 January, 1913. It would seem unlikely they would have travelled over the Christmas period without Dad remembering this detail.

There was an entry in the shipping records for a Percy Taylor, who travelled on board the ship 'Pakeha' from Liverpool to Sydney, departing on the 4 February 1913. He was described as a fitter, aged 44. The date, his age and his occupation are about right, but Mr Taylor was usually known as Joseph rather than Percy. However, perhaps this is what the Ship's Purser might have entered on the roster if given the full name of 'Percy Joseph Taylor'.

If it had been Mr Taylor's original intention that he and Dad travel together to Australia, then considering Dad was definitely in Liverpool in the Hostel of Hope by early January of that year, a boat booked to depart in early February would have meant a month's stay in Liverpool for both of them. If, however, Dad was left at the Hostel because of some unforeseen event, Joseph Taylor may have had to cancel the original booking in January and spend time in Liverpool before catching another boat in February to Australia.

The sailing immediately before the 4 February was on the 6 January 1913. This boat would have been a much more convenient date for Mr Taylor and Dad if they were leaving together.

There were dozens of other Taylors on other Australia boats and many did not give any age or Christian name, so once again no definite positive identification could be made.

A search of other possible destinations, including New Zealand, Canada, or U.S.A. failed to produce any definite lead. In 1913 alone, there were 323,082 passengers who departed by boat from Liverpool to destinations outside Europe.

A search for the Taylors in Australia from 1913 onwards failed to find any obvious matches, so I moved on.

The birth certificate that Dad later found amongst his belongings was not the original, but a copy requested from the Register Office in 1910, and I wondered if this might be significant. If the original had not been passed on or had been lost, then it might have been obtained when the Taylors adopted him. Alternatively, perhaps they applied for it in order to arrange their travel abroad? At least that would suggest that there was a plan for Dad to travel to Australia. Both explanations are possible.

The letters from the orphanage suggested that the certificate had been more recently obtained, and presumably that means the original certificate was not travelling with him. The letters also give the impression that there was a brisk turnover of children, so Dad probably did not stay there for too long.

Considering how much detail Dad managed to give in his story, it is surprising that he did not mention that Christmas of 1912. Christmas is such a big event in any six-year-old's life. In fact, Dad states that nothing of note happened in Liverpool! It could either have been his last Christmas with Mr Taylor, or had been spent with his Macclesfield friends or relatives, or spent in the Hostel of Hope.

All seemingly important events in his young life. The memory must have been suppressed by shock.

There are so many questions without answers.

In summary, the most likely scenario from the evidence thus far was that Mr Taylor and Dad arrived in Liverpool sometime in late December 1912, with the intention of travelling to Australia to join Mrs Taylor. For whatever reason, Dad was left in the care of the Hostel soon after their arrival. Mr Taylor had to cancel their booking and take a later sailing to Australia.

In recent years, I have found other evidence that helps produce a pretty reasonable theory about what happened, and we will look at this later in the book.

The letter from the Hostel to 'Mrs Sergeant' dated January 6, 1913 states *'the little boy has already been offered, and if not accepted will let you know'*. The fact that this letter remained with Dad's paperwork implies that he was *'the little boy'* mentioned, and was not taken by the previous applicant. If so, Dad must have been in Liverpool for several days before January 6 in order for letters to have been exchanged with this previous applicant. So, December 1912 seems much more likely than January 1913 for their arrival in Liverpool.

There were obviously other letters from the Hostel between that of the January 6 and the next of the February 13, as by that latter date a reference had been exchanged and the date was fixed for Dad's 'delivery' to Hull. This was set for *'next Tuesday Feb-18, arriving about 12.30.'*

So Dad spent a minimum of six weeks in the care of the Hostel and possibly longer, perhaps spending Christmas there. As I noted before, his story certainly skates over this period despite the length of time and the festive season.

It may have taken Mr Taylor some time to try to sort out the problem that had occurred with Dad. Dad's story implies he arrived in Liverpool and was left almost immediately, but this was not so.

The only likely passenger found in the lists is the Percy Taylor who sailed on the 4 February, 1913.

That would mean Mr Taylor was also in Liverpool for 5 weeks or so. What did he do during this time?

Whilst writing up the story, and even during fallow periods when I was too busy to write, I continued to nibble away at those missing parts of the story, like this one, where there were gaps.

In late 2012, whilst reading a family history magazine, I came across an advert placed by Swan Genealogy from Western Australia. Lorraine and Cherie offered to research family history anywhere in Australia. Their charges seemed reasonable; I had made no progress, so I set them the task of finding the Taylors.

Given the minimal information I had, they were able to identify the Taylors' stay in Australia very quickly. That was galling, considering the length of time I had been gnawing away at this problem.

However, I felt a real sense of relief to find that both Taylors had actually reached Australia. The discovery scotched several of my conspiratorial theories about Dad's abandonment. I will give more details of their fate later.

Having confirmed they both reached Australia, though it was still possible that leaving Dad had been a calculated act, it seemed more likely that Dad's embarkation had been thwarted in some way. The most plausible explanation was that the Taylors lacked some paperwork, perhaps even just the missing original birth certificate.

If this had been the problem, Joseph Taylor would first have tried to find a way round the problem. Then, on finding that there was no alternative, he would have had to try to find somewhere safe to leave Dad in Liverpool. He would have cancelled the original bookings and taken a later boat.

I checked with the Australian immigration authorities who thought the lack of an original certificate should not have caused a problem for Dad's entry, but perhaps the ship's officers thought differently.

Certainly today, a man on his own named Taylor, trying to take a small boy named 'Harrod' on a trip to Australia without the original birth certificate, or any adoption paperwork, would be viewed with suspicion. Formal registration of adoption in the U.K. did not begin until 1926/1927 and there was no legal documentation in most cases prior to that date.

The available records for the Hostel of Hope were rather confusing.

The 1911 Gore's Directory of Liverpool lists dozens of children's homes and other charitable institutions for the poor or destitute, covering some ten pages, but there is no mention of the Hostel of Hope or any of its branches.

Nevertheless, the street directory for the time lists 140 Bedford Street South as the Hostel of Hope and the Matron as Beatrice Chanler, and this is confirmed by the 1911 census.

The letters that accompanied Dad to Hull were written on paper headed 'Hostel of Hope'.

Like the correspondence described by other researchers of the Hostel who I came across, they apparently came from Miss Whishaw, at the Children's Branch of the Hostel of Hope, though they requested a reply to the Secretary. They were signed by E.E. Martin, Secretary.

One of the printed cards was from Constance M. Whishaw and Hy. (Harry or Henry) Goldstone.

The last card was from Miss Whishaw at Sunny Bank Orphanage, Arnside, near Carnforth in Cumbria. Arnside is a small town south of the Lake District, on the Morecombe Bay estuary. The card was overprinted with 'Office of Children's Branch, Hostel of Hope', with again another overprinted request to reply to Miss Martin at her address in Liverpool.

Sunny Bank in Arnside was obviously, at least for a while, the children's branch of the Hostel of Hope, whilst the office was still based in Liverpool.

The address of the Secretary of the Hostel of Hope, E. E. Martin, who signed the letters retained by Dad was 47, Colebrook Road, Aigburth Road, Liverpool.

The 1913 Liverpool Street Directory confirms that this house was indeed occupied by Miss Elizabeth Martin. Colebrook Road is a street of Edwardian terraced houses probably built between 1901 and 1911, and number 47 is now a private residence.

The first letter held by Dad, dated the 6 January, 1913 was actually addressed back to 'Mrs.' Sergeant. As Mr Sergeant subsequently proved to be a single man, I can only presume that he had used someone as a front for his application.

In Dad's account, he gets a little mixed up about the letters. He lists the 1st letter as the letter of February 13, addressed to Mr Seargent (yet another spelling), and arranging the meeting in Hull. He does not mention the letter of January 6, which suggested that Dad had already been offered, and offered another 18-month-old boy on trial. The letter does say that if the older boy is not accepted, she would let Sergeant know. The older boy was Dad, and he must have been rejected by the first applicant and so became available for Sergeant.

The third letter gives a more specific time for the meeting in Hull, 12.28 p.m., and though listed by Dad in his story, is missing from his paperwork.

The last two letters, containing routine information about the birth certificate and name registration, were actually sent on the 31 March, six weeks after Dad had arrived in Hull. The wording on the letter from the Hostel which gave a warning not to try to trace the parents of the children would have been enough to put most people off, it almost put me off when I first read it! Perhaps it put Dad off.

The property known as Sunny Bank appears to be missing from the 1911 census. The house was on High Knott Road and was later re-named 'Windrush'. It was converted at some stage into a holiday home for children from another orphanage, St. Margaret's Home, in Upper Parliament Street, Liverpool. Later, sometime around or after 1987, it was converted into 3 residences, and can be viewed today on Google Earth.

A document was discovered on line which contained the end of year accounts for 1907 for Sunny Bank, Arnside, confirming that it was used as an orphanage at that time.

The Hostel of Hope at 140, Bedford Street South, was in the 1911 census revealing a substantial property with 11 rooms, so it probably had six or more bedrooms.

The home is listed in the Telephone Directories of 1910 and 1911, then again after a gap from 1922 to 1941, still at the same address in Bedford Street. From 1922 onwards it was listed as a Women's Hostel.

The 1927 Liverpool Social Workers' Year Book reveals that in that year the Hostel of Hope was a home for girls and young women, in connection with Police, Court and Probation work.

The Hon. Secretary and Treasurer was Henry Goldstone, from the Probation Office, Crosshall Street, and the Matron, Miss Martin. Henry Goldstone, named on the earlier Hostel correspondence, later became the Chief Probation Officer in Liverpool. The Matron Miss Martin was almost certainly the same Miss Martin who formerly was the Secretary.

The Hostel was damaged in severe bombing on the night of the 2 May 1941 and later became derelict. The site now forms part of the University of Liverpool campus.

More information was hard to come by. Many of the records which might have revealed more about the Hostel were destroyed in the Second World War. Contact with Social Services in Liverpool, the Liverpool Police and many local charity organisations did not reveal any other information about the Hostel of Hope. No-one had even heard of it.

I had reached another dead-end. The Hostel of Hope in Liverpool was seemingly the place Dad was taken in 1912, but in later years it was involved only in the care of young women. The children's branch was in Arnside, some miles away from Liverpool, but had closed in 1909 before Dad arrived.

I felt I was destined not to discover much more about his stay in Liverpool, but there must be a logical explanation.

His next journey began, once again involving a train, and this time it took him to Paragon Station, Hull.

Chapter 5
The Canon

Late 1905

William Humble-Crofts would have been excited, looking forward to Christmas 1905.

As the long-standing incumbent at All Saints Church, in Waldron, a small village in East Sussex, he always looked forward to Christmas. It was a time of celebration in the Christian calendar and William loved putting on a good show.

For the first time in some years, though several of his children lived away from home, most of his family would be home for Christmas.

He could reflect on a comfortable and successful life as he and his handsome wife, Bridget, had been the focal point in both the social and religious life of the small community.

Photograph 1: Canon William Humble-Croft in old age

Photograph 2: Bridget Humble-Crofts in old age

He had arrived in Waldron in 1882, 23 years previously, and admitted that he had not been an instant success. A petition of about 50 villagers was presented soon after his arrival, asking him to leave. He won them all round and became an institution.

William was a descendant of a long line of Humbles, many of them Church of England clergymen.

The family originated near Bamburgh, in Northumberland, and they had become quite prosperous during the 18th century. Education at Cambridge followed for the next generations and led many to the priesthood. William's father was a Rector in Sutton Scarsdale in Derbyshire. William, who was the eldest son, was born there in 1846. He broke the family tradition by going to Oxford where he proved himself to be a good scholar, sportsman and historian, missing a blue at cricket and rowing because he split his time. All these traits followed him through into his later life.

Remarkably, William played cricket for three counties, Derbyshire. Yorkshire and Nottinghamshire, though his figures, by modern standards, were poor. His Wisden obituary called him a useful batsman and good cover-point. His county average was 8.55. Surprisingly, or perhaps not, he did not get his blue at Oxford. The whole family were cricketers. All his sons played and his distant nephew by marriage, Archibald White, was club captain of Yorkshire between 1912 and 1918.

William became a curate at Worksop Abbey, Nottinghamshire, when he met his future wife, Bridget White. What a good choice. Not only was she a striking woman, with a forthright manner, but she brought with her the possibility of a large inheritance. A perfect match for a young curate.

William and Bridget were married in 1876, in Worksop. At about this time, William took up the post of Vicar at Clayton with Frickley, in South Yorkshire. Soon after, he moved to Waldron. They had eight children, six of whom survived into adulthood.

In 1905, Bertie, the eldest, aged 27, was away most of the time, working as a ship's officer in the Merchant Navy in the Indian Ocean, and was to be at home on leave this Christmas.

Gunny, the second son, aged 25, worked in London as a Jobber in the Stock Exchange, but would be home as well.

Cyril, the third son, aged 24, was working as a solicitor in nearby Uckfield.

Arthur, the fourth son, aged 22, had recently come down from Oxford, having completed his studies, and was thinking about starting work as a teacher.

Una, their first daughter, aged 16, was still at school and lived at home, and

Maud, the second daughter, aged 13, was also still at school and lived at home.

They were all single in 1905.

William was particularly pleased he would see Bertie again; it was three years since his last leave. The bonus was that Bertie would normally get about 6 months at home each time, and he had been back since August. The officers worked their passage back home from India, which usually took about 40 days, had their leave, and then worked their passage back again.

Bertie had always been a bit of a worry for William and Bridget. As a youngster, he was always the one the one in trouble and had critical school reports. He would write home from boarding school to the family nanny asking her to persuade his father to send more money.

Having been sent to a naval school, and then on college at Dartmouth, he was refused entry to the Royal Navy.

Fortunately, he looked at an apprenticeship in the Merchant Navy and was accepted initially by the Shaw, Savill & Albion Line, being appointed Midshipman on board a four-masted barque, the 'Hinemoa', sailing on the service between Glasgow and London to Otago in New Zealand, returning with frozen sheep carcasses. She was one of the last windjammers. After a couple of years, he joined the British India Steamship Company, who were based in Calcutta. He had risen through the officer ranks, passed all his exams, and became a well-respected and efficient merchant seaman, even if he did still have a twinkle in his eye.

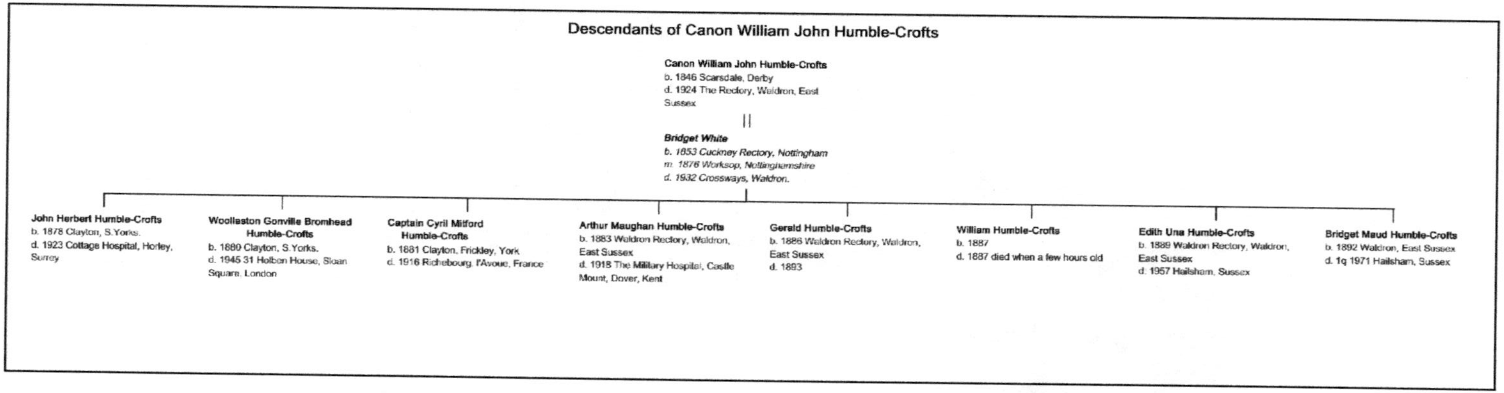

Descendants of Canon William John Humble-Crofts

Canon William John Humble-Crofts
b. 1846 Scarsdale, Derby
d. 1924 The Rectory, Waldron, East
Sussex

==

Bridget White
b. 1853 Cuckney Rectory, Nottingham
m: 1876 Worksop, Nottinghamshire
d. 1932 Crossways, Waldron.

John Herbert Humble-Crofts
b. 1878 Clayton, S.Yorks.
d. 1922 Cottage Hospital, Horley, Surrey

Woollaston Gonville Bromhead Humble-Crofts
b. 1880 Clayton, S.Yorks.
d. 1945 31 Holbon House, Sloan Square, London

Captain Cyril Milford Humble-Crofts
b. 1881 Clayton, Frickley, York
d. 1916 Richebourg l'Avoué, France

Arthur Maughan Humble-Crofts
b. 1883 Waldron Rectory, Waldron, East Sussex
d. 1918 The Military Hospital, Castle Mount, Dover, Kent

Gerald Humble-Crofts
b. 1886 Waldron Rectory, Waldron, East Sussex
d. 1893

William Humble-Crofts
b. 1887
d. 1887 died when a few hours old

Edith Una Humble-Crofts
b. 1888 Waldron Rectory, Waldron, East Sussex
d. 1957 Hailsham, Sussex

Bridget Maud Humble-Crofts
b. 1892 Waldron, East Sussex
d. 1q 1971 Hailsham, Sussex

Chart 2: Descendants of Canon William John Humble-Crofts

Photograph 3: Bertie in summer kit, British India Steamship Company,
1899–1901, age 20

Whilst Bertie was home, he was due to apply for his Master Mariners (Steamship) Certificate in London at the end of November, which he did successfully.

William and Bridget took a very active part in the sporting, social and religious life of the village.

He and his children played cricket for Waldron, and some also played football. They took part in amateur dramatics, the choir, bell-ringing, cycling holidays for parishioners and school work.

William's idyllic life would eventually be disturbed by events.

Like many British families, World War I would wreak its havoc on the young men of the country, and the Humble-Crofts were not immune to this.

Chapter 6
Beatrice Martha

May 1958

Three months after making her will in February 1958, Beatrice Martha's health deteriorated rapidly, both physically and mentally.

A she became increasingly difficult to manage due to dementia, and was aggressive at times, she was admitted to the Priory Nursing Home in Roehampton, where she died on the 21 May 1958.

One night near the end of her life, she somehow managed to summon a taxi and 'escape' from the hospital. She went to an apartment belonging to a friend of her daughter Bridget.

Though she had been estranged from her daughter-in-law, Anna, for some years, it was Anna who was eventually called upon to come round and look after her overnight, pending her re-admission to hospital the following morning.

Anna told me about this episode to me when she was discussing what she had known about Beatrice.

'It was not until very much later that she began to tell me something about her family...it all happened one night when she had absconded from the Home in Richmond' (Roehampton), *'where she had been living, and was eventually found wandering about London in her nightie and dressing gown, and finally landed up in the flat of a great friend of Bridget's, whom she had known. She had taken a taxi from the home, and went back there afterwards. It was only me who was available at the time and who could spend the night with her, and I had to sleep on a rug on the floor. She was very muddled and spoke French the whole time to me. Fortunately, my French was pretty good at that time and so I was able to answer her back in French. It was then that she told me quite a lot about her family. We became friends and she told me then how she could say all sorts of things to me, which she was unable to tell her daughters and what a help I was etc., etc. Poor Beatrice – I really felt quite a fondness for her then.'*

When I talked further to Anna about this conversation, she herself was elderly and a little confused on occasions. She told me that during Beatrice's French ramblings, her mother-in-law had admitted that she had given birth to an illegitimate child, but would give no further details. This was not known to anyone in the family at that time and was even denied by Anna at a later meeting.

Anna, of course, told her husband, Beatrice's son Michael, the next day. He was shocked by this revelation, as you would expect, and he confronted his mother during his next visit to her when she was back in the hospital. All Beatrice would say was, *'You will have to trust me over this'.* Nothing further was said and Michael did not know what to believe.

So, the secret was out, but Michael knew nothing more. The secret remained dormant for many years after Beatrice's death, and it would be 30 years later, and more than 80 years after the event that the truth would be revealed. Even then there was more to tell.

Chapter 7
Stanley Sergeant

13 February 1913 –

I left the story that my father wrote at the end of an earlier Chapter, when at the start of 1913 he was about to travel from Liverpool to his next life in Hull. He was six and a half years old and had no idea what he would be facing. I will take up his story again.

Chapter 2. Enter: – Stanley Sergeant.

I well remember Tuesday February 13th., 1913, not of course as a date or day of the week, but certainly clearly can I hear the sound of the train from Liverpool arriving at Paragon Station – Miss Martin, the secretary, who had accompanied me on the journey, and I alighted on the platform, and walked towards and met a man stood by himself, and obviously expecting us.

He was Leonard Sergeant – a tiny sized man of not 5ft. in height.

After brief preliminaries of introduction, Miss Martin lost herself into a past world as far as I was concerned, to join all those who had passed before, and I stood on the station with my new "guardian" old enough to feel within myself, that I really stood alone – and the new world was not mine.

I remember with nostalgia, the clothes I wore that day. I was very clean, and new, and smart. I had dark navy-blue suiting, a deep Eton collar, with a red velvet bow.

I was instructed to address my new guardian as "Uncle" and Uncle he remained until the day of our separation approx. 11 or 12 years later.

We travelled on a tram-car from the station, to Witham, the east side of Hull. On alighting from the tram, and crossing the road, we approached to where another man stood on the pavement, quite obviously awaiting our arrival, and to whom Uncle spoke. The man, Freddy Smith, of whom more anon, was another midget size, almost identical height of Uncle, though younger in years. He had purposefully waited, in the hope of meeting me for the first time, before returning to afternoon work at Earles Shipbuilding Co.

After this brief encounter, we proceeded for the short distance to my new home. For some strange reason, although it would have been much quicker as I found out later to have approached the front entrance of the house, we took quite a long detour round a square block of streets to enter by the back door.

How I remember it – through a small back-yard – I was ushered inside –
where stood a tall woman whom Uncle introduced as his sister Mrs Bielby – and
then came a dramatic though at the time – a seemingly simple moment:
Uncle said to me: – "What do they call you." I replied, "Stanley Taylor."
Uncle said, "From now on, your name will be Stanley Sergeant."

Dad's story stops abruptly at this point. There were a lot of blank pages left in his notebook, and Dad had plenty of time to complete his story. Though I do not know for certain why he stopped, it is pretty easy to work out. He had obviously intended to write more, as evidenced by his statement in the fourth paragraph from the end, when talking about Freddy Smith, he says, *'of whom more anon'.* There was no more anon.

My eldest brother Peter remembers being shown the story by Dad, during a visit back home, at which time Peter was married and living in Surrey. He asked Dad about the rest of the story. His reply was in essence that the memories were too painful, and that life had been awful. My middle brother, Eric, had conversations with both Dad and Mum about those lost years. Though there is no absolute proof, there can be little doubt that he was abused during his stay with "Uncle". He told Eric that he used to dread coming home from school and then having to wait for Sergeant to come home from work; he knew what would follow. If Sergeant was accompanied by Freddy Smith, he knew that it would be worse.

This was the start of the darkest part of Dad's life, following as it did his 'second' abandonment.

At the time it is pretty certain that Dad did not know that he had been adopted, and assumed that the Taylors were his real parents. He knew his paper trail existed, but he had no idea what they contained. Being abandoned by the person he thought was his 'real' father would have been devastating.

After the trauma of having been left behind in Liverpool, he might have been forgiven for thinking that the worst had already happened, and that he could hope for to a new start in Hull. He would have changed his mind about this fairly quickly. Though he was only six years old, he seems to have had insight into his predicament. As he said tellingly in his own account, he told himself that he was *'old enough to feel within myself, that I really stood alone – and the new world was not mine.'*

Sadly, I never talked to Dad about his early experiences; I did not know about them until I read his story myself for the first time. I was too young to be involved in the earlier discussion with my brothers, and then I was off to London to College and the subject was never brought up again.

I grew up in Hull and the surrounding area to the west, but the district of Witham in the east was not well known to me. Visits later in life showed me that, once again, Dad's description of the location were accurate.

Witham is in the older part of East Hull, north of the main commercial dock area and east of the River Hull, which flows north to south to empty into the

River Humber. The River Hull marks the boundary between East and West Hull, and East Hull was then generally considered to be 'the wrong side of the tracks'. The swing bridges over the River Hull were the main crossings and had to open and close frequently to allow vessels passage up the river, though new bridges now span the river. A new and unique pedestrian swing bridge was opened in 2013.

The Hull is tidal and several times a year the housing immediately on either side of the southern part of the river used to get flooded. Since 1980, protection has been improved with a tidal barrier near the entrance to the River Humber.

The oldest part of the whole city, containing the original financial quarter and Holy Trinity Church are just on the other west side of the River Hull. Holy Trinity is the largest parish church in England. The more modern town centre is further to the west again.

The tram to Witham from the city centre used to run from Queens Dock in the old city, along Charlotte Street, across North Bridge, one of the swing bridges, and then down a road named 'Witham'.

Sergeant's house was number 19, Kingston Terrace. Old maps of the area show that the house was one of a row of terraced houses that ran round three sides of Kingston Wesleyan Chapel and Sunday School building. Kingston Chapel was situated at the eastern end of 'Witham' on the north side. The houses were reasonably spacious and inhabited by working folk and small shopkeepers. Number 19 was on the north-west corner of the Chapel.

Each house had a small garden at the front and a yard at the back. The houses were usually entered via the front garden from a wide walkway round the Chapel. There was also a back entrance to each house from a small alleyway between and around the houses and entered from the street to the north by a small archway between the houses. This was the way Dad went in.

The house had six rooms, with a kitchen and two living rooms on the ground floor.

Neither Kingston Terrace nor the Chapel exist today.

Leonard Sergeant and his friend Freddy Smith both worked at Earles Shipbuilding Yard, an easy walk from the house, less than a mile away south-east across some railway lines and the Hedon Road.

Earles employed thousands of workers during the early twentieth Century. They built and repaired ships, including naval vessels and several ships for the locally famous 'Wilson Line'.

Leonard John Sergeant was born in 1874, in Preston, a small village north of Hedon, east of Hull. He called himself John. He never married.

His surname was usually spelt as above, but is recorded on occasions as Sergeant and Sergeant.

His father was also called John Sergeant, though no name appears on Leonard's birth certificate. His father was born in Lincolnshire, and became a shoemaker. Leonard's mother was named on the certificate as Charlotte Neal, seemingly unmarried at the time of his birth. His father appears to have had three wives in total, all from Hull, and Charlotte was the third.

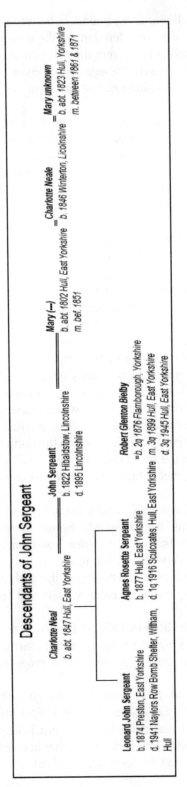

Descendants of John Sergeant

John Sergeant
b. 1822 Hibaldstow, Lincolnshire
d. 1895 Lincolnshire

Mary (—)
b. abt 1802 Hull, East Yorkshire
m. bef. 1851

= **Charlotte Neale**
b. 1846 Winterton, Lincolnshire

= **Mary unknown**
b. abt 1823 Hull, Yorkshire
m. between 1861 & 1871

Charlotte Neal
b. abt 1847 Hull, East Yorkshire

Robert Glenton Bielby
= b. 2q 1876 Flamborough, Yorkshire
m. 3q 1899 Hull, East Yorkshire
d. 3q 1945 Hull, East Yorkshire

Agnes Rosette Sergeant
b. 1877 Hull, East Yorkshire
d. 1q 1916 Scullcoates, Hull, East Yorkshire

Leonard John Sergeant
b. 1874 Preston, East Yorkshire
d. 1941 Naylors Row Bomb Shelter, Witham, Hull

Chart 3 : Descendants of John Sergeant

In the 1911 census, two years before Dad arrived in Hull, Sergeant was living at 14, Wilton Street, 200 yards east of Kingston Terrace, together with Frederick Smith, then aged 14, who was listed as his 'nephew'. Sergeant obviously used the word 'nephew' as a euphemism to explain the presence of a young man alone in his household, much as he suggested the word 'Uncle' for Dad to use.

No family connection has been found between Sergeant and Frederick Smith.

Sergeant's occupation is given as *'Iron Driller, Shipbuilding'*. Sergeant moved to 19, Kingston Terrace in 1912 and lived there until 1933.

Some years later, in 1939, Sergeant was living by himself at 74, Naylor's Row and Frederick Smith was living alone 2 doors away at number 70.

Freddy Smith's family was found with ease. His father Frederick was a cab driver and groom, who was born in Norfolk and lived in East Hull. Freddy Smith was born, like Sergeant, in Preston. Hence, he may have known him when as a young child, and Freddie was just 16 years old in 1913 when Dad arrived.

Sergeant's sister was Agnes Rosetta Bielby. She was actually his half-sister and was born in Hull just over two years after Leonard, in 1877. She was tall, whereas her brother was short, presumably the legacy of a different mother. She had, I assume, taken on the role of 'Mrs Sergeant' during the application process for the adoption.

Agnes married Robert Glenton Bielby in 1899. He worked originally as a fisherman in Flamborough, North Yorkshire, and moved to Hull to work as a labourer. She had six children, and she and her husband lived about half a mile away from her brother, in the direction of the River Humber. At the time of Dad's arrival in Hull in 1913, five of the children were alive and several around Dad's age. Agnes Bielby died three years later in childbirth, in 1916, aged 40. Her husband Robert died in 1945. Four of their six children reached adulthood and all married and lived in Hull.

I did manage to make contact with some of the descendants of Sergeant's half-sister, Agnes. Though they had no personal knowledge of my father, some had heard of him, but they had had no direct contact with Sergeant. They confirmed that Sergeant had gained a reputation for adopting young boys from orphanages; he had probably 'adopted' at least four of them during his adult life.

Whilst in Sergeant's care, Dad duly went to school locally and later to the Technical College in West Hull. Dad had little alternative but to knuckle down and wait for an opportunity to get out. He had nowhere to go, no safe refuge.

He worked hard at school and learnt quickly. He did well in most subjects, especially mathematics and technical subjects.

There were several Bielby and Smith families in Dad's life, all of them unrelated to each other. Despite the expected rarity of the Bielby surname, the 1911 census shows that there were at least 5 Bielby families in Hull at that time, and several others in the surrounding parts of East Yorkshire. Chance dictated that Dad was destined to come across two of them during his childhood.

He met a fellow pupil at school called Alf Bielby, who became his best friend and his saviour a few years later. Alf's family were not related to Sergeant's sister's family of Bielbys.

Dad left school at the age of 14, in September 1921, and apparently at this time made an attempt to get away from Sergeant, but was brought back. In the early 1920s, the age of consent and the age of majority had both risen to 16 years, and the legal consequences of having a 'Lawful Guardian' were more complex.

The possibility of further education or an apprenticeship depended to an extent on Sergeant's continued goodwill, and any move would also require the agreement of an employer.

Hence Dad started at the Young People's Institute branch of the Hull Municipal Technical College, then based in Charlotte Street, just over the River in West Hull.

During his first term there he gained an apprenticeship with Mr Benn Franks, an Optician whose premises were at 44, Saville Street, very much part of the main up-market shopping area.

The start of the apprenticeship required Sergeant to sign a letter of acceptance on Dad's behalf. This was signed by Sergeant as 'Lawful Guardian', and by Dad as his 'Adopted Son'. The copy later retained by Dad was un-dated and un-signed, but another letter from Benn Franks showed the date.

In the agreement Dad was referred to as Stanley Harrod Sergeant. Benn Franks added to the bottom of the agreement in his own handwriting: *'This boy's real name is John Stanley Harrod. I have seen his birth certificate.'* Dad would not have been able to see this addition when he signed his copy and so at this stage did not understand the significance of the 'Harrod' part of his name, and still had no knowledge of his origins.

Benjamin Franks and his wife Helena hailed from Salford, Manchester where his father had also been an optician. Benjamin was aged 58 in 1921 when Dad joined. Benn Frank's business in Hull was termed by him, 'Scientific Opticians' and it had been in existence for some years already. He had other branches in Hanley, near Stoke on Trent, and Doncaster.

So, on the 14 November of that year, 1921, Dad started his six-year apprenticeship whilst continuing his studies at the evening classes.

The contract stipulated that his weekly salary for the first year was 10 shillings, rising gradually to 25 shillings per week by the sixth year. A clause restricted Dad's right to practise as an optician, other than with Benn Franks, within 10 miles of Hull Town Hall, for a period of two years after he finished his apprenticeship. This type of restrictive clause was quite common in professional agreements at the time and continued until late in the Twentieth Century.

In July 1922, when Dad was aged 16, he was still living with Sergeant and was given a prize certificate at the end of his first year at the Technical College. He was studying Technical Drawing, General Elementary Science, Calculations and English. Listed in error as Stanley Harold Sergeant, he obtained a 1st Prize worth 10 shillings, a week's wages!

He was well-liked by staff and patients at Benn Franks, and did very well. His wage rose each year allowing Dad to formulate a plan to seek his independence at some time in the future.

By 1924, when Dad was aged 17, he was in the 3rd year of his apprenticeship. With the encouragement and aid of his friend Alf Bielby and Alf's family, Dad decided to make a move. He would have needed to get the agreement of his employer. With his high standing at work, a short explanation would have been pretty certain to gain that agreement.

The Bielby family attended Albion Congregational Church, in Albion Street, Hull. Dad had joined them and became very involved with many church activities. I suspect he had advice from the Minister and took strength for his escape from his deeply held religious belief. This force stayed with him throughout his life.

Alf, or Alfred Arthur Bielby to give him his full name, was born in Hull in December 1906, so was only ten weeks younger than Dad. His parents were Arthur Bielby, an ironmonger, born in 1875, in Lambeth, London, and Gertrude Eleanor Jubb, a milliner. Alf had an older sister, Lillian Olive, who was four years older.

The Bielbys lived in Severn Street, in the Summergangs area of Hull, further east along the Holderness Road.

Alf Bielby in mid-life was rather a chubby chap; to me as a child he was always linked to my mental picture of Dicken's Mr Micawber. He later became the manager of a large grocery shop, Cussons, which had several local branches.

Alf was definitely not a decisive man. He had a very long courtship with his wife to be, Marjorie Chaffer, which lasted something like 20 years or more. They did not marry until 1965, shortly after the death of Alf's mother, who was a formidable woman and the probable cause of the delay.

Alf and Dad remained lifelong friends. They were friends of the family and fellow worshippers at Albion Congregational Church before and after the war. Alf died four years after Dad in 1975.

With the offer of temporary accommodation from the Bielby family, Dad decided to leave Sergeant. Dad broke into Sergeant's desk, where he had kept Dad's documents, and made good his escape. Alf's parents must have had sympathy for his plight as Dad stayed with them for some time until he became fully independent.

Dad was always grateful to the Bielby family who gave him a foothold to start the next phase of his life. I guess he would have left eventually anyhow, but a safe haven must have been a huge blessing for a 17-year-old. Perhaps he should have left earlier, but he might have lost his apprenticeship and would have had nowhere to live.

What Dad discovered in those stolen documents was to be a complete revelation to him.

Chapter 8
The Grocer

1905

Charles Digby Harrod, Grocer and Tea Dealer, was a very special man.

He was born in January 1841 at 4 Cable Street in East London.

His father, Charles Henry Harrod, had opened his drapery shop in Southwark, South London, in 1824.

This had not been an entirely successful venture, with a dissolved partnership, a financial crash and stiff competition. After struggling on until 1832, he decided to move north of the Thames, prompted by the development of the docks east of London Bridge and the sudden opening up and growth in the tea trade. It was a very astute move.

He opened a grocery and tea shop in Cable Street in 1834 and later a wholesale business in Eastcheap.

Charles Digby grew up in the area living in Cable Street and then in nearby Rosemary Street. He would have been involved in the business from a young age.

By the time Charles Digby was born, his parents had already lost two children to illness.

Sanitation was poor, and the run-down area was near the docks, with visiting seamen and many foreigners.

Cable Street was a relatively deprived area, even for the era, and was inhabited by serial waves of immigrants. It runs from the Tower of London in the west to Ratcliff in the east, and was so named as it was originally the standard length of hemp rope, twisted into a cable, required for sailing ships; – a cable length.

The business was modestly successful and grew steadily over the ensuing years. In 1851, when Charles Digby was ten years old, his parents moved them all to the then green suburb of Bethnal Green, away from the river and the smell and disease. He was sent off to a small school in Edwardstone, Suffolk, for a few years.

His father's best ever decision was to buy up an ailing grocery business in Brompton and move the retail business and the family there, to live behind the shop. That was in 1854 and was the base for the foundation of the Harrods store. On finishing school aged 16, his education in the business continued with a spell with another grocery in the city and work at the wholesale business in Eastcheap.

By 1860, Charles Digby was raring to go. He was 19 years old and was full of ideas as to how he would like to run the store. In 1861, his father, then aged 62, agreed to let him take over the day to day running of the business.

During his time as a single man, he worked hard but still managed to find the time to play hard, being singled out by Punch Magazine with two of his local friends as *'the three best-dressed young blades of Knightsbridge'*. There was young Mr Tattersall, one of several generations of the Tattersall dynasty. They had been in the horse auction business since 1766, and had been thriving in Hyde Park Corner until the lease ran out and in 1865, they moved to Knightsbridge. The site of their business was almost opposite Harrod's shop on the Brompton Road. The other young man was James Chatten, a local General Dealer and Hansom cab owner. James Chatten's great granddaughter, Patricia Pitt Chatten Waters was the source of this information. A James Chatten, presumably either the same individual or a relative, ran dining rooms on the north side of the Brompton Road, in Middle Row, just east of the Tattersalls site.

In 1864, not long after completing the buyout from his father, Charles Digby married Caroline Godsmark, who he had met at the local Chapel. Caroline's father was an established Grocer in London, and her step-father was another.

With an eye for detail and innovative ideas, together with firmness but fairness with his staff, and an ability to charm his customers, he went from strength to strength. He sold cheaply and in quantity, cutting out incentives to servants who often acted as middle men to the wealthier clients, and offering quality goods with value for money. He was an early exponent of large shop window displays and was the first to take out a whole page newspaper advertisement in The Times.

As he bought up the surrounding properties around his shop the footprint of the present store gradually evolved.

Even a major fire in the shop in 1883, just before the Christmas rush, was turned from a disaster into a triumph and allowed him to rebuild a bespoke new store. By the late 1880s he was a wealthy man, and had moved to a 'modern' family home in leafy Sydenham.

Charles Digby and Caroline had a productive marriage, always taking a full part together in local affairs and charitable causes. He worked extremely hard, usually longer hours than any of his staff.

Despite being 'in trade', and therefore excluded from the more exclusive echelons of affluent society, the family had a very comfortable and privileged existence.

They produced eight children and unusually for the era, all survived childhood.

Sadly for Charles Digby who must have hoped for a successor to continue the fledgling dynasty, they had seven girls and one boy. Of the girls, five made good marriages and gave him grandchildren, but none of the girls or their husbands were interested in the family store. Eventually they had 20 grandchildren, but only nine were born during his lifetime and not all of them survived into adulthood.

Photograph 4: Charles Digby Harrod in middle age – photograph c/o JW

Charles and Caroline's only son Henry Herbert Harrod went to Cambridge and trained as a lawyer, but never practised. He remained single and must have frustrated his father by never earning a penny during his life. He spent much of his time as a young man writing fairy stories and reading them to children. He accumulated over his lifetime an enormous collection of pictures, prints, paintings and books, and rather incongruously, historic firearms. The former was bequeathed upon his death to the Victoria and Albert Museum as the 'Harrod Collection', though the 'V & A' only retained 1,600 of the 20,000 pictures in the collection and sold the rest. His unique firearm collection was dispersed around the time of his death.

Photograph 5: Caroline Harrod nee Godsmark in middle age

When he was only 50 years old, in 1891, a combination of circumstances, the lack of a successor, the death of his father, and probably a deterioration in his health, led Charles Digby to sell the business after 30 years of work. Rather surprisingly for a lifelong 'townie', he retired with his wife and unmarried daughters to Morebath Manor in rural North Devon. He knocked down the original building on the site and erected a substantial house, at substantial cost.

Once installed, he took a keen interest in the large amount of land and numerous tenancies that came with the estate, metamorphosing seamlessly into the country squire.

He threw himself into local life, becoming a J.P., a local Councillor, a stalwart of the local Liberal Party and a supporter of good causes.

After 10 years in Devon, according to family legend, Caroline persuaded Charles how much she missed London life and the rest of the family, and they moved back to the south of England, within easy reach of London. He seems to have been easily persuaded.

In 1901, whilst the sales and purchases were being completed and alterations to the new house were underway, Charles and Caroline, and their unmarried daughters went away on holiday abroad.

Then back from their travels, in 1902, they moved to 'Culverwood', a large country house near Heathfield in East Sussex. As in Morebath, he and the family entered into the local life to the full over the ensuing three years. In the same year as they moved in, 1902, he was elected a Liberal member of the Sussex county council. He also served as chairman of the local school's attendance council.

Despite his earlier ill health, he and Caroline were enjoying life. He was a well-loved family man.

Their two eldest daughters had been married for some time by 1905, nearly 20 years each, the eldest daughter, Fanny, with her Shipbroker husband, had given Charles and Caroline five grandchildren, aged between 17 and seven. The next daughter, Grace, had married a Solicitor and they had three children aged between 15 and nine.

Their five other daughters were in good health but as yet unmarried, their son, Henry, now aged 34, though a lovely kind and gentle man, was a disappointment to him. He was definitely not a chip off the old block.

So, life was busy. He was pretty active and the grandchildren were a delight to him. He had had a hectic life in the shop, but this was now in the capable hands of Richard Burbidge, the Managing Director of Harrods Limited, and the shop was now even bigger and more prestigious than in his day.

In August 1905, he was looking forward to the annual garden party for the local schoolchildren, which he and Caroline had started three years previously. This was held in the ground of Culverwood and had proved a great success.

Chapter 9
John Herbert

1905

First Officer John Herbert Humble-Crofts was nearing the peak of his career.

In June 1905 he was working on board the S.S. Onda out of Calcutta. She was a typical ship of the British India Steamship Company. She was a modest size, 5,294 tons, and had been in service since 1895.

He was looking forward to his leave, which came round every 3 years and allowed him to work his passage back to England, spend 6 months at home, and then work his way back again to Calcutta.

He had joined B.I.S.Co. in 1898, at the age of 20, after a short period with another line. His work was almost exclusively around the Indian sub-continent.

The Company ran services from Calcutta and Bombay to Indian Ocean ports and the Gulf, using local coal and with a subsidy from the government of Bombay. Most of the services ran weekly.

There were fortnightly sailings to London from Calcutta, via Madras, Colombo, Aden, the Suez Canal and Naples, and return; and to Australia every 5 or 6 weeks via Singapore, Batavia (Dutch East Indies), Port Darwin, Brisbane, Sydney, Melbourne and Adelaide.

Later there were services to New Zealand and eventually to East Africa and the Far East.

The Company secured the coveted Royal Mail contract which guaranteed a minimum revenue beyond the carriage of cargo and passengers. Competition for such contracts was keen, often cut-throat, but once won, could make or break a company.

I found a description of the Company which embodies the pride in merchant ships of the era,

'British India's sombre livery of black hull, funnel and boats, dark brown masts and dark varnished deck houses was enlivened only by a white sheer line and two narrow white bands separated by a thin black line that ringed the funnel. The house flag was a white swallow tail burgee emblazoned with the cross of St Patrick in red and the crest was among the most symbolic imaginable, the figure of Britannia backed by the British lion with one paw resting imperially on top of a globe. There was something else about these ships: the polished copper steam pipes, the glistening black varnish of the lifeboats, the bleached white teak decks

and vessel names like Cashmere, Kurrachee, Satara and Coconada that bespoke a pride of purpose and place, as belonging to the British India Line of Royal Mail Steamers. The service and discipline provided by British officers and Indian crews was renowned and wearing the company uniform was an object of immense pride.'

The early steamers had auxiliary sails. The ship 'Baghdad' once *"sailed from Mombassa to within a day's run of Aden without the propeller having turned once"*. In addition to being essential in case of a breakdown, sail was routinely employed to get extra speed during the monsoon and to steady a vessel heavily laden with deck passengers. Indeed, B.I. ships used auxiliary sail right through to the First World War and occasionally into the 1920s.

The coastal steamers round India were according to legend called "umbrella ships", that were originally summoned into minor ports, so it is said, to collect cargo or passengers by a merchant hoisting an umbrella, or later a flag, to attract the captain's attention.

B.I. gained a reputation for regularity and safety when the Indian coast, Bay of Bengal and Persian Gulf were among the most precarious waters in the world, each with its own special problems and geographic conditions. There were pirates in the Gulf, inter-racial or other religious fights among deck passengers, as well as the 'burra sahibs' (meaning the most important people, those respected, so in context the white colonials), in Saloon to cater for.

The pattern of trips sailed by an officer like Bertie was that every couple of months he would undertake a trip that would last several weeks, then have a break of a week or two before the next. Bertie was obviously competent and gradually rose through the ranks, starting from 4th Officer to 1st Officer. During his six-month home leave every three years or so, he took and passed his various certificates to help the progress of the promotions.

Despite his history in childhood and his reputation as a naughty boy, he seems to have been well thought of at his work. He received some touching accolades, including one below.

In his papers was the following

'This is a copy of an address presented to me by coolie passengers from Nagapatan to Penang with the request that they might put it in the paper.'
"Sir,
We the undersigned representatives of the ignorant coolie passengers of S.S.Lawada that arrived at our port today from Nagapatan beg to request that you will kindly be pleased to insert the following in your valuable periodical, as one poor thanks for the multifarious kindnesses that we received on our voyage down here from the chief and medical officer: To redound' (old word meaning to add to), *'the glory and honour of Mr Humble-Crofts, the Chief Officer of the ship, we beg to represent to you dear editor that he spared no energy of his in supplying our various habits in the sea at this rough state of the weather.*

Not only had he entered each and every hatch where we were located but also inspected and actually at times present during our meals to find out any grievances and rectify them there and then.

Many a time he came with the doctor to see us and encourage him to give medical comforts to us. The doctor also continually coming and enquiring our welfare with fraternal affection. Our chief officer on board when finding our ship rolling in the middle of the sea ordered two sails to be opened of course with the permission of the commander to steady the vessel thereby preventing us from fear and anxiety.

On the night of the 13th inst. when there was a cyclonic state of the weather in the sea our chief officer came every hour and then and inspected and encouraged us.

In conclusion dear Editor we ask you unanimously to convey our best thanks and regards to the Chief Officer, Medicine Officer and the officers in general of the S.S.Lawada thro the medium of your valuable periodical and to inform them that however poor we are, never spare to pray to our heavenly father to give forth the shower-like blessings upon all the officers who treated us kindly on our voyage.

For which we shall feel highly thankful.

We are dear Editor,"

'Here follows about 30 signatures in English and Hindustani after which comes,' "and all the ignorant coolies on board".

Bertie was born in September 1878, in Clayton, South Yorkshire. He was the eldest child of The Reverend William and Bridget Humble-Crofts. Like his father, he was born with the single name 'Humble', but more of that later.

According to Maud, his sister, Bertie was a 'bit of a lad'. He was the naughty boy of the family, though Maughan, his nephew, added that all of the Humble-Crofts boys were rather naughty. He even listed a scale of naughtiness; Bertie 8/10; Gunn 4/10; Cyril and Arthur 2/10.

Bertie started school boarding at Winchester House School, Eastbourne before the age of five. That seems very young, but Eastbourne was not far from home. Either he was indeed very, very naughty or they just wanted him to start early.

He went next to Stubbington House College, in Fareham, Hampshire. Stubbington House was a very popular school for future naval entrants. Previously known as 'Fosters Naval Academy', it was reputed to be the oldest 'Prep.' School in England. One of many famous alumni of the school was Scott of the Antarctic, and the school boasts six Victoria Crosses.

Whilst there, Bertie used to write home to Nanny to get money when his funds ran out, and the letters were sent to other addresses in the village to avoid his father finding out. The Nanny, Mary Ballingall, was said initially to have gone to Waldron for six months when one of the boys was born, and ended up staying for 65 years! Maughan said, *'She knew <u>everything</u> about the Humble-Crofts family.'* What details she could have told us!

In 1894 Bertie, aged 16, left Stubbington House and moved to the Naval Training College, 'H.M.S. Britannia', based in Dartmouth. Bertie was a very popular and handsome young man.

Photograph 6: Bertie Humble-Crofts about 1895, age 17

I have had access to a series of letters written home by Bertie when he was at each of his schools.

From Winchester House, the letters were initially written by his teacher with an accompanying letter attempted by Bertie. The first, written on the 1st Sunday in Lent, 1883, when Bertie would have been about four and a half years old. The teacher's letter was full of reassurance for his mother and a story that he was popular with the girls, even at that age.

Bertie's letter was a good attempt for his age, with a few spelling errors, and was written on his own.

'Wimch house.
my Dear Mother,
    wen is Father comaing to see me. I have not gone to Church today because I have got a cold tell gnoye (Gunny, his brother) *thath I football yesterday. geave mly* (Emily – we think this must have been a family dog or horse) *1 kiss + ten to Father and ten to you and six to Nurse.'*

Apparently, the envelope was rather grubby.

Bertie looks as though he is being taught to be self-reliant early on.

By 1885, now aged 6 and a half, Bertie's writing, spelling and grammar were much improved, but the content still reflected his age. He was missing home at his new school, asking to see his mother or father, telling his younger brother he would like school, and listing the children and activities he liked and disliked. Another shows how he has settled.

'Quinquagesima 1885 (Latin for the Sunday before Lent)
My dearest Mother,
    Mrs Richards (teacher) *gave me a pocket book for a Valentine. There came lots of great rings at the bell and then we went in and found parcels on the door step. I could not make out where they came from, but the boys say it was Louisa, our maid and they saw her once...we all had parcels of oranges, raisins and ginger biscuits too.*
    It was such fun yesterday as we went to Beachy Head. Alex asked the coastguard man to let him look through his telescope, but he said it was so thick that no one could see anything...ask Father to come and see me and tell Emily if she doesn't behave herself, I'm very strong now and I shall ask Gunny and Cyril to help me knock her down. And if she doesn't do what I tell her, she'll be punished but don't tell her what I'll do.
    4 million kisses to you and
    4 million kisses to Father and 1,000 to Gunny, that's not half as much, and half a thousand to Cyril and 1 to Emily and 10 for nurse and 11 for Mary and 12 for Jennings and 6 for Mrs Lucas and 8 for Mrs Lewis and 2 Frank.' The other names are household or estate servants.

The teacher's covering letter, also retained, tells a slightly different story. It seems they keep the children and parents apart for a while on purpose. The Humble-Crofts were missing Bertie as much as he missed them.

'Winchester House School. Eastbourne. Jan 27, 1885.
Dear Mrs Humble-Crofts,
    I quite sympathise with you about parting from little Bertie. He is very good and quite happy...I think it will be a little trying for him to see you just yet as it might unsettle him but I think that at the end of next week it would do. Half

holidays are generally the best days for parents to come and from 12 to 3 does not interfere with lessons or games...With kind regards, I am, Yours very sincerely, Marion Richards.'

By September 1892, now just aged 14 years, he was still at Stubbington House. He sounded like a young man now. Now dealing with father, not mother.

'Sept. 7, 1892
My dear Father,
*   I felt very sorry to have my birthday away from home.*
*   I hope that you are having good sport...*
*   I had a very kind letter from mother yesterday which nearly broke my heart it touched me so.*
*   Mary Foster is going to take me partridge shooting tomorrow.*
*   Much love, I remain, Bertie.*

In 1894, he was now at H.M.S. Britannia at Dartmouth. It was a harsh life.

Two moored ships were the sleeping quarters and classrooms. Britannia itself, converted in 1869 from a 121-gun, screw-propelled, first-rate three-decker, line-of-battle ship of the Royal Navy previously called 'Prince of Wales', and the two-decker Hindustan, added some years before to provide extra space, and joined by a covered gangway.

Bullying was a constant problem and may have prompted the decision for Princes Albert Victor and George, sons of the Prince of Wales, to be educated there in 1877. There had been a widely publicised case of bullying and sending the Princes there was seen as a vote of confidence.

Prince Albert, the eldest son was to die tragically in 1892 aged 28.

Prince George, later King George V, later wrote of his time as a Naval cadet:

'It never did me any good to be a Prince. The Britannia was a pretty tough place, and so far from our benefiting, the other cadets made a point of taking it out of us, on the grounds that they would never be able to do it later on. There was a lot of fighting among the cadets, and the rule was if challenged you had to accept. So they used to make me go up and challenge the bigger cadets. I was awfully small then, and I'd get a hiding time and again. But one day I was landed one on the nose that made me bleed. It was the best blow I ever had, as the doctor forbade me to fight any more.'

Bullying was again a problem in the 1890s and changes were made.

In the early 1900s the training became land-based.

Numbers varied depending upon the number of Lieutenants needed in the Navy, but there were about 100 entrants each year. The Entrance Examination included the following subjects, arithmetic, algebra, Euclid, French, Latin, English, history, geography, any living language with the exception of French, and elementary drawing. Latin had been dropped in 1869.

An 1894 letter began,

'My dear mother,
This is a very jolly place as soon as I get settled down.
Old fellows came back this morning, fainted at drill, don't know why... Like the hammocks...Awfully low roofs but very jolly with the old fellows. Learn dancing. Been ashore...Awfully hard punishments...Much love dear old mother...'

He also sent a letter to his brothers Gunny and Cyril with more detail,

'Not bad grub. Good deal of work and play. Mostly nice boys...I have not been out with the beagles yet' (Britannia formed a beagle pack in 1878). *'Lots of seagulls here. Ship lighted with electric light.'* (The first practical use of electric light in a building was courtesy of Joseph Swan and was also in 1878) *'250 boys on board. There are some awful fools on board. There is an awful lot of fagging and bullying here. It is awful fun here'*

Who was he trying to convince?

Some records suggest he had flaws. After Naval College he tried for the Royal Navy which would usually be almost automatic, but failed to gain entrance. At some stage during his young life, someone wrote a critique of Bertie's character which ended up in the family papers. There is no evidence as to the identity of the author, and it must be assumed that it was one of his teachers or officers'. It is both perspicacious and revealing, and reflects his strengths throughout his life.

'Bertie. Brains well placed. Sharp and clever – too much so sometimes – steady – industrious, intellectual – rather than social or friendly – great tenacity of life – with ability to bear pain. Wanting in patience and continuity – too fond of change – soon tiring of anything undertaken – great love of possessions – admiration for all things artistic – great refinement – good at language and able to express himself well. Good imitative ability – quick at buying and keen insight into the value of things – therefore make good auctioneer – good as barrister or doctor – practical – enquiring turn of mind – faith in the unseen – where provoked would show great firmness – where tempted, weakness – great activity – restlessness.'

After failing to get into the Royal Navy, he decided to become a Merchant Sea Officer.

He served first as a midshipman on board a four-masted steel barque, the Hinemoa. She was a fast ship, built in 1890 in Greenock, length 278 feet and displacement 2,283 tons.

She was probably the first four-masted barque to visit New Zealand, when she arrived at Wellington on December 28, 1892, after a voyage of 78 days.

According to the New Zealand Maritime Record, she was reputed to be the only sailing ship built with freezing-machinery for the transport of up to 20,000 carcases of mutton from New Zealand, but she carried general cargo as well. This machinery was later removed and she then carried many thousands of immigrants to that colony. She was reported as being a handy, well-behaved ship with a good turn of speed.

According to Basil Lubbock in his book 'The Last of The Wind Jammers', she had a bit of a chequered history. One of her captains went mad, another was dismissed for criminal offenses, while still another became such a hopeless drunkard that at one stage the crew took over the running of the ship. A later captain was found shot with a revolver by his side, while his successor also died a violent death, though not aboard the Hinemoa; he shot himself while on a minesweeper off Lowestoft.

She was eventually sunk during a voyage from Australia to Great Britain by a German submarine, 35 miles WSW of Bishop Rock on September 7, 1917.

Bertie, now an experienced sailor aged 20, wrote home from the Hinemoa in 1898.

'April 28th., off the Lizards.

I am writing a line to you in case any fishing boat comes near enough. We have a dead head wind and cannot beat up against it...If we get a southerly wind, (which is unlikely) we can be home in 24 hours. All well and had a fine passage. Longing to get home to you all. Have such lots to ask you about...come and meet me...and bring...some good cigarettes. Have not had any bread or potatoes for weeks. Very short of all ordinary food. But plenty of meat and biscuits. No time for more as a small ship close to us and may take my letter.'

Later in 1898, Bertie joined the British India Steamship Company and developed his career with them.

He gained his Second mate's Certificate in the same year.

Over the following years he gained experience and rank, rising to 1st Officer.

In June 1905, he was on board the S.S. Mombassa, bound for London, working his passage as 4th Officer to go back for his three-yearly leave.

Bertie was on his way home. All was well with the world. He was a free spirit and enjoying his life.

Chapter 10
Beatrice Martha

21 September 1906

In the September of 1906, Beatrice Martha Harrod found herself temporarily back in London, having been living for some months in Tunbridge Wells. She was 29 years of age, single, and heavily pregnant.

Were it not for her predicament, she might have found London very exciting.

King Edward VII had been on the throne for five years after a very long wait as the Prince of Wales. London was buzzing with new construction, extensions to the Underground and the new Vauxhall Bridge. The Suffragettes were in full flow.

1906 had been the hottest September in living memory with temperatures in some parts of the country up to 97°F, (36°C). It would have been very uncomfortable for anyone in her condition.

She was installed in a Nursing Home in Kensington, at 22, Cheniston Gardens, ready for the birth of her child. She had had to run away from her home to stay with her sister in order to hide her condition, and someone in the family, probably her brother Henry, had found this home run by Miss Emily Perks.

Beatrice's father had died suddenly in the August of the previous year, 1905, and I suspect this event may have had some influence on her behaviour over the following months, during which time she became pregnant.

It seems as though she never revealed the name of the father to her family, and from what I have found out since, the father himself never found out about the pregnancy.

In the early Twentieth Century, an illegitimate pregnancy for a girl of Beatrice Martha's social status was disastrous. Though adultery amongst married women was more frequent in the Victorian and Edwardian middle and upper classes than history might suggest, sexual liaisons amongst unmarried women were not common until the First World War. There was no such thing as a legal abortion, and though illegal back-street terminations of pregnancy were easy to find, they carried a huge risk to the mother and were not infrequently fatal.

Many discrete advertisements were to be found in publications, advertising potions and powders, laxatives and tonics that contained thinly veiled suggestions that they might help a girl out of a difficult situation. They were almost always ineffective. Amongst working-class women, the folklore was rich. Purgatives were a popular choice to try to induce a miscarriage, pennyroyal (a herb), aloes and turpentine were all used, as were very hot baths and gin, extreme exertion, and occasionally in desperation, a fall down a flight of stairs.

Beatrice Martha may have tried some of these 'remedies' when she discovered she was pregnant. Though missing a period was the obvious sign, most women of this era had to wait several months to confirm they were pregnant because of the lack of any simple tests for pregnancy.

Approaching a doctor for help and confirmation would have been very difficult for her. As a single girl in 1905, her range of knowledge about sex and pregnancy would have been limited to what she had learnt from her older sisters and friends. Books and articles about the subject were intended for married women and often gave incorrect advice to judge by today's standards. I can remember seeing a 1920s 'Health Manual' which got the 'safe time of the month' and 'the time to get pregnant' completely the wrong way around!

In some families, especially middle- and working-class families, illegitimate babies might be 'absorbed' into the family and passed off as the children of sisters, cousins, aunts or even on occasions, the baby's grandmother. This choice was not available to Beatrice Martha.

She would have had little alternative but to try to disappear for the later stages of the pregnancy, have the baby and then hope to find an adoption agency. Any thoughts of keeping the baby would have been foolish and would have made her a social outcast.

So, she duly gave birth to the child in the Nursing Home on the 21 September 1906 and arrangements would have been made for an adoption. One assumes this would have been as soon as possible after the birth. However, the records show that Beatrice in person registered the child locally in mid-October, 19 days after the birth, giving the address of the Nursing Home.

A 'lying-in' period of 14 days or more would have been the norm at that time, so it must have been unusual for her still to be at the Nursing Home with the baby that long after the birth.

She named the baby John Stanley Harrod. Later research showed that John was the first name of his father, though this was not the name by which his father, or the child, was usually known. Stanley was a name with no obvious connection to Beatrice or her relations. It is not a name associated with many famous people, but was at its most popular in the early 1900s. There was Henry Morton Stanley, the journalist who 'found' Livingstone in Africa in 1871, and reputedly greeted him with the phrase, 'Dr Livingstone I presume'. He died in 1904. He was incidentally, also was an illegitimate child.

What happened immediately after the registration is not clear. The discovery of Dad's baptism record produced more questions than answers. He was christened C. of E. on the 2 November, 1906, at St. Peter's Church, in the small Gloucestershire village of Frampton Cotterell, just north of Bristol.

He would have been six weeks old.

Oddly, according to the original record, he was christened John Reginald Stanley Harrod. His mother's name was given as Beatrice Martha, but there is no other information in the record.

This might suggest that he was still in the care of his mother at this point, six weeks after his birth.

Try as I might, I could find no connection between Frampton Cotterell and the Harrod family, their friends or servants, to account for the choice of this village. Nor does the name Reginald feature in the family, or in any of the residents of this village in the 1911 census who might have had a connection.

I thought it possible that 'Reginald' was a transcription error from the baptism before or after Dad, but this proved not to be the case and Dad was the only child baptised at that church on that day, so confusion would be unlikely. I thought the alternative explanation might be that he had already been adopted by a family who wanted to add Reginald to his name.

A more recent search of Frampton Cotterell records revealed an orphanage in the village in the 1911 census, a finding confirmed in the 1901 and 1891 censuses.

The St. Michael's Cottage Orphan Home, Frampton Cotterell was opened in 1881 as an overflow offshoot of a similar institution in the nearby village of Winterbourne.

Information from www.childrenshomes.co.uk run by Peter Winterbotham, and from the Frenchay Museum Archives who hold the Winterbourne Parish Records, have revealed more information.

The home was set up in some conjoined cottages known at Step House, Penny Lane (now Park Lane) in Frampton. It was run by an order of C. of E. nuns called the Sisters of Mercy. Having opened in 1881, it eventually closed in 1921. The initial Superintendent, Sister Emily Dufar Clark, ran the home for several decades.

The Home was listed in the 1888 Charities Register as a home for the reception of orphans, destitute, friendless, illegitimate and suffering children of both sexes. That is guaranteed to pull the heartstrings of donors.

Children were admitted from birth up to 8 years for boys and 10 years for girls, staying to the ages of 14 and 16 years respectively.

They were given an education, a secure environment and then discharged with new outfits when situations were found for them. Most of the girls went into service and the boys into a trade. Money was always in short supply, and though the worst cases were looked after for free, many others were 'paying' guests. They relied heavily upon donations of money, food and clothes.

By the mid-1890s, they were more frequently admitting unwanted babies and starting to arrange adoptions to deserving childless couples. The Parish Records available only go up to 1895, so for the moment nothing more can be found.

This would certainly explain Dad's baptism in Frampton. I have presumed he was a 'paying' entrant to the home soon after his birth registration, and at some stage between 1906 and 1910, probably earlier rather than later, he was adopted from there.

The connection between Beatrice Martha and the home in Frampton remains undiscovered, though doubtless she or her family would have been paying for the service provided.

Though the Sisters' order had a branch in London in 1881, there was no orphanage attached there.

It is possible that there was an arrangement between the Nursing Home in Cheniston Gardens and St. Michael's Home, but nothing has been found to confirm this.

Sometime after his stay in Frampton, Dad found his way to Manchester and into the care of the Taylors.

I have no doubt that when Beatrice Martha made these arrangements, she thought she was securing a safe future for her baby. She was not to know the way things turned out.

The birth certificate for Dad that was issued in 1906 in Kensington must have gone astray at some time between its issue, and Dad's arrival in Hull, as the certificate that he discovered with his other papers in Sergeant's drawer was a copy obtained in November 1910.

Dad, as we know, eventually found this documentation. Together with the letters from the Hostel of Hope, the certificate would for the first time have given Dad some inkling of his origins. He found out that he was actually called John Stanley Harrod, that the Taylors were not his real parents, that he had been born in Kensington to a woman who came from a 'very respectable family' and that his father was a Merchant Navy Captain.

Quite a lot to find out in one go.

It is difficult to imagine the train of thought this find would have set in motion in the mind of my 17-year-old father. It must have made him want to find answers to at least some of the questions posed.

Though Dad always suggested to his family that he was not interested in his origins, there is some evidence to suggest that he may have made attempts to find out more, perhaps during one of his trips to London in later life.

He knew that he had been born in a nursing home. Unless this was just a guess, it was something he could only have discovered from the London Street Directories or the telephone directories of 1905 or 1906, which identify 22, Cheniston Gardens as a nursing home.

My attempt to find out what had happened started in 1986 with only the same documents as those available to Dad.

The obvious place for me to start the research for Dad's origin was his birth certificate copy, it was the only important lead that I had.

The early stages of the investigation proved very exciting as new information was found. During those first few years I spent a great deal of time travelling across the country, visiting large records offices and laboriously wading through index books and paper records. I wrote hundreds of letters for information and help to anybody who seemed to be in any way connected. This style of research is all but finished these days. There is so much available now on the internet; that makes research less exciting but a great deal easier.

The birth certificate states that his mother Beatrice Martha Harrod was 29 years old at the time of Dad's birth. The address in Kensington, so close to Knightsbridge and the Brompton Road, raised my hopes that perhaps there was a 'Harrods' connection, something that had only been whispered between us as part of Dad's ancestral mythology.

I made an initial visit to London with my wife and daughter Jo and this proved very rewarding.

We started by looking at 'Births, Marriages and Deaths', in the paper records in huge index books at St. Catherine's House, on The Aldwych.

We soon found Dad's original birth entry and a birth certificate for Beatrice Martha. It was astonishing to find that her father was Charles Digby Harrod, a Grocer and Tea Dealer, living at that time in Sydenham.

Though there was almost nothing available on line in 1987, other non-digital records were available, and the paper census records proved a godsend. They were kept at The Family Records Centre in Myddleton Street, London, on microfiche, with paper records available to order for a later date. It was a simple, but time-consuming task, to trace the whereabouts of most of the Harrod family up to 1881, which was the latest census date then available under the 100-year rule.

The other useful source of information was the probate records and wills. The Probate records are created by the distribution of a person's estate after death. Since 1858 they have been stored centrally, and those prior to 1858 were available in records offices around the country.

The records post-1858 were stored at the time in Somerset House, on the south side of the Strand. The index could be searched, and then paper copies of the probate documents and the will were ordered. These records were not only interesting in their own right, but the wills produced a 'spray' of previously unknown relatives and other names to trace elsewhere, plus some insight from the possessions bequeathed into the life of the individual. They were very helpful.

Using the censuses and wills I was able to piece together a really good picture of the family.

The explosion of results confirmed that our Harrod family was indeed the 'Harrods' family. Charles Digby's father, Charles Henry Harrod was the founder of Harrods.

We found Beatrice Martha had one brother and six sisters, and discovered Charles Digby's brothers and his family connections. We soon realised that I and my brothers were the only living descendants of Charles Digby Harrod who still retained the surname Harrod.

The rationale was simple. Beatrice Martha's sisters had either married, their children therefore taking their husbands' names, or in two cases remained unmarried. Her only brother, Henry Herbert Harrod, had never married, nor had any children. Beatrice Martha's illegitimate child retained the Harrod name by default.

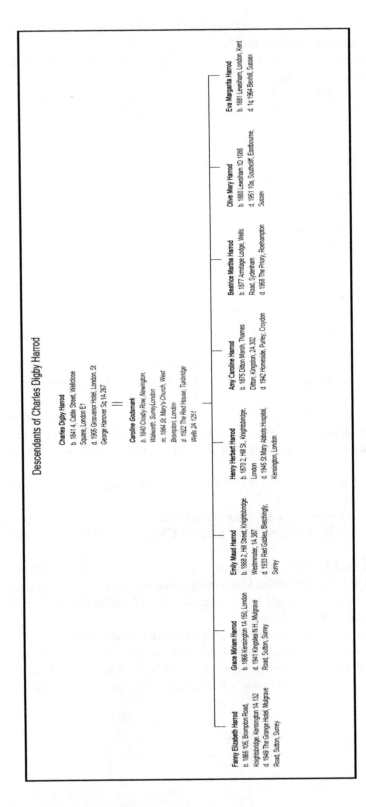

Descendants of Charles Digby Harrod

Charles Digby Harrod
b. 1841 4, Castle Street, Welldose
Square, London E1
d. 1905 Grosvenor Hotel, London. St
George Hanover Sq 1A 267

=

Caroline Godsmark
b. 1840 Crosdry Row, Newington,
Walworth, Surrey.London
m. 1864 St. Mary's Church, West
Brompton, London
d. 1922 The Red House, Turbridge
Wells 2A 1251

Fanny Elizabeth Harrod
b. 1865 105, Brompton Road,
Knightsbridge, Kensington 1A 132
d. 1949 The Grange Hotel, Mulgrave
Road, Sutton, Surrey

Grace Miriam Harrod
b. 1866 Kensington 1A 150, London
d. 1941 Kingsles N.H., Mulgrave
Road, Sutton, Surrey

Emily Maud Harrod
b. 1868 2, Hill Street, Knightsbridge.
Westminster, 1A 387
d. 1933 Red Gables, Bletchingly,
Surrey

Henry Herbert Harrod
b. 1870 2, Hill St., Knightsbridge.
London
d. 1945 St.Mary Abbots Hospital,
Kensington, London

Amy Caroline Harrod
b. 1875 Ditton Marsh, Thames
Ditton, Kingston, 2A 302
d. 1942 Homeside, Purley, Croydon

Beatrice Martha Harrod
b. 1877 Armitage Lodge, Wells
Road, Sydenham
d. 1958 The Priory, Roehampton

Olive Mary Harrod
b. 1880 Lewisham 1D 1066
d. 1951 10a, Southcliff, Eastbourne,
Sussex

Eva Margarita Harrod
b. 1881 Lewisham, London, Kent
d. 1q 1964 Bexhill, Sussex

Chart 4: Descendants of Charles Digby Harrod

The biggest mystery was Beatrice Martha herself. Try as we might; and by this stage 'we' included most of my immediate family and my two brothers, we could find no trace of her marriage or death, or any other children she might have had.

I had hit a brick wall. I could not find any further trace of her.

Given her age, 29 when she gave birth to Dad, I began to assume that in that strait-laced era, she might have remained unmarried following the trauma and shame of her illegitimate child. This did not explain the lack of a death certificate, unless she had changed her name or lived abroad.

As often happens during family history tracing, a sideways step eventually revealed the answers.

I contacted the Harrods Archivist of the time, Natalie Hansen, who was very interested in our connection and very helpful. I started to trace the living descendants of Beatrice Martha's siblings, and tried to get in touch with them to see if anything more was known by them about my father.

In the same year, 1987, we visited the address on Dad's birth certificate, 22, Cheniston Gardens, Kensington, which Dad had correctly thought was a Private Nursing Home. The house was in a rundown condition and in multiple occupation. It was south of Kensington High Street, in the Parish of St. Mary Abbots, and a stone's throw from Knightsbridge. In 2008, when I visited the property again, the house had been renovated and was in much better condition.

My research in Street Directories and Electoral registers at the Family Records Centre showed the listed resident at that address between 1904 and 1909 to be a Miss Emily Perks. The property was quite large, it had 12 principal rooms.

A search for Miss Perks elsewhere was unsuccessful. There was a professional nurse of the same name working in private houses outside London in the 1891 and 1901 censuses, and another at the City of Westminster Infirmary, in Fulham, in 1920 and 1921. There was not enough information to link any of these ladies to the Nursing Home. The Central Midwives Board records for 1906, stored at Kew, show no registered midwife of that name. I guess she either may have been an enthusiastic amateur, or just the resident owner.

I continued my research whenever I could, but the time available was limited by some rather important distractions. I was working full time as a general practitioner with long hours and regular nights on call, my wife was working full time, we had three growing girls and we were trying to complete the renovation of our large Victorian house. Looking back, I do not know how I managed to do any research at all.

Most of the further work was done at home. I wrote a lot of letters. I looked for anything and everything connected with the Harrod name. I posted my interest in a number of genealogical publications and joined genealogical societies. I had dozens of replies from worldwide Harrods, most of who were certain they would find a link to the Harrods of Knightsbridge. I talked to and corresponded with researchers in the U.S.A., Sweden, Australia and New Zealand. I ended up with a lot of disparate Harrod family trees, but none of them linked to our family.

New Zealand researchers sent details of William Digby Harrod, an unmarried son of Charles Henry Harrod, who had emigrated to New Zealand in 1863 and subsequently died there. I was even sent photographs of his grave. I found out all sorts of information about other Harrods and the shop, most of which was interesting, and some of which was useful.

There was a (now no longer connected) branch of Harrods in Buenos Aires.

There was a defunct but connected branch of Harrods in Winchester.

There was a very distant relative, James Harrod, who was the first European to get through the Kentucky Gap in the U.S.A. (Harrodsville in Kentucky was named after him in 1774). He sadly and literally met a sticky end when the native American Indians he had fought against finally caught up with him, and relieved him of his scalp.

There were the other sons of Charles Henry Harrod, all of who had 'Digby' as their middle name.

I found an entry in 'Who's Who' listing a Major General Lionel Alexander Digby Harrod. He turned out to be in his late 60s, a great grandson of Charles Henry Harrod, and the son of one of Charles Digby's brothers. He was an illustrious soldier, still very active and involved in Army recruitment. At last, I thought I had made a breakthrough, I had found a living related Harrod to question.

He was not at all fazed by my approach and our tenuous connection, and readily met with me, my family and my brothers. He was a delightful man and we enjoyed one another's company. However, he did not have any information about my branch of the Harrod family.

The real breakthrough came after further visits to Somerset House to look at the Wills of various members of the Harrod clan. The married names of the Harrod sisters, and hence some of their descendants became traceable.

Once the initial log-jam had been broken, there followed several years of detailed tracing of the family. I was able to make contact with descendants of most of the married sisters of Beatrice Martha.

They were all interested in the story and were welcoming to us, despite us being latecomers to the family. Sadly, none of them knew anything about the existence, let alone the birth, of my father.

The culmination of my Harrod research was a meeting I arranged for all the known (and available) descendants of Charles Digby Harrod in Bath in 2009, where I presented a brief resume of my findings. Interesting, but no new information was forthcoming.

I was determined to put down on paper everything that I had discovered for future generations.

This included my research into other branches of my family, and my wife's family. The writing started in 2008 and I was finished by the end of 2011.

The publication was more extensive than I had envisaged, running to over 300,000 pages with more than 1000 illustrations and photographs. It could only be produced and distributed as a CD.

It was definitely a reference document, and not one I expected anyone to read.

Despite all this effort, inevitably there remained many unsolved mysteries, as you will see, and these continue to be investigated. Family research has no final goal and continues as Parkinson's Law decrees, to expand to fill the space available.

I will give a brief resume of the Harrods I have found so far.

The earliest direct Harrod ancestor I have found is William Harrod, (who was born about 1769 and died in 1812). He was an Exciseman who worked in Suffolk and later Essex. He was my great, great, great grandfather.

An exciseman, also known as a gauger, was employed by the Board of Excise (an early precursor of H.M.R.C.) in order to ensure that people, especially traders, paid their taxes. He would have travelled on horseback in small groups, or rides, to chase up tax payments.

Excisemen were not popular, hence they were quite well paid, were not usually employed in their home district, and were seldom employed for too long in any one place.

William Harrod married a local Suffolk girl, Tamah Mason, (who was born in 1776 and died in 1811), in her home village of Hartest, and they had at least five, and possibly six children, born in the various parts of the country where William was posted at the time. These children became orphans when their mother died in 1811, followed soon after by their father in 1812. Their causes of death are not known.

The eldest surviving child, Charles Henry Harrod, (born in 1799 and died in 1885), was reputed to have started life as a Miller in Clacton, Essex, though there is no objective evidence to confirm this.

The first written record of him after his father's death in 1812 was running a Draper's shop in Southwark, South London in 1824. Later records show that he was caught up in the 'Panic of 1825', an economic crisis caused by a stock market crash. He was in partnership for a while with a William Wicking, but this was dissolved in 1826. Despite these setbacks his listing in Southwark continued until about 1831. During this time, in 1830, he married Elizabeth Digby, a Miller's daughter from Birch, Essex, just south of Colchester. She was born in 1810 and died in 1860. William had worked around this area for about 10 years and may have met her there some years earlier.

This finding of this first 'Harrods' shop in Southwark was a new discovery, unknown to the Harrods store or previous Harrod historians. Harrods had always prided themselves that Harrod was the first of the major London store owners to have started his life as a grocer, rather than a draper. Sadly, they were now proved wrong, and were not especially thrilled to hear about it.

In 1832, he opened premises for the first time north of the Thames in Upper Whitecross Street, near Old Street, and then settled in Cable Street in Limehouse, East London with his wife and family,

With the move to the north bank, he opened a retail business as a grocer and tea dealer. Cable Street is where the accepted 'Harrods' story began.

After an apparently barren five years, Charles and Elizabeth had a child in 1835 and eventually had five children, three of who survived. Charles Henry went 'missing' for a few years from 1836, spending time in prison, as you will see in a later chapter, and during this absence his brother Frederick took over the shop for him.

He had 20 successful years in East London, running both a retail and a wholesale business.

The wholesale business, as a *'Dealer in Colonial Goods'*, was from premises in Eastcheap.

On the back of his financial success, in 1854 he made a decisive move to premises in a then run-down and rather peripheral area of West London, the Brompton Road, where he took over an existing grocery business. He recognised the potential of the area as the London population spread westwards following the Great Exhibition of 1851 in Hyde Park.

This was the start of the Harrods store and empire that we know today.

He made slow progress initially, living above the shop at 9, Middle Queen Buildings, and slowly expanding his range of goods. The pace of change may have been governed, not by lack of ambition as some have suggested, but by lack of finance after the purchase of the premises and business.

His eldest surviving son, Charles Digby Harrod, (who was born in 1841 and died in 1905), joined him in business as a teenager and eventually bought out his father in the early 1860s. By this time, Charles Henry had been in business over 40 years. He had gradually expanded and modernised the business and was probably happy to let go of the reins. The solid base laid by Charles Henry was enhanced by the vision, vigour and ambition of Charles Digby, who transformed the business from just another grocery store into a hugely successful department store. The rate of change went from 2nd. gear into overdrive.

Charles Henry's second son, William Digby Harrod, (born in 1842 and died in 1907), was the oddball of the family. He seemed to have had no interest in the business. In 1863, with some members of his mother's Digby family, he emigrated to New Zealand, where they all became farmers.

William fought in the Maori Wars for which he was granted land by the Government. He never married, and lived and died in New Zealand.

The youngest surviving brother, Henry Digby Harrod, (who was born in 1845 and died in 1915), initially joined his father and brother in the Brompton Road shop. It looks as though Henry did not get on well with his brother Charles, and so he left and branched out, and supported by his father, opened several small grocery shops in other parts of London over the course of several years.

Henry married Caroline Wade, an Ironmonger's daughter from Suffolk and they had 12 children. They moved to Winchester where Henry ran a successful grocery and tea dealing business. One of his children, Frank, a teacher by profession, had a rather distinguished army career in World War I.

One of his grandchildren, Lionel, who was already mentioned earlier, also had an army career, ending up as a Major-General.

The 1860s had proved to be a momentous decade for the three Harrod brothers. Charles Digby took over the shop from his father, Henry Digby started the process of setting up on his own, and William Digby emigrated to New Zealand. These three events may well have been related to each other.

As we saw earlier, the only son, Henry Herbert Harrod, was not interested in the business and went his own way.

In 1891 Charles Digby decided to retire and sold the store to a Limited Company.

He began his well-earned retirement.

The family's settled existence was shattered in August 1905 by Charles Digby's sudden death. After the annual garden party in Heathfield, Charles Digby and Elizabeth went up to London to take a break in his favourite hotel in London, the Grosvenor in Victoria. He suffered a heart attack during his stay. The family were devastated, and nothing was going to be quite the same afterwards.

Beatrice Martha Harrod, the fifth daughter of Charles Digby and Caroline born in 1877, was resident in December 1905 with the family at Culverwood for their first Christmas without her father. It would have been a sad occasion, the first Christmas without his dominant figure in their lives, and the last the family would spend in the area before their move early the next year to Tunbridge Wells. It was during this festive period that the liaison which resulted in my father's birth took place. The father of the child remained a mystery to all apart from Beatrice Martha until over 100 years later, in 2007.

Prior to 1905, Beatrice Martha seems to have led an uneventful early life as far as I have been able to learn. Her appearances in the censuses of 1881 and 1891 at the various residences of the family are some of the few sources of information.

During her early life in Sydenham, her father would have been much involved in the business so that she may not have seen a lot of him. As an affluent family, her mother had plenty of help in the house and she had several sisters at home to keep her busy. Beatrice's paternal grandmother and maternal grandfather had died many years before her birth, and her other grandfather, Charles Henry Harrod died when she was eight years old.

She and her sisters were very close to their maternal grandmother, Caroline Godsmark, and her family, the Kibbles. Her Godsmark grandmother had been herself widowed after only 10 years of marriage in 1849 but had then remarried a lovely man, Beatrice's step-grandfather, Robert Jones.

During her teenage years she and some of her sisters spent time with the Kibbles, and also with their Harrod cousins, the children of her Uncle, Henry Digby Harrod.

Beatrice is missing from the 1901 census, when aged 24, as are her mother and father, and some of her unmarried sisters. No reason was discovered at the time to account for this; missing information in the censuses is not uncommon and it seemed logical that if one entry was missing, then the whole family might be missing from the same address. However, when it later became available on line, a search of the Find My Past website for passport applications between 1896 and 1901 revealed the reason.

In January 1901, Beatrice Martha, her mother, and two of her sisters applied for passports. Charles Digby had obtained a passport at an earlier date.

They went on holiday together. During that period of time between the sale of Morebath Manor and their move into Culverwood, in Sussex, the family were homeless and went off abroad for a while. No passenger lists were recorded for cross-channel journeys, the records that exist are for boat traffic beyond Europe, and they do not appear in these latter records. My assumption is that they went off for a European Grand Tour.

Chapter 11
Countess Marie

Late 1909

Things were getting more difficult for Marie.

Money was the problem. She seems to have been struggling for a number of years despite her skirmish with the aristocracy 17 years earlier.

She was born in Yverdon, Switzerland on the 28 February 1862. Some records give 1864 as her year of birth, but the majority opt for 1862. Yverdon-les-Bains is a town in the Vaud canton at the southern end of Lake Neuchâtel. The surrounding area has been occupied since the Neolithic Age and was settled by the Romans. The Spa which flourished there in the 18th century had fallen into disrepair through neglect in the mid-1800s and was not renovated until the late 19th century.

There were about five thousand inhabitants at the time of Marie's birth. The area is French speaking and there was a significant Protestant population including Marie and her family.

She gave her name at her marriage to the Count in 1892 as Irma Marie de Joly, however, despite extensive searching, no-one of that name or similar are listed in the births or baptisms in Yverdon between 1862 and 1864. Upon her marriage she became the Countess Irma Marie Grotta zu Grottenegg.

I know from her later history that she was not averse to telling porkies. (Cockney rhyming slang: lies – pork pies – porkies). So it is possible that her name, date and place of birth are a fantasy. She might have been born elsewhere and with a different name, or have been previously married. I cannot be certain.

There were several families called Joly in the Yverdon area at the time, including a family of restaurant owners, a baker, a lawyer and a President of the local State Council. Other Joly family members are known to have emigrated to Canada between the World Wars.

It would certainly not have been beyond her capabilities to add the 'de' to her name in the lead up to her marriage to her count.

There are individuals to be found elsewhere with the name de Joly. The most famous was Marie Emillie Thérèse de Joly, known as Mademoiselle de Cloin. She was a mistress of the Grand Dauphin, son of Louis XIV. Born in 1670, the daughter of a Baron, she was a lady in waiting, lover and morganatic wife to the Dauphin, who was called 'Grand' because of his size. They produced one child, a boy, who died early in childhood. There are still some de Jolys in Paris who may be related to Marie Emillie. I found one de Joly in Switzerland, Etienne, who was a teacher at a private Catholic school in the first half of the 20th century.

Perhaps Marie may have added the 'de' after reading about the royal mistress in order to invent an aristocratic background.

That first sighting of Marie in the records that I have found was at the death of the Count in 1893, and as she later in her life acted as a nurse, I have made a guess that she became entangled with the Count because of her occupation. I have not been able to document or explain her move from Switzerland to Vienna nor how she met the Count. I have not been able to find a record of the wedding but it was acknowledged and her details were given in an announcement of the Count's death.

Nurses in that era were often not trained or qualified in any formal way, but became skilled after working with other nurses and gradually gaining experience.

After the death of the Count a year after their marriage, Marie may not have been left financially secure. The money and property passed by the terms of the family Trust to his sons, and though she may have been left an individual bequest, this was unlikely to have lasted very long, and she may have reverted to her nursing to make a living.

Her next recorded sighting was in Vienna in 1902, living in Lazarethgasse, in the IX district, house number 3. From 1908 she was at number 29 and in 1909 at number 18. Most of these buildings in Vienna were tall apartment buildings, with several flats on each floor.

During a visit to Vienna a few years ago I managed to find some of the many apartments that she had lived, some of which were still in existence.

They were certainly no longer 'smart' places to live, and I suspect never were.

She moved about frequently in the subsequent years, and her whereabouts could be followed using the Vienna archives.

Number 18 Lazarethgasse, where she resided in 1909, is now a busy modern medical clinic named the Goldenes Kreuz (Golden Cross) Clinic. The clinic occupies a very much altered old building in number 16 and 18. The clinic now specialises in obstetrics.

My research showed that in 1909 Lazarettgasse 18 was still a private address, and not yet a nursing home. The Clinic did not open until 1913 when number 16 was purchased and number 18 was not added to the clinic until some years later. The site was originally in the grounds of Vienna's old Lunatic Asylum, and according to the 'Graphic Guide to Vienna, 1873', the site of some spa springs.

What little evidence there is suggests that Marie was living at number 18 whilst working as nurse.

Though I am now entering the realm of total guesswork, this is based on a mixture of my admittedly limited knowledge of some of the characters and some vague rumours voiced by the families involved.

There is some circumstantial evidence which suggests a continuing link between Josef Grotta, the Count's second son, and Marie, after the death of Josef's father in 1893 and brother Friederich in 1895.

I suspect they were both devious and untrustworthy characters and would have been drawn to each other. Josef would have played the swashbuckling ex Cavalry Officer and Marie the widowed Countess. They were both probably short of money.

The Golden Cross organisation was founded in 1893 for Officers of the Imperial Army and was supported by the Imperial Household. They bought the property in Lazarethgasse in 1910 to turn into a clinic for the civil service courtesy of a donation from Heinrich and Therese Wieser. By completion in 1913, the clinic had 31 rooms and 45 beds. It was used as a hospital for the wounded during World War I.

One of the court cases in Vienna against Count Eduard Grotta, in 1893 and shortly before his death, involved some sort of fraud of a Civil Service Association Consortium supported by the Austrian Monarchy. It was reported in the newspaper *Wiener Zeitung*, on the 10 June 1893.

My translation is not accurate and so there may be no connection at all.

Additionally, and perhaps even more tenuously, an occupant of Lazarethgasse 16 at the same time as Marie was in number 18 was Rudolph Krassnigg, a writer and journalist, known for his humorous stories about military life. He was born in Klagenfurt in 1861 and died in Vienna in March 1909. It is likely he would have known or known of the Grotta family; whose family estates were in Klagenfurt.

Marie remains a rather mysterious character with little information about her life. One way or another, she ends up playing a large part in the life of Beatrice Martha.

Chapter 12
Beatrice Martha

12 December 1909

In the December of 1909, Beatrice Martha Harrod was in Vienna. She had travelled there from Paris a few days earlier.

She was staying in an apartment, the residence of the widowed Countess Maria Grotta zu Grottenegg.

Were it not for her predicament, Beatrice might have found Vienna very exciting. Her condition would mean she was not in the mood to take a trip on the Wiener Riesenrad, Vienna's giant wheel.

The beautiful old-world city of Vienna, then the centre and capital of the Austro-Hungarian Empire, ruled by the much-loved Emperor Franz Josef, was at the pinnacle of its growth and sophistication.

The Empire stretched from the Tyrol to Transylvania, from Albania to Prague and Krakow, and Vienna was a very wealthy city.

The magnificent circular boulevard, the Ringstrasse, had been built in 1865 and was followed by the construction of magnificent public buildings around the road over the following 30 years.

By the time of his death in 1910, the Mayor of Vienna, Karl Lueger, known as handsome Karl, had transformed the city. In addition to the grand showy buildings, he had built homes for the poor and elderly, expanded the pipeline bringing Alpine water to the city and built a municipal gas works.

Sadly, he also had become known for his anti-Semitic views and racist policies against non-German minorities.

The population had risen rapidly over the previous three decades, and though the Empire itself was on the wane, Vienna was still a city with the buzz of opportunity.

It was a very fashionable city, a centre of high culture and modernism, cosmopolitan and artistic.

Vienna played host to composers such as Brahms, Bruckner, Mahler and Richard Strauss.

According to the 1910 census, the population of Vienna was around 2.1 million, and the city was expected to expand further to as much as 4 million. It was the sixth largest city in the world at the time.

Vienna was also an immigrant city, with Czechs and Jews leading the way.

Alongside the development of the city, the economy also experienced an upswing. Historians often describe the last years before the war as a 'second Gründerzeit', a period of economic expansion in the 19th century. The streets of Vienna were paved with culture and the city was awash with architects, actors, painters, musicians, psychoanalysts and philosophers.

At the same time, Adolf Hitler, Leon Trotsky, Joseph Tito, Sigmund Freud and Joseph Stalin all lived within a few miles of each other in central Vienna, and many of them were regulars at the same coffee houses.

Hitler moved there from his hometown of Braunau am Inn, near Linz, in 1908, with the goal of attending the art academy and becoming a great artist. He was 20 years old in 1909 and was struggling to make a living due to a mixture of his laziness and a lack of talent. He was at a low point in his life. That December he moved for the first time into a shelter for homeless men.

The author and historian Manfried Rauchensteiner was prompted to say:

'We believe that humanity is entering into a long and blessed period of peace' – an assumption that was soon to prove hugely incorrect.

The discovery of this part of Beatrice's life was pure chance. As with a lot of family history research, it was found because of persistence, luck, coincidence and serendipity.

In 2008, almost a hundred years after the events, I found by chance some documents in the National Archives that described the events in 1916 which were the result of Beatrice's trip to Vienna in 1909. Later research furnished me with the details, which are covered in a later chapter.

How and why Beatrice Martha chose Vienna for the birth of her second illegitimate child remains a mystery.

There must have been a historical connection between her and the Countess, and though no evidence exists, I have formulated a rational explanation that until proved otherwise remains the best guess.

The records show that Beatrice travelled abroad with her family to Europe in 1901/1902 on what was probably the equivalent of the old European tour. They would likely have visited Paris and Vienna amongst many other European cities. Beatrice spoke fluent French.

She did not seem to appear in any U.K. records between 1902 and 1905, nor between late 1906 and her appearance in Vienna in late 1910. That is not as unusual as it may sound. Between those dates there were no censuses, and women did not appear in the Electoral Register or in documents related to the ownership of property.

She was eventually found on one occasion during those dates, courtesy of British Newspaper Archives, listed as a guest at her sister Amy's wedding to Arthur Weightman on the 30 October 1907. Otherwise nothing.

My guess is that after having tasted the European life, Beatrice spent time there during part of those dates. If the Countess Marie was trying to earn a living as a nurse, their paths may have crossed.

There is some flimsy evidence that Marie may have worked on board some of the ships giving Mediterranean cruises during this time. The Oceana was one of those ships; she called regularly at Trieste, only 75 miles from Klagenfurt and 250 miles from Vienna.

The possible wild card in the story is the Count Eduard Grotta zu Grottenegg's second son, Josef, who was destined to become the next Count upon the death of his brother in 1895. The Countess Marie was his stepmother and may have kept in touch with him after his father and brother's death. Looking at what I have found out about their characters, both Josef and the Countess were 'chancers'.

As we have seen before, Josef was a dashing Cavalry Officer, and like the father of Beatrice's first child, had a reputation both as a lad and becoming involved in financial difficulties.

Is it possible Josef and Beatrice's paths crossed? She might certainly have been attracted to another happy go lucky man in a uniform Could Josef have been the father of this child? This could explain the connection to the Countess and Vienna.

There is some verbal history to support this speculation. According to family mythology, the father of this baby was supposed to have met Beatrice on a ship in the Mediterranean, and to have been from the aristocracy. However, as I have often found, family mythology is wrong as often as it is right.

As we shall see in later correspondence, Beatrice was able to remain in touch with the father of the baby at a later date, and this might be significant.

Sadly, I have no descendants of Josef to be able to use DNA once again to clarify the issue.

The Vienna Archives list a Beatrix Harrod, given as born in London in August 1880 (she was actually born in April, 1877), as a resident of Lazarettgasse 18, apartment eight, between the 16 December 1909 and the 21 January, 1910. She was listed as Anglican, and a resident of London.

The record states she arrived from Paris and left after her stay for Paris once again. It also stated that this information was given by the Countess Grotta zu Grottenegg, the tenant of the property. The date of birth given is not correct and the date of arrival is 4 days after the date of the birth of the child at that same address, suggesting the Countess may not have known Beatrice's date of birth, or Beatrice lied about it. Not knowing when Beatrice arrived is a bit odd, but perhaps reflects the date the information was given to the Vienna Police Department. More surprisingly again, when the child's birth was registered, the name and date of birth given were incorrect.

Perhaps Beatrice actually arrived on the 16 November, and this is a transcription error. Beatrice would then have arrived three+ weeks before delivery, a reasonable safety margin, and stayed at the apartment a little over nine weeks, until the child would have been 6 weeks old.

It is possible that this information was given by the Countess sometime after the event, and she could not remember the dates exactly.

On balance, I go for the likelihood that she actually arrived on the 16 November and stayed with the Countess for nine weeks.

Beatrice's arrival from and departure back to Paris was unexpected.

Paris may of course have been only an intermediate destination on a train journey from England. A journey from London with cross-channel steamer to Calais, might travel via Paris, then leaving the Gare de Strasbourg, (now Gare d'Est), on the Orient Express via Strasbourg; or direct from Ostend.

I have no information about her whereabouts between 1907 and 1909. I had supposed that with her fluent French she might have lived in Europe for some time but had no information about a stay in Paris.

A search of the Paris City Archives and the Paris Police Records produced no result for Beatrice.

So, on Sunday, 12 December, 1909, at 7.30 in the evening, at the apartment occupied by the Countess Marie, Beatrice Martha gave birth to her second child, once again a boy.

At the time that I discovered this event in 2008, I had no information about the child's name, sex, father's name or subsequent history. It would be several years later, and another chance finding, that would give me that information and more.

Chapter 13
The Countess and Vienna 1916

1916

In 1916, the Countess Marie was still living in Vienna.

Beatrice Martha had returned to Paris in early 1910 and by 1916 her life had moved on in dramatic fashion, as we shall see later.

Marie remained at the same address as in 1909, IX Lazarethgasse 18, until about the summer of 1911, so a total of two years, and then moved around frequently over the following few years, living in at least nine different residences. One or two were in poor areas, and one in a well-known red-light area.

Most of her apartments were in the same district VIII, more so after 1912, and her lengths of stay varied between two weeks and nine months, probably reflecting her parlous state of finances.

By 1916, she had been in VIII Floriangasse 60 for a year or so.

In the Vienna Archives, Beatrice Martha's child is recorded as being with the Countess from April 1912 to February 1913, at four different addresses during those ten months. They may have been together outside those dates as the records are incomplete, and some only list the principal adult resident. However, the lack of certainty about the child's whereabouts raises some possibilities about what was happening.

The presence of an extra mouth to feed would have added to Marie's woes.

Now aged 52, she was almost certainly in more serious financial difficulties than she had been before.

Her situation reflected what was going on in Vienna after two years of the Great War.

The National Archives website tells us that since the early 18th century, with naval supremacy, blockades had been one of the tools often used by Britain. This supremacy was still very much intact when war broke out in 1914, and the British government moved immediately to strangle the supply of raw materials and foodstuffs to Germany and its allies.

British naval ships spent the war patrolling the North Sea, intercepting and detaining thousands of merchant ships thought to be harbouring cargo bound for enemy shores. This aroused considerable anger in neutral countries, many of whom enjoyed strong trading links with the Austro-Hungarian Empire.

Britain declared the North Sea a British 'military area' in November 1914, and despite some discussion about the legality of this, most neutral merchant ships agreed to put into British ports for inspection. Cargo bound for Germany was confiscated and the ships were escorted through the British-laid minefields to their destinations.

The blockade was very effective, helped by a French blockade of the Adriatic ports.

The enemy countered the blockade with a new weapon in the form of submarines or U-boats, with a devastating effect on Allied shipping. The sinking of the Lusitania in May 1915 shocked many neutrals as well as allies and proved counter-productive. The effects of the U-boat threat were limited by the convoy system and eventually provoked the U.S.A. into entering the war.

The British blockade continued unabated and by 1916 the occupants of the Austro-Hungarian Empire often went hungry, though few actually starved. Their system of rationing was, in fact, no less efficient than the systems used in France or Britain.

Apart from food, there was a shortage of raw materials such as coal and various non-ferrous metals, and the blockade cut off vital fertiliser supplies.

Staple foodstuffs such as grain, potatoes, meat and dairy products became so scarce by the winter of 1916 that many people subsisted on a diet of ersatz products that ranged from so-called 'war bread' (Kriegsbrot) to powdered milk. The average daily diet of 1,000 calories was insufficient even for small children. The effects of malnutrition in the form of scurvy, tuberculosis and dysentery were common. The shortages caused looting and food riots, not only in Germany, but also in the Habsburg cities of Vienna and Budapest, where wartime privations were felt equally acutely.

In larger cities, 'war kitchens' provided cheap meals en masse to impoverished local citizens and this together with other rationing had some limited success.

The police reported long queues for certain products. Bread and flour coupons were introduced in April 1915 as the first incisive rationing measures, followed in March/April 1916 by coupons for sugar, coffee, milk, and fat or butter. In spite of the fixing of price ceilings, speculation and hoarding drove prices upwards, with 150 per cent inflation in 1915 and 200 per cent in 1916. Petrol, candles, coal and wood were not to be found.

The district courts were full of cases of profiteering and looting. The names of convicted profiteers were announced in 'pillory lists' or posted in public.

The website of ww1.habsburger.net gives extensive information about the effects and conditions during the war.

'Vienna was not a combat zone, and the population was therefore never confronted directly by the war. This was one reason why the city at the end of the war had not changed much externally. The war nevertheless left its mark in many different ways. The inhabitants had to make great sacrifices on account of the increasingly dire supply situation. More and more people were caught up in a vicious circle of undernourishment, disease and frequently death. The war found its way into everyday life and changed customary habits such as shopping, cooking or heating, had an effect on clothing and fashions and demanded new time planning on account of the hours of queuing. The first waves of refugees increased the mood of hostility towards foreigners, with thousands of Jewish refugees being targeted in particular. When the patriotic euphoria began to wane, the militarisation and years of shortage made themselves felt in the form of an increasingly aggressive mood, and in petty criminality and violence.'

By March 1916 there were thousands of war wounded in Vienna. The city was the centre of war activity. There were eight new 'barracks' military hospitals, all increasing the incidence of tuberculosis, smallpox and typhus and worsening the hunger, dirt and poor hygiene. Even this wasn't enough, and so a number of public buildings were converted into temporary hospitals and clinics. According to a Vienna police report in March 1915, there were 266 "other hospital facilities" alongside the forty genuine hospitals.

260,000 war casualties were treated in Vienna in 1915. Orphanages were emptied and families were paid to house the children. A few children were evacuated.

The dismal everyday lives of the Viennese marked by hunger and deprivation turned the once glorious capital of a great empire of 53 million and imperial residence into a "dying city". The city was afflicted more and more by demoralisation and exhaustion, drained by the mobilisation of all energies and resources for the front.

The cold winter of 1915 just exaggerated the situation.

The Countess Marie was, hopefully, using her nursing skills for the war effort. But like many other aristocrats left penniless in the city, she decided to resort to another method to raise some money.

Chapter 14
Beatrice Martha

12 October 1910

On Wednesday, the 12 October, 1910, ten months after giving birth to her second child in Vienna, Beatrice Martha was in London. She boarded a P. & O. ship, the S.S. Caledonia, bound for India. She was travelling alone.

There were 291 other passengers on board, 243 of them bound for Calcutta.

The boat was no means crowded, it could carry 800 passengers, but she was fortunate to have the means to be able to travel First Class. For this journey there were almost more crew than passengers.

The Caledonia was a twin-funnelled steamship which had been built in Greenock in 1894. When launched she was the largest ship in the Peninsular & Oriental Steam Navigation Company fleet. She carried the U.K. mail service to India and in 1907 had broken the London to Calcutta speed record.

The boat set sail the next day for Calcutta, a journey of about 40 days. It would have been a very exciting journey were it not for the import of her impending daunting task in India.

She was due to arrive in Calcutta on about the 22 November.

Most of the passengers were going all the way to Calcutta, but some were disembarking in one of several stops made on the voyage.

As they headed south, the passengers would have been thinking about the potentially difficult journey through the Bay of Biscay, but they were lucky, as the weather was kind. They were more fortunate than they might have realised at the time. The S.S. Abhona, a new boat sailing without passengers from Plymouth to India a few days later, was caught in a storm and sank, with the loss of all aboard.

As the journey progressed, the warmth of the Mediterranean would have been very welcome after the chilling October Atlantic weather, and they docked at Marseilles to disembark some passengers, and pick up others who had travelled through France rather than endure the journey through the Bay of Biscay. The passage continued eastwards through the Mediterranean to the next port of call, Port Said, in northern Egypt. It was a crowded, bustling and very smelly city.

The excitement of passage through the Suez Canal would follow. This brilliant engineering achievement, completed 40 years earlier, revolutionised the journey to the east and made it both shorter and cheaper. What an experience this would have been for Beatrice and many of the others on board who were used only to European life. This would be their first taste of the exotic middle-east, with scenes straight from the Bible unfolding before their eyes.

The next few days, sailing through the Red Sea, with Arabia on one side and Ethiopia and north-east Africa on the other would lead into the Arabian Sea west of the Indian sub-continent.

The ship travelled on south to Colombo in Ceylon, (Sri Lanka), followed by the penultimate port of call, Tuticorin. This is a less well-known port of call, but was one of the oldest cities and most important ports in India. It was known as 'The Pearl City' because of the local pearl fishing industry.

Beatrice was one of very few women travelling on her own, but her 'advanced' age, then 33, would have made it more acceptable that she should travel without a chaperone. Some of the single women would actually have been travelling for the same reason as her, to go to India to seek a husband. They were known at the time as the 'fishing fleet'.

In contrast to Beatrice, who had a particular man in mind to catch, the 'fishing fleet' were going to join relatives or friends already abroad who would help match them to the many single British men in India; in the Army, or working for the Indian Civil Service, or farming 'up-country'. They were lonely men, stranded in a social system where contact with eligible European women was extremely limited and contact with local females would make them outcasts.

At last, in mid-November, on a beautiful clear day and with a modest temperature of 86°F, (30°C), they arrived in Calcutta. Thankfully it was the beginning of the cooler and drier season; the monsoons had just finished in October.

All the talk and discussion on board about what to expect would not have prepared Beatrice for the teeming mass of people and activity that awaited her at the Chandpal Ghat on the Hooghly River. The noise, the clamour and the smells would have been overwhelming, even for someone as well-travelled in Europe as Beatrice. Calcutta was a city of a million people, the commercial hub of Imperial India and until the following year, still its capital city.

Her task in Calcutta was to find, pursue, woo and marry John Herbert Humble-Crofts, known to all as Bertie.

He could be found based at the Head Office of the British India Steamship Company in Calcutta. He was on shore leave between trips as a Merchant Sea Officer with the Company.

Though I have very little information about her stay in Calcutta, it would have been impossible for Beatrice to arrive there without a contact in the city; if not Bertie himself, then almost certainly a friend of her family. Hopefully the friend and their house boy would have met her, shepherded her and her luggage off the boat and into transport to reach their destination. She would not have managed without them.

No-one back home had supported her decision to chase to India to find Bertie. His family were horrified at the match and her family thought it foolish.

But she was a determined lady; she had few alternatives, and was making her last stand for a family life.

She had first met the Humble-Crofts family when the Harrods moved to Heathfield in Sussex in 1902.

She had previously been living what would have been quite a restricted life in Devon.

However, in the gap between selling the house in Devon and completing the alterations to the new house in Heathfield, the extended trip to Europe must have opened her eyes to a world outside of her relatively sheltered life. In 1902, she was 25 years old and still single, so she must have desperately hoped that the move closer to London might help her to find a husband and settle down.

Canon William Humble-Crofts, Bertie's father, had been the incumbent at the nearby Parish Church in Waldron for 20 years. The Harrods began to worship regularly at Waldron Church.

Bertie was away most of the time working abroad and the only Humble-Crofts children left at home were the youngest son, Arthur, who was aged 18, and the two young girls who were at school.

She would almost certainly have had a first look at Bertie when he came home from India on extended sick leave soon after the Harrods arrival at Culverwood. He had been suffering from a tropical illness and was sent home in late 1901, spending six months off work in the end. What a dashing figure he would have cut in his uniform He was very handsome man, was of a good height at 5'10", with a high forehead, brown eyes, a Roman nose, a firm mouth, a square chin, a dark complexion, an oval face. Rather exotically for rural Sussex, he had tattoos on both arms.

Though their paths crossed but transiently, she could have fallen for him there and then. He probably hardly noticed her, and soon after he was back off to India.

In the ensuing three years, she might have thought about him at times, but he was inaccessible and a long way away, so life went on much as before.

By the time of his next leave in late 1905, life had changed drastically in the Harrod family and Beatrice was three years older, aged 28.

Beatrice's older married sisters, Fanny and Grace, both had families who were all growing up rapidly. Her nephew Jack Conder was already 17 years old. She had some catching up to do.

Her father, Charles Digby Harrod, was his usual busy, munificent and beneficent self, thoroughly embedded in the local community in East Sussex despite having lived in the area for only three years.

In August of that year, Charles and his wife Caroline had hosted their now regular annual garden party for the local school children and their teachers.

On Friday the 11 August they had entertained 290 children and 33 teachers at Culverwood, their substantial home near Heathfield, with its extensive grounds. There was cricket, swings and sports at 2.30 p.m., tea at 3.30 p.m. and tea for the teachers and helpers at 4.30 p.m.

Charles and Caroline travelled to London on the Monday for a bit of relaxation at their favourite hotel, The Grosvenor in Victoria, near the station.

On the following day, Tuesday the 15th., news came back from London that Charles had collapsed and died at the hotel. He had not been in robust health for some years, but this would have been a surprise and a major blow for the family.

Following the spread of news of his death, there were hundreds of messages of condolence and support from far and wide, and the funeral a few days later was a magnificent affair. Charles Digby had been a well-known figure in London for many years, and Harrods had continued to prosper after his final departure from the shop in 1891.

Most funerals were male only affairs at the time, so Beatrice's only brother, Henry Herbert Harrod, was the only member of the immediate family at the funeral and represented the close family. Also present were other male relatives; Charles Digby's two sons-in-law, Rennie Conder and Herbert Martin; and Charles's brother, Henry Digby; and his nephews.

The newspapers, both local and national, were full of the story and touchingly loud in their praise of Charles's work and achievements.

Charles Digby had been such a huge influence in the family that life at Culverwood would have been very flat for the following few months. Things would not have been improved by the decision that the remaining family must soon leave and find a new home.

They were to spend their last Christmas at Culverwood that year, before they moved to a rented house in Tunbridge Wells. It would be slightly nearer to London and some of the family, but further away from their friends in Sussex.

The Reverend Humble-Crofts took Charles's funeral service. Both the Reverend and his wife were very caring and thoughtful people, and would have given a lot of support to the Harrod family.

Then, in the middle of her grief, back into Beatrice's life comes Bertie Humble-Crofts, a dashing knight on a white charger. Well, perhaps not a charger, but perhaps in his white summer uniform.

His regular leave was due every third year and he promptly arrived back in England that same August in 1905, eight days before the death of Charles Digby, with seven months leave to come.

Bertie spent some of the early weeks in London where he took his Master's Certificate, so he would not have been able to spend much time with his own family until a while after the funeral.

How, when, and where the relationship between Bertie and Beatrice changed from being a family friend to a lover is not known. Was this a spur of the moment fling, or had she been hoping to start a relationship that might lead to marriage?

Their illicit liaison, working from my father's date of birth, must have happened sometime before Christmas 1905, probably around mid-December.

A very ancient resident and gossip from Waldron who I met in the 1980s swore blind they 'got up to some hanky-panky in the woods'. I checked the weather for December 1905. It was dry, but quite cold, so this was unlikely. It also struck me that London might possibly have been the venue for their 'fling'.

Bertie spent some time in London during his leave, and perhaps they arranged to meet there if Beatrice took a trip to town to shop or go to the theatre. Her father had earlier kept a flat in London when they had moved away, but I think by 1905 that was long gone.

Soon after Christmas the Harrod family moved to Tunbridge, and Bertie was gone again. He got back to Calcutta on the 6 April, 1906, so he would have had no idea about the panic that overtook Beatrice when she had missed two periods.

Fortunately, once the Harrod family moved to Tunbridge, very few local people would have known them or their business, so Beatrice would have been able to keep the pregnancy secret for some time.

However, it would not be long before it would be obvious to her sisters and mother. She would be a disgrace.

An elder of the Conder family believe that as things progressed, she ran off to Croydon to stay with one of her married sisters, almost certainly the eldest, Fanny, and someone later helped her to find the Nursing Home where she was to give birth. Though she gave the child Bertie's first name, John, it looks as though she never revealed the name of the father to her family. Certainly none of her descendants heard anything about it.

The rest of that story has been told already.

What happened in the ensuing years after the birth is a mystery. It is very likely that Beatrice's life might have been more restricted by her mother. Her penance would be to live the life of a dutiful single and disgraced daughter.

To add to her misery, her sister Amy married Arthur Weightman in 1907 to become her third married sister. She was being left behind.

During the European tour with her family in 1901, Beatrice had probably acquired friends and contacts abroad. Her mother might have condoned a trip to stay with a trusted family friend.

Some years later in 1909 she was certainly in Paris, and returned there from Vienna a few weeks later in 1910.

In 1909 she was aged 32 years old. She was on a threshold. Either she knuckled down to the life of a spinster daughter, as two others of her sisters had done, or she must make an attempt to change her life.

She decided to make an effort to rescue the mess that her life had become. She might have tried to correspond with Bertie, and he may even have known of her intended travel to India.

Her next move would have been a shock to everyone. She bought a one-way passage from London to Calcutta.

The Humble-Crofts family version of events is that Beatrice 'chased' Bertie out to India to get married. Michael said that she *chased him in no mean manner*. Was this a decision made in desperation or a calculated plan as a result of correspondence between the pair?

The delay of several months between Beatrice's arrival in Calcutta at the end of November 1910 and their wedding at the end of April 1911 suggests her trip to India was not planned well in advance.

Pinning down Bertie in India would not have been made easy by his irregular and sometimes extended disappearances from Calcutta on board ship. As an officer with the British India Steamship Company, his trips were along the coast of India and Burma, the Persian Gulf and East Coast of Africa, and then back again. Most of these trips lasted 3 or 4 weeks. About a week after her arrival in Calcutta, Bertie was promoted to Acting Commander and sailed off to Rangoon on the S.S. Kistna.

During his absences, she may have stayed with friends, or lived in the Y.W.C.A., or one of the clubs frequented by Europeans. It would be impossible for a single lady to live in the city by herself.

He was on shore leave during the Christmas break of 1910, and this would have been an opportunity to press her suit, but he went off to sea again early in January.

Her task was to take her almost five months. But she succeeded.

By the April of 1911, though he was initially rostered to travel aboard the S.S. Katoria as First Officer, this was cancelled so that they could marry.

On the 22nd of April, 1911, after the reading the Banns locally, they were married at St. John's Cathedral Church, Calcutta, with just a few friends present. No photographs of the wedding exist, nor any record apart from that held in the church in Calcutta and at the British Library.

Beatrice had completed her task.

During my first research of Beatrice's life, the trail had come to an early end when I could not initially find any records of her marriage, any children or her death.

The breakthrough came after several visits to Somerset House, on the Strand, to look at the wills of various members of the Harrod clan. The married names of all the Harrod sisters, and hence some of their descendants were found in this way.

In particular, I found the wills of Henry Herbert Harrod, Beatrice Martha's unmarried brother, and Olive Mary, one of her two unmarried sisters. Both listed a bequest to a Beatrice Martha Humble-Crofts!! Well. No wonder we had not found any more about her searching under the Harrod name.

So much of my life and time became involved in the family research, that to my friends any absence whilst I was furthering my knowledge of the family was henceforth known as 'Humble-Crofting'.

As usual, the new discovery produced more questions than answers. Every time an apparent breakthrough was achieved, another brick wall appeared. But brick walls, I discovered, can be broken.

Having discovered the name Humble-Crofts, there appeared to be absolutely no trace of any living Humble-Crofts anywhere. There were no finds for the name on an internet search at that time. Nor could I find any sign of a marriage in the manual records then available.

A thorough inspection of every local telephone book for the whole country in my local library produced not a single Humble-Crofts. Sadly, there were no telephone lists available on computers 20 years ago, so it was necessary to laboriously go through every book. The reasons for the lack of any positive findings became apparent sometime later. The only living Humble-Crofts in the world were invisible to me. One of them moved house so often in England that he never made it into any current U.K. telephone directories; the other lived in Australia. The rest had either died or married and hence had a different name.

However, with the name Humble-Crofts now available to search, Beatrice Martha's husband, John Herbert Humble-Crofts, known as Bertie, was easily found in the records. Astonishingly, the records also showed that Beatrice Martha and Bertie had produced three children.

To make Humble-Crofting more confusing, I found that Bertie had been born with the name 'Humble', not 'Humble-Crofts'; that he and Beatrice Martha had married abroad; and that Bertie had died prematurely, when aged 44.

The records showed that of the three children of Bertie's and Beatrice's marriage, the two girls had already died, and the youngest child, a son Michael, born in 1918, was alive and had two children of his own. One of Michael's two sisters had been married, and had a daughter, Jane.

So my search was then focussed on finding Jane or Michael and his family.

Jane was found first, running a hotel in the farthest reaches of the north of Scotland. It had taken a rather devious route for me to find her. Her mother's will mentioned a bequest to a Dr Lord, though it was not clear whether he was a relative or friend.

However, his address was in the Medical Directory and a letter was dispatched to him, more in desperation than hope. The reply, from Mrs Lord, informed me that Dr Lord was, fortuitously, Jane's Godfather, and gave her married name and address.

Once contacted, Jane was able to help with some information. She was not aware of the whereabouts of her Uncle Michael, but she did give a married name for Michael's daughter.

This daughter was by then divorced from her husband, though he still lived and worked in Hong Kong and so might be found there. I decided to see if he could help and sent him a letter whilst I continued with other lines of research.

My persistence paid off. I found, once again in the Cheltenham Library, a copy of 'Who Was Who 1969' which contained a lead.

Listed there, was *'Major Michael John Muschamps Humble-Crofts M.V.O. 5 Class 1942'*. A few bits of information about his regiments and service were included, but no recent address.

What was this M.V.O.? I had no idea but it was easy to find out that this meant 'Member of the Royal Victorian Order', and to discover that this was an award given for service to members of The Royal Family. I saw another possible lateral approach.

I wrote an open letter to 'The Keeper of the Privy Purse', who I had identified as the repository of M.V.O. records. I explained the reason for my enquiry, hoping they kept records of past M.V.O.s, and more importantly, kept in touch with them. I received a reply from Major General Rice at the Central Chancery of the Orders of Knighthood, in St. James's Palace. He suggested I send a letter which they would send on to Major Humble-Crofts and allow him to reply if he wished. Hopefully the letter would find him alive at his last known address.

The letter I wrote to Michael in early 1988 aimed to attract his interest without scaring him off with the whole story at once. I did not reveal the true relationship that I suspected.

At this point in the research, I had no idea whether Michael had any knowledge of my father at all.

At about the same time, I had a reply from Hong Kong with an address for Michael's daughter.

The worry about whether my letter to Michael might cause offence was totally unnecessary. Within a short time of sending it, there was an enthusiastic telephone call from 'Uncle' Michael, as he soon became known. I told him I thought he was my father's half-brother.

He was not fazed in any way; in fact, he was excited by the idea. I was to discover later that he had suspected there might be another child, but had no further information. A follow up letter gave him all the details, and several photographs. He sent several in exchange.

He accepted very equably the fact that his mother had another child before she had married his father.

The photographs of Michael and my father looked remarkably alike. More like brothers than half-brothers.

The gem of an idea, a hypothesis, began to form in my mind. Perhaps Bertie was my Dad's real father, so that Michael would be my father's full brother, not a half-brother.

It seemed too far-fetched from a logical point of view; but was very attractive emotionally.

Michael was quite moved about the possibility of having had a brother, but equally very sad that they had never known each other. There were several clues to suggest that my hypothesis might be a possibility.

The letters that accompanied my father from the home in Liverpool said that *'His mother came of a very respectable family, and his father was a merchant captain'*. It was quite a coincidence when I discovered for the first time that Bertie had been a Merchant Marine Officer.

We soon arranged a meeting with Michael and were introduced to several members of his close and extended family.

I decided that it was paramount to try to find out if Bertie had actually been Dad's mystery father.

Until the mid-1990s, whilst I continued research into the Harrod family, looking for the origins of Charles Henry Harrod and the descendants of Charles Digby's children, much of my time was spent on this problem. It seemed unlikely that I would ever be able to prove it, but I was determined to try, and the research filled a lot of my spare time.

Was it likely that a girl from a good middle-class family, in early Edwardian England, having had an illegitimate child in 1906, would marry the father of that child 5 years later?

I needed to go through the 'when, where, how and why' of the theory.

I investigated the possible dates when they could have met after the Harrods moved to Sussex. They were few and far between. Bertie was at sea most of the time.

During the time that the Harrods were in the Waldron area, Bertie only had two periods of leave from India. Both lasted a few months, but he may of course not have spent all the time in Waldron.

The first leave in 1902 lasted about seven months, and Beatrice Martha had only arrived in the area during the latter part of that leave. There would not have been much chance to get to know Bertie well. The second leave was in 1905, for about seven months. By then, Charles Harrod was already a respected local benefactor and Beatrice Martha would have been 28 years old. It is during this leave that any 'affair' must have taken place.

My wife and I paid several visits to Waldron and met as many elderly residents as we could. A lot of unsubstantiated gossip was gathered. The incumbent at the church published an appeal for information in the Parish Magazine and I crossed his palm, well the church's palm, with silver. Though many interesting stories about both families were sent to me, there was no useful specific information about Bertie and Beatrice.

Was it possible to show that Bertie and Beatrice were in the right place, at the right time, somewhere around the end of 1905, in order to conceive my father? Both of them must have either stayed in Waldron for Christmas or stayed in London around that time.

Bertie's Merchant Navy records were found at the Brass Foundry at Woolwich Arsenal, and the dates of each of his trips and leaves were noted. Bertie had joined the British and India Steamship Company as a 4th Officer, aged 20 in 1898, and worked mostly on coastal trips around the Indian Ocean. He was given leave back in the U.K. every three years.

Passage home on leave was normally worked on one of the Company's own ships, and in total usually lasted between three and six months.

An amazing bit of evidence about the 1905 leave was found by a piece of complete luck.

I had followed one of my brothers into collecting old postcards. My speciality was the ships of The Isle of Man Steam Packet Company. It had started during trips to see my in-laws who lived on the Isle of Man. The boats were sea-worthy little tubs full of polished wood and brass, and were very attractive. These were the days before the Ro-Ro. The postcards were relatively easy to find.

I went to Postcard Fairs from time to time. At such events, the cards are listed and displayed by subjects of interest and geography. Inevitably, after looking under 'Merchant Shipping', I would look at places I or my wife had known well. I also looked at places connected with my family history research, mostly small villages in Sussex. At a Postcard Fair held in the Town Hall in Cheltenham in 1988, whilst browsing through 'Sussex Villages', I was astonished to come across a postcard with a photograph of 'The Rectory, Waldron, Sussex'.

It was postmarked with the date of the 28 February, 1906 and was addressed to a younger single sister of the Canon called Edith Humble. It read:

'Miss Edith Humble,
Maisonette,
College Road,
Harrow.'

On the top, a message to the postman, stating, 'Please forward if away'. The postcard read:

'B. leaves us tomorrow – and sails on Saturday for Calcutta.'

It was signed: *'B.H.C.'*

At the time this card was found, I did not know that Bertie used his second Christian name rather than John, so I had no idea who 'B' could have been.

'B'., I later found was short for Bertie, and 'B.H.C.' was his mother, Bridget Humble-Crofts. 'Tomorrow', would have been the 1 March, and a Thursday. 'Saturday' would be the 3 March, the day Bertie's boat sailed. It was written by my great grandmother.

I made the mistake, being so excited by the find, of telling the seller of the postcard my connection – with it. Inevitably, having done that, bargaining over the price, a normal feature of card sales, was of no use. Needless to say, I have searched every Postcard Fair I have visited since, looking in the 'Sussex, Villages', section, without any further similar finds.

Bertie's records subsequently confirmed that he left India on the 26 June 1905 aboard the 'Mombassa', and was at home on leave by the 8 August. He returned to duty the following year, after seven month's leave, departing England on board the 'Manora' on the 3 March 1906, bound for Calcutta. Where did he spend his leave? Was he in Waldron?

Thanks to paperwork provided by the Humble-Crofts family, I found that Bertie had been sitting his Master's Examination in London around Christmas 1905, but I could not be sure how long he had spent there. He would naturally have gone home to Waldron soon after his arrival in August and then travelled to London for his examination. The dates on his certificates clarified the timing; he had taken the examinations on Wednesday the 29 November and Friday the 1 December, and the certificates were issued on the 2 December. So, I guess he was at home for Christmas, probably overjoyed by his success of his examination results. The postcard confirmed that he was in Waldron before his departure back to India.

Now the hypothesis was not just possible, but probable. Bertie was in the country, and was likely to have been in Waldron before and around the time of Christmas 1905.

So I had the 'when', and probably the 'where'.

'How and why' go together. Had the conception been part of a prolonged affair during the leave, or a one-off quickie? Bertie was 27 years old and it is difficult to imagine that a Merchant Seaman of some seven years standing was without sexual experience, whereas I assume that Bea was at this stage of her life still likely to be a virgin.

Michael described his father as, *'quite a boy',* an opinion shared by other relatives I asked.

Bea was 28 years old, certainly past the first flush of youth, but not yet on the shelf.

I searched for ways to confirm that Bertie was the father.

In 1989 when I started looking, genetic testing as such was in its infancy and was based on blood groups. A colleague from my college at The London Hospital agreed to test some blood samples to see if he could confirm any relationship between me, my brothers, and members of the Humble-Crofts family.

The tests would consist of blood grouping and the detection of so called 'private' red blood cell antigens which are virtually confined to some families. This might provide strong evidence of a common ancestry, but could never offer proof. A rare gene, might however, help the case.

I and my two brothers, and a Humble-Crofts cousin offered samples but the results were disappointingly negative. There were no unique features, no private antigens.

That was as far as I could go. I resigned myself to never being able to prove my hypothesis.

The investigation remained at this suspended stage for several years. Michael was convinced that he and Dad were 'full' brothers; I remained more sceptical but fervently hoped that he was right.

Bertie was the only traceable person in the frame to be my paternal grandfather.

By 2007, DNA testing, or genetic fingerprinting, had improved dramatically and was increasingly used in both forensic police work and paternity testing. It had become possible to get this done privately and at a reasonable cost. Using a company in the U.S.A., I and one of my brothers (just in case of paternity issues in our family), and Michael's son in Australia took samples and sent them off.

Our 'Y-chromosome DNA analysis' showed that all 3 of us shared 23 out of 23 markers. This is as near to 'proof' as one could get at that time of a common male ancestor. By 2010, it was possible to show 43 markers in each of our original samples. We found we shared 43 out of 43 markers. Q.E.D.

So, Bertie really was the father of Beatrice Martha's illegitimate child and our common grandfather. Michael really was Dad's brother and our Uncle! I should be called Robin Humble-Crofts!

Sadly, by 2007, neither Michael nor Dad was alive to join us in our celebration.

Following the later findings about the 'Austrian connection', the possibility was raised that Bertie might have been the father of the 1909 baby. The family of that baby told me stories about Beatrice being on board a ship in the

Mediterranean with her lover, who was a merchant ship's captain, so it seemed a possibility.

Though most of Beatrice's movements after 1906 were not known, Bertie's were well documented in Merchant Navy records. I looked at Bertie's dates of travel in 1909 with the likely date of the baby's conception, probably about early March, 1909. Though he had a further six months leave in 1909, the dates when he could have been home do not match the conception date. He arrived back in England in late July 1909, returning to Calcutta in late January 1910. I suppose that Beatrice could have been travelling on board with him in March 1909, but wives were not usually taken and mistresses definitely not.

Beatrice's letter to the Foreign Office in 1916 confirmed later that Bertie, then her husband, knew nothing of the second pregnancy

The only other possibility was that Beatrice might have gone out to India in 1909, but this is not supported by shipping passenger records.

Hence, it was pretty well impossible that Bertie could be the father of the second child.

I needed to look elsewhere for the missing father.

Beatrice had trapped her man at last, but the future was not going to be a bed of roses.

Chapter 15
Beatrice Martha

Mid 1916

The National Archives are now housed in splendour at Kew, South London. They are a frequently used and invaluable source of documentary evidence. They house the country's records and archives deposited by individuals, government bodies and departments, local government and private organisations. One can look up and read the original passenger manifest of the Titanic, old County records or minutes of Government meetings not held back for reasons of security.

Especially useful is the ability to search on-line, not only their own Catalogue, but documents held in County Record Offices and other repositories, such as university libraries. I have used them frequently during my research, in particular for finding old maritime records.

As new records are added regularly, I frequently re-enter topics for research that I have looked at before. I had discovered by 2008 that Beatrice Harrod had given birth to an illegitimate child, my father, and had sometime later become Beatrice Humble-Crofts. I knew nothing about any Austrian connection or a Countess.

One day, throwing Beatrice's name once again into the National Archives search index revealed an entry not previously seen, listed under a Foreign Office document code FO383/123.

Under the heading of Humble-Crofts it read:

'Austria-Hungary: Prisoners, including: Herbert Marsh, British subject: his death of tuberculosis at Prague General Hospital. Hans Brandeis, Austrian subject, interned in Britain, and Albert Edward Jones, British subject (formerly of the Whitehead Torpedo Works) interned in Austria: Austria-Hungary refuses proposed exchange because of Jones's expertise, but are willing to exchange Brandeis for James Fraser Ross, British subject interned at Baden, Austria.'

The entry was intriguing, but baffling. The extract was obviously only part of the document and did not include the name Humble-Crofts, so the heading did not seem relevant. It has changed since. Several members of Beatrice's Humble-Crofts family had fought in World War I, but there had been no previous suggestion that any of them had been made a prisoner of war. Perhaps the family had been involved in charitable work for prisoners? The reference was noted, and added to a list of documents to look up whenever I next visited London and the Archives.

Some months later my brothers and I spent some time at the Archives, chasing other records. At the end of an exhausting, and not especially productive day, one brother asked if there was anything else he could order from the basement store. I sent him off to retrieve the Foreign Office document and what an exciting find it was. It proved to be a goldmine.

The heading regarding prisoners of war related to the adjacent documents.

The correct file consisted of 17 letters and memos held by the British Foreign Office since they were written in 1916, referring to payments due from Beatrice Martha to a Countess Maria Grotta zu Grottenegg. In essence, Beatrice Martha had some unknown years before 1916 given birth to another illegitimate child, who was 'adopted' by this Countess in Vienna. Detailed examination revealed an amazing set of documents. The correspondence was between the Austro-Hungarian Foreign Ministry in Vienna, via the U.S. Embassy in London and Vienna, (who during the hostilities acted as intermediaries), to the British Foreign Office. It included a letter from Beatrice Martha explaining the circumstances of the adoption, and a plea for secrecy. The American Embassy was involved to by-pass the block on communication between the two parties in W.W.I., the Austro-Hungarian Empire and Britain.

I will go through the documents at some length as they are quite important.

The first 'Note Verbale', (in diplomatic language, an unsigned, usually non-urgent message), came from the 'I. and R., (Imperial and Royal) Ministry for Foreign Affairs' in Vienna, dated the 3 June 1916, No. 58228/11.

It was sent to the American Embassy in London, requesting that they

'*inform Mrs Beatrix Humble Croft, nee Harrod, of Waldron Rectory, Sussex, that Countess Mary Grotta zu Grottenegg of Vienna, VIII Floriangasse 60, is in urgent need of the money due to her and that she requests Mrs Croft to remit this money to her through the American Embassy in London.*'

The response, dated the June 30 1916, and couched in the usual diplomatic terms and niceties, is from the American Ambassador, Mr Page, to Sir Edward Grey, the British Foreign Secretary transmitting the Note Verbale and asking, '*whether Mrs Croft is in the position to pay the amount in question, and whether His Majesty's Government are willing that this amount should be remitted to Countess Mary Grotta through the American Embassy in Vienna*'.

The next document was an F.O. internal advice memo sent two days later, asking someone higher up whether H.M.G. should allow the remittance through the U.S. Embassy at Vienna, and instructing the recipient that they should copy the correspondence to Mrs Croft, saying that if she wished to remit, (the money), she should apply to Parliamentary Counsel, stating the circumstances.

The fourth document, five days later, was an F.O. memo with the draft of a letter to Beatrice Martha.

It commences, *'The Under-Secretary of State for Foreign Affairs presents his compliments to Mrs Croft...'*, sending the correspondence and continuing, *'Lord Hardinge of Penshurst'* (Sir Charles Hardinge was the Under-Secretary), *'is to state that should Mrs Croft desire to remit monies to Countess Grotta she should apply for the necessary leave to the Parliamentary Counsel to the Treasury, explaining fully the circumstances of the case.'*

It is not difficult to imagine how the receipt of that letter from the F.O. in 1916, especially addressed to the home of her in-laws, would have set the cat amongst the pigeons for Beatrice, who was married and settled.

What followed next was a letter from Beatrice Martha to the F.O., sent from another address. It was quite a surprise.

'Ref 129/81/1286
Caville, Dunster, Somerset. July 9ᵗʰ 1916
Sir

In reference to the letter regarding monies due to Countess Mary Grotta zu Grottenegg, at the outbreak of war I was remitting to her through a third person the sum of 5/ – a week for the maintenance of a child, I discontinued the payment then as it was not known through what source to send it.'

(That was quite a modest but not insignificant amount, about £20–25 in today's worth. That would have been just over £1,000 per year now.)

'When she accepted the care of the child some years back, she agreed to do so without payment but soon after my marriage I had demands from her for money. I wrote to the father about it but he refused to help me and I was told I could not force him to do so except through the law courts and for me this was an impossibility, as my husband knows nothing about the matter. I believe I am legally responsible for the sum of 5/ – to be paid her per week. I am willing to remit this sum to her through the American Consul on hearing from you in what manner this can be done. I should be very grateful to you if you could help me keep the matter as secret as possible, I am happily married and have two little daughters. My address (permanent) is Mrs J H Humble Crofts, Limworth Lodge, Bury St Edmunds, Suffolk, and I should be glad if you could correct the error of addressing any communication to Waldron Rectory which is where my husband's people live. I am staying here through until the end of September.

Yours truly
Beatrice Humble-Crofts.'

The next document is an internal F.O. memo on three pages in response to her letter, headed:

'Wishes to know if can be paid through U.S. Consul.'

It states,

'Mrs C. is under no liability to pay the Countess 5/– per week if the latter agreed to take the child without payment. It is unfortunately a case in which blackmail could be levied with great facility.

The child is no doubt English-born and we could authorize the remittance if necessary, without referring the matter to Sir. A. Thring.' (Sir Arthur Thring was a member of the Parliamentary Counsel, a specialised team of lawyers based in Whitehall. Their main work was, and still is, drafting Government Bills for introduction into Parliament and related Parliamentary business.)

'Perhaps we could write privately in the first instance to Mrs C. asking whether it is really her wish that authority should be given to enable her to send the remittance to Austria which she mentions in her letter. If she does not wish to send the money, we could refuse authority officially and so inform Mr Page. This would be effective as long as war lasts.'

A comment added to the memo was addressed to its author, Mr Watkin.

'I see no harm in doing this in the first instance, but if authority is ultimately to be given, I think Sir. A. Thring should be consulted, unless we have any authority for not doing so in special cases. This should be done without disclosing the lady's secret.'

A final comment by H.R., dated the 11 July, gave the definitive instruction, 'Write privately to Mrs Humble-Crofts in the first instance as suggested.', and is overwritten, 'done 11.7.16. (see within).'

What follows on the same day is the letter to Beatrice Martha. It is headed 'unofficial'. It reads:

'Madam,
I should be glad if you would inform me whether it is really your desire that authority should be given to enable you to send to Austria the money mentioned in your letter to the Foreign Office of the 9th inst., or whether you would prefer that authority should be refused.

Yrs. Truly,
H.B. Warner'

Handwritten underneath this was a note:

'Mr Yeatman called 14.7.16 on behalf of Mrs H-C. and in reply to this letter, copy overleaf, and suggested that the best course was to take no action.'

Signed H.B.W. 14.7.16.
The whole correspondence had covered just six weeks and ended there.

The Foreign Office had tried really hard to help Beatrice. It had given her the option to use the war as an excuse to refuse payment until the end of the war, or to continue payment using the permission of the Government. It looks as though Beatrice Martha became anxious about the whole business, and had decided to accept the status quo.

It is interesting to speculate who Mr Yeatman might be. He would be, of course, someone trusted by Beatrice Martha, and might be someone who is not known to this story. It is very likely that the intermediary was actually one of her brothers-in-law, Arthur Weightman, who worked as a European Agent. His name over the phone could easily be mistaken for Yeatman.

Arthur John Weightman would have been 52 years old in 1916, a man of some experience, and already involved as a Merchants' Agent in the transfer of funds abroad. He would have been the man Beatrice would have consulted if she needed to transfer money abroad before the war.

A second illegitimate child was a revelation. The documents gave no clue as to any details of the child's birth; there was no date of birth, no place of birth, and no name or sex for the child. In the correspondence, the F.O. had presumed that the child was 'English-born'.

It was suggested by one person in the Harrod family that one of Bea's sisters, thought to be her eldest sister, Fanny Conder, who was 12 years older than Beatrice, had been involved with an illegitimate child. The rumour alleged that she had taken Beatrice in during her pregnancy. But with which of the pregnancies had Fanny been involved? This one, or my father in 1906?

Perhaps her sister Amy, two years older than Beatrice, and the wife of Arthur Weightman, had been involved as well as her husband? None of the descendants of either the Conder or Weightman family who have been contacted during the research knew anything about either pregnancy, so things had been successfully kept very quiet at the time.

Anyhow, the wheels of diplomacy marched on in the correspondence from Vienna.

The I. and R. Ministry of Foreign Affairs in Vienna sent a further 'Note Verbale' to the American Embassy in late July 1916, gently reminding them that they had received no reply about Mrs Crofts. In response, the Austro-Hungarian Division of the American Embassy at 18, Belgrave Square, London, sent a further note to H.M.G. in August.

'The American Chargé d'Affaires presents his compliments to His Majesty's Secretary of State for Foreign Affairs, and...has the honour to enclose herewith three copies of a Note Verbale of the Austro-Hungarian Foreign Office, dated July 25th last, No.74.787/11 respecting this subject.

Mr Laughlin would be grateful for an answer on the subject at Lord Grey's convenience.'

The internal memo in response to this note was:

'?Reply thus – the case is not one in which H.M.G. feel able to grant licence to remit.'

Translated into diplomatic speak, this became a memo to the U.S. Chargé d'Affaires in early September:

'Viscount Grey would be grateful if the U.S. Amb. at Vienna would be so good as to inform the Austro-Hungarian Govt. in reply that the case is not one in which they feel able to grant the necessary licence for remittance from this country.'

H.M.G. had decided to go along with Beatrice Martha's wishes and refuse any further payments.

The exchange of letters and memos reveal a lot about the workings of the Foreign Office. It is obvious they were sympathetic to her case and trying to help, in a case that they viewed as akin to blackmail.

As usual, the whole business raised more questions than answers.

It was bad enough at that time, certainly in middle-class society, to have had one illegitimate child. To have fallen pregnant twice must have been devastating for Beatrice and this correspondence would have frightened her.

Who was the father of this pregnancy?

When and where was the child born?

How and why on earth was an Austrian Countess in Vienna involved?

What happened to the child in 1916 and thereafter?

Did the payments resume at the end of the war in 1918 or 1919?

Did I have a half-uncle or aunt somewhere out there, either in Austria or back in Britain?

Between 2008 and 2013, despite spending a lot of time and effort on research, no definite answers were found to any of these questions.

I did not know the child's date or place of birth, its sex, its name, or the name of the father. The lack of records on-line in Austria meant that any further research was going to be very difficult if not impossible, particularly with my lack of German. It transpired that even searching the manual records would require as a minimum details of the age and religion of the child in order to yield a result.

I started to try to narrow down the range of possibilities, starting with the possible date of birth.

The age of consent in Britain in 1916 was probably 21, though boys of 18 were allowed to join the army during the First World War. Hence, I supposed this child must have been aged 18 years or less in 1916 to be viewed as a child in the F.O. correspondence. The child must have been born before Beatrice Martha married in 1911, as that is when the Countess started to demand payments.

My father was born in September 1906, so that would rule out the time covering that pregnancy and lying in period, a year or more from the winter of

1905 onwards. Her letter of 1916 says the child was accepted by the Countess 'some years back', suggesting quite a few years ago.

Using these details, I could conclude that this child must have been born between either about 1898 and 1905, or between 1907 and 1910. The child was probably born with the surname 'Harrod', as the father was not admitted by Beatrice, but this was not definitely so, as the father might have consented for the child to take his name on any certificate.

Other questions remained.

What was the connection with the Countess and Vienna?

Where had Beatrice been between 1906 and 1910?

Was the father a friend or relation of the Countess's? It was obviously not Beatrice's subsequent husband as she was insistent that secrecy must be maintained from him and his family.

How did the Countess know that Beatrice had become married? It suggests some continued contact between them. Why did the Countess wait until 1916 to begin the attempt to recover the money? The payments must have stopped two years earlier at the onset of the war.

Beatrice declined to name the father, but was obviously still able to get in touch with him in 1916 to see if he would help. His refusal suggests that either he also was in a position where discretion was paramount, or that he was just not inclined to help.

The fact that she had been advised that the father could only be forced to help her by recourse to the law courts, tells us that she had some sort of legal advice, and that the father was theoretically subject to the British law.

Could the legal advice have come from another of her brother-in-law's solicitor Herbert Martin?

In order to try to pin down a date, a place and a name, I began a search of U.K. births to a Harrod mother, without a father's name on the certificate, during the period 1898 to 1910. It proved time-consuming, expensive and fruitless. Sadly, the index of births in England did not include the mother's name until 1912, so for the possible dates prior to 1912, a search would have to include all Harrod children born.

My searches showed that during the possible dates, 396 'Harrod' children had been born in England and Wales, of whom about half were born in London or environs. It was not practical to purchase and search all of these birth certificates, with such a low probability of success.

I decided that I could reduce the numbers I needed to research by choosing births in the most likely places, and excluding those born to women with other children, those children who were still resident in the U.K. in the 1911 U.K. census, and those children who had died within the time period studied.

It was possible in this fashion to reduce the numbers of the most likely candidates to 70.

These certificates were ordered and examined, but there was no positive result from all my hard work and expense.

Chasing the Countess seemed the next best idea.

There was evidence of the name 'zu Grottenegg' on genealogy websites showing family lines in the 17th and 18th century in Southern Austria and Northern Italy. Contact was made with a Heinz Grottenegg, a physicist, who was found on line, but neither he nor his father knew of the Countess.

Correspondence with a researcher in Vienna unearthed some information, limited a little by language problems.

The Countess was listed as Mary J. Gräfin (Countess) Grotta zu Grottenegg. She had been born on the 28 February, 1864 in Yverdon, Switzerland, at the southern end of one of a Swiss lake.

She was a widow and in 1918 was living alone at Vienna VIII, Stolzenthalergasse 13.

She had died on 20 November 1926; her name at that time was given as Marie Grotha.

Soon after the end of W.W.I. Austria had dropped the use of aristocratic titles, hence the name change.

As stated earlier, by 1916, the state of inflation and severe shortages in wartime Vienna had whittled away resources. The barricade by the British Navy had been very effective. Food supplies were limited and the population was getting desperate. Perhaps poverty had prompted the Countess to act at that time.

She was aged 52 in 1916 when the letters were written, and 62 when she died.

I felt there must be more records in the Austrian files, but I had not discovered the means to gain access to them. The Austrian-related websites available then were searched without success.

Requests for information were posted on Austrian family history sites with no response.

My lack of German language precluded a personal visit to go through records.

I had hit a brick wall and I needed help.

As you will find out, a breakthrough several years later helped me answer many of these questions, but not all of them.

Chapter 16
Eduard Harrod

1909-1912

Eduard Harrod was born in Vienna on the 12 December 1909 at IX Lazarethgasse 18, an apartment rented by the Countess Maria.

He was the second child, the second boy and the second illegitimate child of Beatrice Martha Harrod.

The research that produced this information took place some years after the original discovery of his existence in the Foreign Office records, which had given me no details about the child.

After some fruitless years with no results, I had resigned myself to making no progress in my quest for information about the 'Austrian Problem'. At that stage I knew nothing more about Beatrice's second child apart from his or her existence, and the information found about the Countess in the Vienna records.

Once again, serendipity was my saviour. Two chance encounters helped me to find more information.

Firstly, my interest in Austria was rekindled by an episode of 'Who Do You Think You Are', broadcast on television in late 2013. The subject of the programme was the singer, Marianne Faithful. She had Jewish relatives who had lived in Germany and Austria during the First World War, and some had escaped from the Continent before deportation in the Second World War. As part of the programme, she travelled to Vienna to consult a researcher, William Godsey, who was British. Could he be my link for further research?

I googled him and found that his main interests were Austrian aristocratic families, and the Austro-Hungarian Foreign Office during World War I. He sounded the perfect person to help my research.

With some difficulty I found an e mail address and wrote to him. He replied and passed me on to a colleague, Dr Rita Steblin who was available for research. I was off!

Dr Steblin worked hard and made some major breakthroughs fairly quickly. As I originally wrote this part of the story the information was changing day by day and week by week. An early success led me on to other research with even more dramatic results. It really did confirm that persistently nagging away at a problem would eventually produce results.

Dr Steblin confirmed the earlier results regarding the Countess. For the first time, she traced her husband, Eduard, Count Grotta zu Grottenegg, who had died in June 1893 in Vienna's VIII District.

The Countess was a Protestant – a Lutheran, and was registered in her husband's home town of Klagenfurt, about 160 miles from Vienna.

Dr Steblin had a 'Eureka' moment some weeks later when she found in the archives an 'Edi Harrod', living in Vienna with the Countess during 1912 and 1913. The child was listed as born on the 12 December, 1909.

At last it looked as though I had a name for Beatrice's second child! Though this could have been short for Edith, Edi is also the short version of Eduard in Austria and looked the most likely explanation.

I re-researched the U.K. records for any Edi/Eduard/Edward Harrod born on that date in England and found that there were no matches, so it is seemed likely that he was born abroad.

Edi would have been two and a half years old when he was living with the Countess in 1912, but was missing after 1913. Later findings in the Vienna archives provided more information and hinted at what might have happened to Edi. For a while it looked as though he might have come to an early and rather depressing end.

There are two documents which give information about his birth.

There is an extract from the Vienna birth records, requested and produced in 1913, and dated 22 April 1913. It states that the information is a word for word copy of the records.

It gives the child's name simply as Eduard, and the place, date and time of birth as listed earlier. The birth is recorded as 'out of wedlock' and the mother's name is given 'allegedly' as Pauline Harrod, an Anglican, aged 27 years. The word 'allegedly' was used deliberately, I suspect, as the person who reported the event was not the mother, and was probably the Countess.

The second document is a copy of the Vienna Magistrate's birth records, the document itself undated, and was found in Eduard's military records held at the Bundersarchiv. Over the copy is a written addendum stating that this was from the official records and produced for military purposes, presumably to verify details on enlistment. The record gives the same details as the other.

The name and age of the mother, Pauline Harrod was a bit of a shock. Not only the wrong name, but Beatrice was aged 31.

Naturally I tried to find this Pauline Harrod. The only one in the U.K. records for that period proved to be a lady married in 1873 to Walter Harrod, who was born in 1841 in Norfolk.

Just to muddy the waters, in the censuses, Pauline is listed as having German parentage and in 1911 was running an agency for servants, mostly foreigners. She was based in Frimley, Surrey.

She had been born in Wallach, near Dusseldorf, Germany, in 1851. She died in London in 1920. Despite the obvious possible links, I could not find any connection to Beatrice and she was not a member of the Harrods shop family.

This Pauline would have been pushed to give birth in Vienna in 1909 and be living a different life in Frimley in 1911. In any case, she was aged 58 in 1909, not 27 as stated, so was not Eduard's mother.

As a final twist to this false lead, Pauline Harrod had three children, one of who was called Mabel Pauline Harrod. She was born in 1875 in London, so would have been 34 years old in 1909. She had married in 1900 and would have been Pauline May by 1909. In the 1911 census, she is living in Lambeth, London, with her husband and daughter. Another red herring.

It was impossible that both a Pauline and a Beatrice Harrod had given birth at the same address on the same day to a child called Eduard.

Why was this name given in the document? Perhaps Beatrice gave a false name to hide her identity. But why lie about her age, when she was actually 32? Perhaps Pauline was a transcription error; Beatrice's signature on letters I possess could easily be misread as Pauline. Perhaps the Countess, who almost certainly gave the information, was trying to hide Beatrice's identity from future investigation. She was almost successful!

The Vienna Police Archives give the dates of entry and departure for Beatrice, those being the 16 December 1909 and the 21 January 1910 respectively, as discussed earlier. Her whereabouts from early 1910 for the following nine months are not known.

Beatrice states that the Countess initially offered to look after the child for no charge. I find this difficult to believe unless there already was a connection between the two women, founded upon a common factor, perhaps Josef, the Countess's stepson, or previous acquaintance. Even then, you would have to have had a close relationship to look after someone else's child.

Eduard does not appear again in any records until 1912.

The Countess obviously knew that Beatrice had married in 1911. This could not have been by chance.

There were no announcements as the wedding took place in Calcutta. There must have been continuing correspondence between the two, presumably enquiring about Eduard's state of health, etc., or perhaps the information had been given to Eduard's father.

If, as Beatrice said in her letter to the F.O., 'soon after my marriage I had demands from her for money', Beatrice would certainly have wanted to know from the Countess that the child was safe and well.

The Countess, and presumably Eduard, moved about over his first few years. She was at the birth address until mid-1911, then in several apartments in district I, staying for short periods only.

Eduard appears again in the records when he is baptised, on 6 April, 1912, in Christchurch, Vienna.

This church was the official church for the British Embassy in Vienna, the Embassy Chaplain presided, and several other British children were baptised on the same day. The other children were all a few months old, whilst Eduard was two and a half years old.

Christchurch is located in the III district, some distance south-east from Edi's birthplace or the Countess's known residences. It is close to the British Embassy and near the Belvedere Palaces and Gardens.

Eduard can only have been presented for baptism by the Countess, as Beatrice was in England eight weeks after the birth of her daughter.

The listing reads:

Baptised: 6 April 1912, born Dec 12, 1909 No. 545 Child's Christian Name: Edward Maria Parent's name, Christian: Beatrice Surname: Harrod No father's name is given. This is always put in the register if known. No address in Vienna given or occupation.

He was baptised by Arthur P. Hill, Chaplain.

No information is available about who attended the ceremony, but on this occasion, the correct mother's name was given by the Countess.

Why has Maria been added to Eduard's name? It is not all that unusual as a boy's name in Austria, but it is also the Countess's name. Was she putting her 'stamp' on him?

Why was Eduard's baptism delayed until this date? Does the document give a signal to Beatrice that the child is alive and still with the Countess?

Soon after the baptism, in fact three months later, Eduard's name starts appearing in the archives at the various addresses occupied by the Countess. His name is given in the archives as Eduard Harrod, with a correct date of birth.

This occurs at four addresses over the following eight months and then he is no longer listed.

This might not be significant. The records for some dates were from the Vienna Archives, which lists all residents, but these are incomplete. Other dates were from Lehmann's Directory. The latter, a fantastic resource for researchers of Vienna, lists names and addresses of only the principal owners and tenants by street from 1859 to 1942. It was digitalised by the Vienna Library and has been available on line since 2011.

The next piece of information is the copy of the birth record, ordered on the 22nd April, 1913.

So...

1909 December – Eduard is born. Name given as Eduard Harrod.

1911 – The Countess starts to demand money from Beatrice.

1912 April – Eduard is christened. Name given as Eduard Maria Harrod.

1912 July – Eduard appears in the Vienna Archives.

1913 March – Eduard no longer appears in the Archives.

1913 April – Copy of Eduard's birth certificate is ordered.

As you will see later, I am certain this sequence of information is important in explaining some discrepancies that occur later.

Chapter 17
John Herbert

22 April 1911

Bertie must have shocked himself by getting married. On the 22 April 1911 he stood in St. John's Church in Calcutta and waited for his bride to walk up the aisle.

Just six months before this, at the age of 32 he would have considered himself, if not a life-long bachelor, at least a confirmed one for the time being, sailing the seas and having unencumbered fun.

Following his wedding, Bertie had a leave lasting 22 days, and then after a short spell of office duties, he went back to work at sea.

Almost exactly six months after they married, in October, 1911, Bertie resigned from the Company. The company records state that he intended to leave the East after November that year and find employment at home.

It may be that Bertie originally intended to continue work in India. On the other hand, they may have decided to leave and Bertie had to work out six months' notice of his resignation. His work schedule would have been fine for a single chap, but difficult for a married man.

To add to his turmoil, and true to previous form, Beatrice was soon pregnant and would have found out about her condition by June of that year. Was Bertie by now a willing participant in future family life or a reluctant partner?

Beatrice would have been quite heavily pregnant by the end of 1911, so they may also have reached the conclusion that life in India with a baby was to be avoided, and that they needed to get back to England as quickly as possible.

Money would not have been a major consideration. Beatrice had some means of her own following her father's death and Bertie knew that he was eventually to be the recipient of a large family Trust.

Passage home was granted at ⅔ the 1st Class rate. After 10 years, six months and nine days service with the Company, (not including leave), he was granted £250, about £15,000 today!

Despite extensive searching, no definitive trace of their return journey from India has been found.

The Company records state he left Calcutta for home on board the 'Golconda' on the 26 October, but they are not on the ship's lists on arrival in London on the 2 December. A possible explanation is that they disembarked in Marseilles, and travelled overland and across the Channel to avoid the winter weather in the Bay of Biscay. This might have been a wise decision as Beatrice would have been seven months pregnant. It would also have provided a honeymoon of sorts travelling through France.

Having returned to England, they moved into a house belonging to Bertie's mother Bridget, 'Little Dumpton', on the South Cliff, in Broadstairs. It had been built in 1909. This was a convenient bolthole on their return from India.

Bridget Joan, the first child of the marriage, was born there in February, 1912.

By the following year, 1913, they had moved to Athelington, in Suffolk, 30 miles or so from Lowestoft. It is likely by this time that Bertie was working on North Sea coastal shipping.

Beatrice yet again confirmed her fertility, as their second child, Margaret Beatrice, was born just 13 months later, in March, 1913, whilst at Athelington.

World War I shaped many lives, and caused the death of many young men, including two of the Humble-Crofts' sons. It provided Bertie with a change of direction. Having been rejected by the Royal Navy after leaving college, he had joined the Royal Naval Reserve early in his Merchant Navy career and as a consequence he served most of the war serving with them on coastal patrol vessels.

During the war, Beatrice and the children initially continued to live in Athelington, and then spent some time with his parents, probably from sometime in 1915 to the Autumn of 1916, as evidenced by her fear of exposure to the in-laws in her letter to the F.O. in that year.

Photograph 7: Beatrice Martha age 38, with the Humble-Crofts family, about 1915. Front row L to R, Beatrice, Rev. Williams, Bridget, Winfred Podd; back row L to R, Bertie, Maud, Arthur, Una, Cyril, Gunny

At the end of 1916, they moved to Bury St. Edmonds in Suffolk.

Later in the war, prompted by Bertie's next posting, they lived in Falmouth between 1917 and 1919.

Bertie's Service records are available at the National Archives, listed under the Naval Lists, and registers of Naval Vessels and Ships Logs.

He served initially in the autumn of 1914 as Sub-Lieutenant on the Armed Yacht, 'H.M.Y. Evening Star', and was put in temporary command a couple of months later. Like most of these small vessels, they were privately owned and 'on loan' to the Government.

'Evening Star' was built in 1894 and was TM (Thames measure) 270 Tonnes. She was hired by the Admiralty from her owner, Lady Alexander Paget, a member of a famous military and naval family. She was fitted with two six-pounder guns and supported patrol flotillas in the North Sea.

In November 1914, he joined the Armed Yacht, 'Eileen', as an acting Navigating Lieutenant under the command of Sir Alfred Paget, K.C.B, K.C.M.G., a brother of Lady Alexander Paget. He was a retired Admiral, who also joined the R.N.R. during W.W.I. and was appointed as the Admiral of Patrols.

Sir Alfred had joined the Navy in 1865 and had an illustrious career. He died in the 'Turf Club' in Picadilly in 1918! It was a club for the aristocratic; catering for social events, equestrianism, sports and cards.

'Eileen' was built in 1910 and her owner was S. B. Joel. Eileen's officers were the captain; Bertie, a sub-lieutenant; an Engineer Sub-Lieutenant; and an Assistant Paymaster.

She carried an unusual gun, a 4.7"/50 (12.7 cm) Armstrong/Elswick, with an interesting history. These guns had been manufactured in Britain for use on four cruisers which were being built in Newcastle, and sold to Brazil around the turn of the century. Brazil only took up one of the cruisers, and the rest were bought by the U.S. Navy. Eight such guns wound up in U.S. Naval hands. They were not well liked as they used non-standard ammunition and spare parts, so in 1903 they were replaced.

In 1907, seven of the removed guns were placed in the Philippines on Grande Island and at the mouth of the harbour at Subic Bay. One gun returned to Britain where it was used on the armed yacht H.M.S. Eileen during W.W.I. They could fire five or six rounds a minute with a range of just over five and a half miles.

Bertie was promoted to the rank of Lieutenant in 1915 on the recommendation of Lord Paget and was posted back to 'Eileen', based at Immingham in Lincolnshire.

He served on the 'Eileen' for two years in total. The 'Eileen' patrolled the North Sea as part of the coastal shipping force, tasked with keeping the Humber Ports open, checking on shipping and challenging strangers. The force consisted mostly of converted yachts and trawlers.

In 1917, Bertie was transferred to H.M.S. Dreel Castle for service on shore in Falmouth, to work in a training capacity. His application for promotion to Lieutenant Commander in April of that year was refused; no reason was given.

That must have disappointed him. It was the second time he had been thwarted by the Navy. Did he have some sort of black mark on his records?

H.M.S. Dreel Castle was a 97-ton Kirkcaldy drifter. A drifter was a small trawler, used in peacetime to fish with large drift nets. She was built in 1897 and seconded to the Navy in 1915. Later in the war she worked around Penzance and the Scillies as a net tender (looking after anti-submarine nets), and then became a Depot Ship at Falmouth. She acted as the base ship for the ships of the local auxiliary patrol and men like Bertie, who were allocated to the ship, would have been based ashore.

She survived the war, and returned to civilian use, and then went on to serve during World War II.

In December, 1917, Bertie was transferred to take command of another Armed Yacht, the 'H.M.Y. Rovenska'. She was a very elegant one funnelled yacht.

At last he was promoted to Acting Lieutenant Commander.

'Rovenska' was built in 1904 in Leith. Her crew were the captain; a lieutenant; a sub-lieutenant; an Assistant Paymaster and a Telegraph Operator.

The ships logs from the Rovenska were found at the National Archives. Her duties were to check, and if needed challenge shipping in the English south-west approaches. The records reveal challenges to several German Submarines. On one occasion they tried to ram a submarine which was submerging, and on another they fired at a submerging submarine. In both instances they were unable to cause serious damage.

On the 19 August 1915 Rovenska saw off U38 after the submarine had sunk the 'Restormel', a collier ship, forcing the U-boat to withdraw. Rovenska rescued the survivors of that encounter.

U38, under the command of Captain Max Valentiner, was the 3rd most 'successful' U boat during the war, sinking 138 ships.

Beatrice told her son Michael in later life that Bertie was the Commander of a Royal Yacht. Although initially I thought this might be a bit of exaggeration, there is more than an element of truth to the story, as can be seen from a history of this interesting boat.

Rovenska had been built for the Archduchess Maria Theresa of Austria, and was named after Port Rovenska, a small port on an island off present day Croatia. The Archduchess owned the ship between 1904 and 1909. She was next owned, between 1910 and 1913, by Sir Maxim Waechter, who lived in Richmond; and just before the war by Gustavus Harry Fradelle Pratt, a London-based Naval Architect and Yacht Broker.

After the war, in 1919, she was bought by Guglielmo Marconi, renamed Elettra, and converted into a floating wireless laboratory. A Neapolitan naval officer, Raffaele Lauro, was appointed as captain, commanding a crew of 30. Marconi travelled between Italy and England, where the vessel was restored to its former glory and fitted out as his personal, floating laboratory, containing very advanced radio equipment for the day. She was given the call sign 1CCM and took part in many of the trials of early sea-going radio equipment. In addition to the wireless laboratory, the yacht had cabins for Marconi and his wife, three guest cabins, four bathrooms and an oak study.

In 1929, the King of Italy gave the title of Marquis to Marconi.

The boat was so loved by Marconi that his daughter, born in 1930, was also named Elettra.

Marconi's wife, the grand Marchessa Marconi died in 1937, and soon Marconi sold the boat to the Italian Government, or more accurately the Italian Ministry of Posts and Telegraph.

She was requisitioned by the German Navy in 1943. Under a German flag, in 1944 she was torpedoed by a British submarine and sunk off the Dalmatian coast. She was raised in 1962 to be cut up for scrap.

There were very few boats that served England in WWI and Germany in WWII.

Bertie must have made it home from 'Rovenska' for spells on leave, as the third child of the marriage, Michael, was born in late 1918 in Falmouth, after a gap of over five years.

In February 1919 Bertie was admitted to Portland Hospital for 14 days with influenza. This illness occurred during the worldwide influenza epidemic of 1919 which killed his brother Arthur later that year. He was fit again for service by March 1919. Two months later he was awarded the Victory Medal and returned to the Royal Naval Barracks in Portsmouth for 'disposal'. At that time, he and Beatrice were living at 11, Weston Terrace, Falmouth. He was demobbed soon afterwards, retaining the rank of Lieutenant Commander.

After the War, it was Bertie's intention to go back into the Merchant Navy as a North Sea Pilot. A passport, number 309964, was issued for this purpose in 1919 when he was aged 39, and gave personal details about him. The passport was a much more complicated document than today, a large folded sheet of paper, counter-signed by the Foreign Secretary and valid for two years. It was endorsed *'Travelling as a Pilot between Great Britain, and ports on the North Sea and the Baltic'*.

Nothing much is known about Bertie's work or life during the period immediately after 1919. I know that the family soon moved to Horley after Bertie had for some reason decided not to continue his Merchant Navy career.

According to Maughan Innes, Bertie's nephew, and an amusing raconteur and gossip about the family, between the end of the War and 1922 Bertie was instrumental in getting money out of a family trust to support a series of failing businesses. Maughan's mother told him that Bertie did this twice.

The Crofts Trust had been instigated by Bertie's maternal great grandfather, Robert Crofts, (born 1783 and died 1868), in order to leave the majority of his extensive Dumpton Estate in Kent to his first-born male descendant using the surname 'Crofts'. Thwarted for some generations by the birth of only daughters and granddaughters, Robert Crofts eventually got his wish posthumously when Bertie Humble became Bertie Humble-Crofts. More details of this complex Trust and its ramifications will be found later.

Descendants of Beatrice Martha Harrod

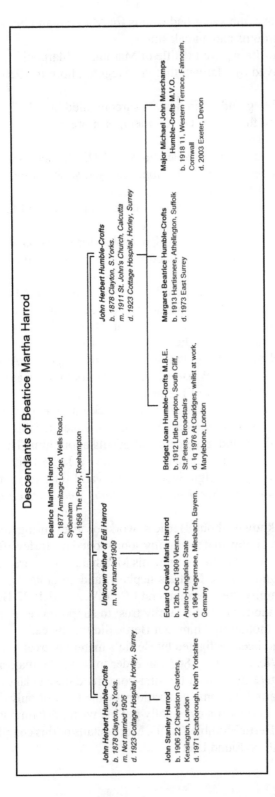

Beatrice Martha Harrod
b. 1877 Armitage Lodge, Wells Road,
Sydenham
d. 1958 The Priory, Roehampton

Unknown father of Edi Harrod
m. Not married 1909

John Herbert Humble-Crofts
b. 1878 Clayton, S.Yorks.
m. Not married 1905
d. 1923 Cottage Hospital, Horley, Surrey

John Herbert Humble-Crofts
b. 1878 Clayton, S.Yorks.
m. 1911 St. John's Church, Calcutta
d. 1923 Cottage Hospital, Horley, Surrey

Eduard Oswald Maria Harrod
b. 12th. Dec 1909 Vienna,
Austro-Hungarian State
d. 1964 Tegernsee, Miesbach, Bayern,
Germany

John Stanley Harrod
b. 1906 22 Cheniston Gardens,
Kensington, London
d. 1971 Scarborough, North Yorkshire

Bridget Joan Humble-Crofts M.B.E.
b. 1912 Little Dumpton, South Cliff,
St.Peters, Broadstairs
d. 1q 1976 At Claridges, whilst at work,
Marylebone, London

Margaret Beatrice Humble-Crofts
b. 1913 Hartismere, Athelington, Suffolk
d. 1973 East Surrey

**Major Michael John Muschamps
Humble-Crofts M.V.O.**
b. 1918 11, Western Terrace, Falmouth,
Cornwall
d. 2003 Exeter, Devon

Chart 5: Descendants of Beatrice Martha Harrod

Maughan said that on the first occasion he shared out equal amounts between all of those who were due to receive bequests, but on the second occasion, with the help of an amenable and allegedly crooked solicitor, he broke into the Trust again to pay off the debts of his failing garage business.

The absolute truth of this is unconfirmed, but when Bertie's mother Bridget died, all the children except Bertie's family received a share. There may have been an earlier settlement which precluded them from receiving any more in Bridget's will.

A rather different slant on the whole Dumpton Estate and Crofts Trust business was given by Michael Humble-Crofts, when he wrote a letter to Maughan Innes. The timings mentioned are different, but the gist of the business is the same.

'Now I will try to put the record straight re the Dumpton Estate. The correct version was given to me by Maud and I still have her details in writing.'

Maud, Bertie's sister, appears to have told Maughan her son, a slightly different tale to the one she told to Michael, her nephew.

'After my father came of age and before he married,' (which would make it between 1900 and 1911), *'our grandmother,'* (Bridget Humble-Crofts nee White), *'and Bertie agreed to "cut the entail" and take out £10,000 from the Dumpton Estate to be divided between Gun, Cyril, Arthur, Una and Maud, after the death of our grandmother.'* (Presumably Bertie was also in the cut. The others were his siblings. Grandmother did not die until 1932, so the question remains as to whether any money was actually divided? I wonder now if Michael really meant 'before the death of our grandmother', otherwise it was pointless.

Entail is a system of fixed succession of land tenure which was introduced by the statute De Donis in 1285, and by which the holder has only a life interest in the land, which passes on his death to his heirs and which cannot be altered by a will. Readers of Jane Austen novels will know that it is also discussed in Pride and Prejudice. The Crofts Trust would have passed the property and estate intact through the generations, with the considerable rents and interest available to the owner of the time.

'My father received an allowance from his mother of £100 per year.'

Hence the children only received the interest on their share until their mother's death. £100 would be worth about £9,000 today, so £10,000 would be about £900,000 today!)

'The whole estate was valued at about £90,000,' (£8M today,) *'and after the first "entail cut" the estate was re-entailed according to Robert Crofts will, i.e. our grandmother was left everything in trust for her life and it then passed to the eldest son, my father. If my father had a son, which he did, me, and if he, my father that is, pre-deceased his mother, which he did, the whole estate would*

pass to his eldest son, me, which never happened.' (Odd to think that in fact my father John Stanley was actually the eldest son!).

'Because unknown to our grandmother, my father with the help of Jack Hodding, his solicitor and grandmother's half-brother, cut the entail again so that he could borrow money from an Insurance Company. My mother knew all about this and our grandmother was terribly shocked, when my father was killed, to learn that the Dumpton Estate was swallowed up by the Insurance Company.'

To translate this, Bertie contrived, with solicitor Jack Hodding, and probably with wife Beatrice, to take capital out of the Trust rather than wait until his mother's death. To do so, he must have given the Trust as surety to the Insurance Company for the loan of money!

To have cut the entail again without his mother's knowledge would necessarily have required forgery. One presumes that Bertie had intended that he would pay the Insurance Company back after his mother's death, but then unexpectedly he died before her. The Insurance Company would have had to wait until Bridget's death in 1932 to get hold of the Estate, but then it would be theirs.

Records held at Kent Archives show how extensive the Estate was, and that parcels of very desirable land were sold off in 1903 and 1919, presumably the dates when the 'entail was cut'.

At the National Archives there are a large number of records relating to the Crofts legacy and the numerous legal wrangles that followed the death of Robert Crofts in 1868. They are contained in the records relating to the 'Court of Chancery'. Despite spending several days sifting through many of these documents at Kew, no great light was thrown on what really happened; indeed more questions were raised than answers found. The National Archives describe what Chancery is about.

'Since the late 14th century, hundreds of thousands of disputes over inheritance and wills, lands, trusts, debts, marriage settlements, apprenticeships, and other parts of the fabric of daily life, were heard by the Lord Chancellor or his deputies. People turned to his court of Chancery because it was an equity court, promising a merciful justice not bound by the strict rules of the common law courts. The procedure was quite different, and involved the gathering of written pleadings and evidence. These still exist in such quantity that today the equity records of the court of Chancery (from 1873 the Chancery Division of the Supreme Court of Judicature) are one of the treasures of The National Archives, and a major resource for social and economic history.

Most of its records are in English: many appear (misleadingly) to be written speech. The initial pleadings are the best known, but behind them is a huge hinterland of investigation (and administration of properties in dispute) by the court.'

It was difficult initially to find the correct documents. After searching under the name 'Crofts' with no success, I discovered that the records are sometimes filed under the name of subsequent litigants. Under the catalogue reference, C16/759/W129, the case of 'White v James' was discovered and followed. White was the maiden name of Bridget Humble-Crofts, and James was one of the original Trustees of the Trust. The initial pleadings, depositions, interrogatories, affidavits and answers, then some of the decrees and orders, could be found and the trail was followed from 1871 to 1877.

These cases often went on for decades before a final conclusion was reached.

It was obvious that there were many more papers which I did not find and I suspect they are filed under yet another name.

The initial Bill of Complaint lists the plaintiffs as,

'CHARLOTTE CROFTS WHITE and BRIDGET WHITE, infants, and CHARLOTTE BATES HODDING, the wife of the Defendant HENRY SWEET HODDING, by the Reverend EDWARD LAMB, their next friend;

Charlotte and Bridget White's mother, the daughter of Robert Crofts, also called Charlotte, had re-married a Henry Sweet Hodding after the death of their father, the Reverend White.

Jack, or John, Hodding, the solicitor who later helped Bertie with the Trust, was Henry's son. The White sisters, named as 'infants, were in fact aged 20 and 18 in 1871!

The details of the Chancery case are long, detailed and baffling, and I must admit I never fully understood what happened.

In short, the Trustees were accused of retaining funds for their own purposes. Names were added to and removed from the list so that by 1877 a completely different list of plaintiffs was used, adding to the confusion. I have still to find the conclusion of the case.

Whatever happened, Bertie, with the help of his solicitor friend Jack Hodding, managed to use his future expectations from the Crofts Estate to obtain money by using it as security with the insurance company. The money was used to buy a house and a business, and probably to bail out a business.

The plan, put into action without the consent of his mother, and hence illegally, was to go horribly and expensively wrong.

In 1920 Bertie took over a garage in Massetts Road, Horley called 'George Norman Motor Repairs'. He renamed it 'Horley Motor Services and Supply Company Limited'. It had a hire business in Victoria Road and the workshop was in Massetts Road.

The National Archives at Kew show that the business had been established in 1919 by five Horley tradesmen and an Engineer, with a bank loan secured by various parcels of land in Horley.

Descendants of Robert Crofts

Chart 6: Descendants of Robert Crofts

In 1920 the Engineer left the business and Bertie then appeared on the list of directors and shareholders. He had 1500 shares out of a total of 7200, so just over 20%. He signed the Company Returns as the Secretary and was also the Managing Director. The assumption is that he invested a lot of money. Whether this was a genuinely reasonable investment or some sort of a scam by the other shareholders is not known.

The relevant page from the Horley Area telephone book for 1920 shows not only the Humble-Crofts' personal entry for their house, at Lovell Oaks, Charlwood, but the business entry and a small advert for the Company. It stated, '3-ton Motor Lorry for Hire. Anything taken from and to anywhere. High-Class Cars for Hire. Repairs by Skilled Engineers.'

An estimate for a wedding car from Horley Motor Service and Supplies Company Limited from 1925 has been found amongst the papers and shows some other details. The car was a Lancia Saloon, and for two journeys and an extra car for the wedding, the total estimate was £2 15s.

Following Bertie's entry into the business it did not do well financially, and everything got much worse for the family in 1923.

At about 7 o'clock on the evening of Saturday, the 1 September, three days before his 45th birthday, Bertie was in collision with a motor coach whilst riding his motorbike, and died two days later. He had officially parted company with the business the day before the accident and was on his way home. Had he been celebrating?

The event is described in the newspaper article covering the story and the Coroner's Inquest.

COLLISION AT HORLEY
HORLEY MAN'S DEATH WHILE MOTOR-CYCLING.
DAY AFTER RETIREMENT FROM BUSINESS.
The day after his retirement from business, Mr John Herbert Humble-Crofts, of Lovell Oaks, Lowfield Heath, and well known in Horley, while riding a motor-cycle collided with a motor char-a-banc and received such injuries that he died. The accident occurred at the junction of Bright Road and Massetts Road, Horley, about seven o'clock on Saturday evening, and Mr Humble-Crofts died in Horley Cottage Hospital on Monday. Deceased was for several years a director of the Horley Motor Services and Supply Co., and the evening before the accident he was presented with a silver cup from his employees as a token of goodwill. He had also made arrangements for a holiday tour. Mr Humble-Crofts was riding out of Massetts Road, and the motor char-a-banc was proceeding towards London. He swerved into the char-a-banc, and his body striking the mudguard, he was thrown against the side, knocking off the handle of the driver's door and also damaging one of the supports of the canopy.' (Most coaches in those days were open-topped, with a canopy like a soft-top that could be raised in inclement weather.)

'Mr F. J. Nightingale, Coroner for East Surrey, held an inquest into the circumstances at the Chequers Hotel on Wednesday morning, and, sitting without a jury, he found that death was due to accident.

Superintendent West was present, and Mr G. L. Patten represented the owners of the char-a-banc and the driver involved in the accident.

Mr John Edwin Hodding,' (Jack) 'of Moro, Plat, Caton, Lancashire, an uncle of the deceased, gave evidence of identification, stating that his nephew was 44 years of age, and was a retired motor garage proprietor.

CHAR-A-BANC DRIVER'S STORY

George Percival Meede, of Risely, Bing Road, High Barnet, Herts., the driver of the char-a-banc, stated that he was driving from Brighton to London on Saturday. He was going slowly past the Church. A gentleman on a motor-bicycle came out of Massetts Road at a high rate of speed. He hit witness's off-side wing. Witness was on the crown of the road.

The Coroner: Why were you on the crown of the road?

Witness: I had just pulled out on to the middle of the road to pass a lady on a bicycle.

The Coroner: Isn't that rather a dangerous thing to do when passing a turning, because it would give less room to a person coming out of a side road.

Witness: I suppose so.

The Coroner: Did the deceased come straight at you?

Witness: He hit the wing of the char-a-banc and knocked the handle of the door right back, and knocked back the bracket where the canopy is fastened.

The Coroner: Did he come straight at you without turning to the left or the right?

Witness: He swerved out of the road and could not get around me.

The Coroner: Do you suggest he was going too fast to turn the corner properly?

Witness: He was.

Witness: continuing, said he immediately pulled up and went for Dr Clarke, and for the Police, and he helped Dr Clarke.

The Coroner: I don't understand why you were going at only 15 miles an hour. Why did you slow up?

Witness: I was passing Gatwick Racecourse, and I knew it was the race day. Witness added that he knew the corner fairly well, as he had driven a milk cart around it.

Mr Patten: Was there plenty of room to have got around you?

Witness: Yes, but deceased had such a speed that he had to swerve right out in the middle of the road to turn the corner.

Mr Patten: Nothing you could have done would have avoided the accident?

Witness: No, I could not have done anything.

Mr Hodding asked the witness if he saw the motor-cycle after the accident, and whether it was badly damaged.

The witness replied that one mudguard was broken or bent, but it was not seriously damaged, and a man got on it and rode it away.

Mr Hodding: In swerving round he did not go head on?

Witness: No. He was going so fast that as he hit the mudguard he left the bike.

Mr Hodding: If he had hit you head on it would have broken the machine up?

Witness: It is hard to say.

Mr Patten: If Mr Humble-Crofts had only struck you a glancing blow it would not have damaged your char-a-banc so much.

Witness: No. There was only a slight impact between the two machines.

EYE-WITNESSES' DESCRIPTION

William James Fraser, of Holmlea, Gatwick, stated that on Saturday evening. He was walking slowly along the footpath near the junction of Brighton Road and Massetts Road. He saw the char-a-banc coming from Brighton towards London, and as it approached the corner a motor-cycle came out of Massetts Road on to the main road. The motor-cyclist was travelling at a very smart pace; he would say at about 25 or 26 miles an hour. He considered it a high rate of speed for him to take the corner. The char-a-banc was coming along at about 15 or 16 miles an hour.

The Coroner: Where was the char-a-banc?

Witness: On the crown of the road.

The Coroner: Did you hear any warning sound – any hooter?

Witness: None at all, until the crash.

The Coroner: Did you see where the motor-cycle struck the char-a-banc?

Witness: Yes; on the offside wheel and the side of the car.

The Coroner: So far as you could see the char-a-banc was being driven in a proper manner?

Witness: Quite in a proper manner.

Dr S. H. Clarke said he saw deceased just before the accident. Deceased was going down the road at a "nice, decent speed". Witness did not see him go round the corner. Witness was going home, and he had reached his gate when the message came to him to return. He saw deceased lying on the road, on the left-hand side looking towards Gatwick. Witness could see that he was absolutely unconscious, and has a fracture of the base of the skull, and a comminuted fracture of the right leg. He saw him at the Hospital, and he telephoned Dr William Turner, of Harley Street, who arrived at a quarter to eight Sunday morning, and he agreed that nothing could be done. Death was due to the fractured base of the skull.

CORONER AND WARNING NOTICES

The Coroner said this unfortunate occurrence had happened at a spot known to be dangerous and representations had been made to the County Council and to the Automobile Association, but no warning notice had been put up.

Sometimes if notices were put up, they were disregarded. This unfortunate gentleman knew the corner as he had been riding around it twice a day, and if one knew it to be dangerous it was incumbent upon him to drive carefully. From the evidence he came to the conclusion that the deceased was going round the corner at a speed higher than he ought to have done, and his finding was that death was due to accident, and no blame attached to the driver of the char-a-banc. He expressed his sympathy with the widow.

Mr Hodding thanked the Coroner and Mr Patten for their sympathy.

The Coroner said that if he had had a jury doubtless, they would have suggested that something should be done to get notices put up, and he would make representations to the authorities.'

The Death Certificate issued states that Bertie was a 'Retired Motor Garage Proprietor'. Death was due to 'Accidental death. Fracture of skull and other injuries caused by collision of motor cycle ridden by the deceased with a char a banc.'

He had been married for 12 years and his children would have then been aged eleven, ten and four.

It is difficult to believe that if the business had been doing well, Bertie would retire voluntarily at his age. He had been the Managing Director and Company Secretary for 3 years. More likely that he was being eased out, or the company had already failed. The silver cup presented to him suggests that there was no acrimony with his staff at the time of his departure. There is no question of his death being anything but an accident, so suicide was not his intention.

John Edward (not Edwin) Hodding, (Uncle Jack), the solicitor who had helped Bertie with the Trust, was Bertie's step-Uncle on his mother's side and was then aged 62. It is odd that he should come all the way from Lancaster to be the person to identify the body and then remain until two days later to represent the family at the Inquest. It was a long way to come when Bertie's father and brother were much closer. Bertie and Jack had been involved in the financial dealings together and Jack may have wanted to keep an eye on the money and his reputation subsequent to Bertie's early death.

If Bertie's family were too upset to perform the duties, the surprise is that Herbert Martin, Bea's brother-in-law, and a London Solicitor, did not do the job for the family. However, the Harrod and Humble-Crofts sides of the family were not close to each other and the rift may have widened following the tragedy.

The tributes at the funeral confirm that Uncle Jack and Bertie were close friends.

There was an outpouring of sympathy and sadness in Waldron. The funeral, which took place the day after the Inquest, on Thursday the 6 September, was covered by several papers. The report from the Sussex Express of the 7 September is typical. Parts of the report follow:

WALDRON RECTOR BEREAVED
SON A VICTIM OF MOTOR ACCIDENT,
BURIED ON HIS BIRTHDAY.

The parish of Waldron was in mourning yesterday (Thursday) afternoon, when the eldest son of the Rev. Preb. W. J. Humble-Crofts (Rural Dean and Rector of Waldron), and Mrs Humble-Crofts was laid to rest in the churchyard. Mr John Herbert Humble-Crofts was the victim of a motor accident at Horley, Surrey, on Saturday evening. Whilst negotiating a bend in the road on his motor cycle, he swerved to avoid a cyclist and collided with a motor coach. He was taken to Horley Cottage Hospital suffering from severe injuries and he passed away on Monday morning.' (This was not quite correct; the coach driver had moved to the centre of the road to avoid the cyclist.)

'Mr Humble-Crofts, who would have attained his 45th birthday yesterday, resided at "Lovell Oaks", Horley. He was educated at Stubbington House, near Portsmouth, and after a period on the "Britannia", he entered the Merchant Service and was with the British India Steamship Co. for about 16 years.' (Actually 13 years in total). *'During the late war he served in the Royal Naval Reserve. For the past three or four years he had been Managing Director of the Horley Motor Services.*

The immediate mourners were Mrs J. H. Humble-Crofts, (widow), Mrs W. J. Humble-Crofts, (mother), Mr and Mrs G. Humble-Crofts, (brother and sister-in-law), Miss Humble-Crofts, (sister), Mr and Mrs Innes, (brother-in-law and sister), Colonel Humble-Burkitt and Mr J. E. Hodding, (uncles), Mr and Mrs Chalk, (uncle and aunt), Miss Humble and Miss E. Humble, (aunts), Mr H. Harrod, (brother-in-law), Miss Chalk and Miss Hodding, (cousins).'

Among others who were listed, some are worth listing, *'Mr E. Blundell and Mr J. Brown, (representing the Horley and District Constitutional Club), Miss Ballingall,'* (Nanny)... *Mr S. Harris and Mr J. Razell, (representing the Horley Motor Services) ...Mr W. Whitmore (Horley).'*

Henry Herbert Harrod, Bea's brother, was the only member of the Harrod family present apart from Bea herself. Bea's mother had died the previous year, 1922.

Other reports tell us that the bearers were all friends from Waldron Parish, where Bertie had lived since aged four. Many names of other mourners were in other reports, most were presumably local villagers, but they also included a Lord Newborough. (This would have been Thomas John Wynn, the 5th Baron Newborough. Thomas Wynn was the same age as Bertie and had attended Stubbington House School at about the same time. He also served in W.W.I. in the Royal Naval Reserve.)

'FLORAL TRIBUTES
Beautiful floral tributes were sent as follows:
"Mrs J. H. Humble-Crofts." (From Bea. Just the name, but no message, unless it was kept private.)

"In ever loving memory of our dear son, I thank God for every remembrance of you." (From his parents).

"In loving memory of a very dear brother, from Una."

"With deepest sympathy, from Gun and Winnie."

"With love, from Leslie and Maud."

"Love for a happy birthday, from Babsie."

"With happy birthday greeting, love from Bridget." (These were from Bertie's two daughters, then aged eleven and ten. His son, Michael, then aged four, would have been too young to be included.)

"From his loving god-mother, Aunt Tootie." (His mother's sister Charlotte.)

"In loving memory of a true sportsman, in every sense, and the best and cheeriest of pals, from Uncle Jack and Auntie Belle, (Mr and Mrs J.E. Hodding)." (This rather confirms their close relationship.)

"Golden memories, Nannie." (Nanny Ballingall.)

"Evelyn Chalk, in great admiration." (Cousin.)

"In loving memory, from Nurse."

"In remembrance, Gertrude G. Ackerman." (The governess at Waldron Rectory.)

"With deepest sympathy, from G. Burbridge, M.A. Burbridge and Percy." (From Harrods)

"With deepest sympathy from Mr and Mrs W. Whitmore, jnr., (Horley)."

"From the Waldron Men's Social Club, as an expression of sympathy."

"With deepest sympathy, from the President and Committee of the Waldron Flower Show."

"In kind remembrance, from the past and present members of the Waldron Cricket Club."

"With deepest sympathy, from the members of the Horley and District Constitutional Club."

"With deepest sympathy, from the staff of the H. M. S. and Co., Horley."

Another notice stated that:

'He was a very gallant gentleman and great sorrow has been expressed at his untimely death'.

There were many others, not listed here as they are not relevant to the story.

Although some of the feelings expressed in the reports may well have been directed as much to the Rector and his family, as to Bertie, they do not suggest any Humble-Crofts family split caused by Bertie's financial dealings. Perhaps they were still as yet undiscovered.

The expressions of love from friends suggest a warm relationship with Bertie who was obviously a very social animal. He was well-liked locally and viewed as a war hero by many.

The lack of any tributes from Beatrice or support from her family, apart from her brother Herbert who was at the funeral, and sister Olive, who sent flowers, is a little surprising.

The warm messages from staff of Horley Motor Services, and the new owner, did not suggest an acrimonious departure.

Bertie's will was brief; he had not expected to die at this age. It was written on the 9 February, 1912, the day before the birth of the first child of the marriage, Bridget, reflecting his recognition of his impending financial responsibilities.

Basically, he left everything to Beatrice Martha, who was also the sole executrix. The will left £2636.4s.8d, about £120,000 in today's value. He was certainly not bankrupt at that stage, but would have been worth a lot more if the Trust had been intact. This would seem to suggest that the business cannot have been doing that badly.

However, by 1925 it is more evident things were not going well for the Horley Motor Company. There was no Bertie involved in the Company, and there was a late submission of the annual return to Companies House. The business was then owned by a single family, the Whitmores, and soon after this it went into liquidation. The Company continued to appear in Kelly's Directory until 1930. The Local History Society told me that the business was taken over again in 1933 and lasted until 1971, then becoming 'Horley Tyre and Exhaust'.

Chapter 18
Eduard Maria Harrod

1912-1933

As we saw earlier, Eduard disappears from the records after early 1913, having added Maria to his name at his baptism.

He does reappear in 1918, when he would have been eight years old.

The Countess appears alone in records, at various addresses in district VIII of Vienna, between those dates, though the Archives and Lehmann's do not always agree on the exact address or dates.

During this period several important events occur.

Beatrice appears to have been paying the Countess a regular amount for her care of Eduard.

At the outbreak of World War I, in July 1914, these payments would have ceased as no money transfers would be allowed between the warring factions.

By 1916, looting and food riots in Vienna as result of the British blockade in North Sea and French blockade of Adriatic ports became increasingly common as shortages began to bite. Hunger and disease became commonplace in large cities.

By mid-1916, the Countess must have become desperate. She enlists the help of the Imperial Foreign Ministry to write to the British Foreign Office, using the offices of the American Embassy, to try to get the payments reinstated.

The Countess knew not only Beatrice's maiden name, but also her married name, and her address at the Waldron Rectory, which was her in-laws' family residence. I am certain Beatrice herself would not have used this address for any previous correspondence with the Countess, so the Countess must have had another source for this information.

I would presume that in order to obtain the help of the Ministry, the Countess must have had some privileged access. I am not sure that any 'Hinz, Kunz und Franz' (Tom, Dick and Harry) could have mobilised them to act on her behalf. Perhaps just being a Countess was enough? Perhaps she still had friends in high places? Her failure to obtain further funds from Beatrice must have made her more desperate. If Beatrice was able to contact the father, who refused to help, would the Countess also be able to make contact and seek help?

The death of Emperor Franz Josef on the 21 November 1916, aged 86, unsettled the army for a while, but had little overall effect on the eventual loss of the war and death of the Empire. They were already lost. His nephew and original heir, Archduke Franz Ferdinand had been assassinated in 1914 in Sarajevo, resulting in Austria-Hungary's declaration of war against the Kingdom of Serbia, which was Russia's ally. That activated a system of alliances which resulted in World War I.

After Franz Josef's death, his grandnephew, Archduke Charles succeeded him.

Whatever happened to the Countess and Eduard personally, over the ensuing two years, things can only have got worse for ordinary folk in Vienna. Despite the privations, the salons of the very rich continued and much of Vienna's talent continued to flourish. Even in 1918, the exhibitions were held, but at the end of that year, Schiele, Klimt and Moser had all died in the flu pandemic sweeping Europe.

There was civil unrest in 1918 with strikes against food shortages and rationing. Most of Vienna was exhausted. The shortage of fuel led people to go to the cinema to get warm and just stay there. A point was made to show no food in the films.

In the midst of all this mayhem Eduard reappears in February 1918, at the same address as the Countess, VIII, Stolzenthalergasse 13/1/5. She remained at this address for the following eight years.

The Countess had moved there that February after three years in VIII Floriangasse.

These periods of residence were the longest stable spells during her appearance in the Vienna archives – does this suggest an improvement in her finances?

By the early 1920s all the sophistication of Vienna had gone. The artists and politicians had fled to Berlin. Vienna was still hungry, but was now the capital of a small country. There was growing nationalism and anti-Semitism. The Austrian writer Karl Kraus called his country the 'laboratory of the apocalypse, dancing towards destruction'. The National-Sozialistische-Deutsche-Arbeiter-Partei (National Socialist German Workers' Party), the precursor of the Nazi Party, was rising and recruiting.

Vienna was in the midst of a great political upheaval. The Grand Coalition of the main parties that had begun in 1920 had come to an end. In 1923 and 1927 there had been violent clashes between left- and right-wing supporters, and by the end of the decade the Social Democrats eventually gained power after more conflict. The French occupation of the Ruhr in 1923, the result of Germany's failure to meet its W.W.I. reparations payments, caused both economic problems and stoked the rise in National Socialism. Hitler, who had led them since 1921, felt the time was ripe for an attempt to seize power. However, this failed, and Hitler was jailed for a several months in 1924.

For the period from 1918 onwards, whilst the Countess had a stable address, Eduard was apparently living at the same address until about 1924, when he would have been 14 years old. It may have just been his 'home' address whilst he was away some of the time.

Eduard's descendants were told by Eduard that he spent time with foster parents in Switzerland, where he furthered his education, and also had a spell in the Foreign Legion. There is little evidence to back this up, and he would have been too young for the Foreign Legion during this period. I shall return to these claims later. Eduard also claimed in a later document that from 1923 onwards, he was acting as a representative for various companies travelling around the country. This may have been so when he was a bit older, but I doubt this started in 1923 when he was 13 years old.

Eduard was certainly back in Vienna in 1924.

The archives state that between July and October that year, 1924, Eduard was living at XIII, St. Veit-Gasse 25, a home for delinquent juveniles.

In the August of the following year, 1925, Edi, as he was called, was 14 years old. He was arrested for fighting and causing damage. He had thrown stones at a Jewish car during disturbances at the 14th Zionist Conference in Vienna and was sentenced to ten days confinement. There was trouble from young Nazis throughout the Conference. The President of the World Zionist Organisation, Chaim Weizmann and his wife rode through taunting crowds accompanied by a police escort from their hotel to the conference hall.

In 1926, he was again in trouble and was discharged by the Juvenile Court in July. At the end of October, he was in police custody and absconded from a Police Youth Centre in early November.

He was last seen in the home for delinquent juveniles in St. Veit-gasse in December.

He had gone off the rails. At this time, it would not have been unusual for a young lad at a loose end to join an anti-Jewish movement. There had been a lot of anger and resentment stirred up in those post-war years about immigrants to Austria, especially the Jews.

In addition, there may have been problems at 'home'.

The Countess was ill at this time and died on the 22 November, 1926. The death of the Countess, his only known 'relative', must have had a profound effect on the youngster. He had been in recurrent trouble in the few months leading up to her death.

Further searches of the records showed she did not leave a will, and at the time of her death there did not seem to be any true relatives or friends involved in her life. The report after her death stated that no relations were known or could be traced. She had lived in the apartment in Stolzenthalergasse consisting of three rooms, an entrance hall, and a kitchen. She was all but destitute, having no cash, and owned only the furnishings in her apartment, estimated to be worth 1000 Schillings. This probably equates to less than £1000 today.

Her burial costs were estimated at 95 Schillings.

All of this information was given to the authorities at the time of her death by a young man who lived with her as her boarder, Eduard Hugetz. He also signed the documents and agreed to pay her burial costs. His profession was given as "Privater" which means that he was living on private means.

It seemed unusual that a lodger would pay for his landlady's funeral expenses and suggested some sort of friendship. Had he moved in when Edi moved out?

As Hugetz had the same Christian name as the Countess's husband, it crossed my mind that there might be a connection. I started to wonder if perhaps Eduard Hugetz was Beatrice's Eduard, and related in some way to the Count.

Hugetz is very rare name, but despite this, research found no trace of this Eduard Hugetz.

I did trace a Hugetz family in Houston, Texas, and encouragingly, the research showed that the man was called Edward (Eduard), as were his father, grandfather and great grandfather before him. The family originated in Slovakia and Hungary and promisingly, were in Vienna in the early 20th century. One of the several Eduard Hugetz had emigrated to the USA in 1914.

My hopes were dashed. Having made contact, Edward Hugetz in Houston knew nothing of the family origins in Vienna or any of the characters I had found.

I found an Ernst Hugetz in Vienna in 1913 and a Fritz Hugetz, a hotel waiter in London in 1911.

No connections to Eduard were discovered, and this line of research gradually dried up.

The Hugetz link was another red herring.

Following the Countess's death, Edi was left with no stable person in his life. He spent the next 18 months or so in and out of Police Youth Centres, latterly in Korneuburg Educational Institution, seven miles from Vienna.

Once again, he is missing between 1927 and 1930. Was this the time he was acting as a representative, or in the Foreign Legion?

After Eduard reappears in March 1930, now aged 20, he then lives in a series of men's hostels, each for a month or so at a time until June, when he was discharged to Salzburg, 180 miles to the west of Vienna. In September 1930, he attended an Employment Conference in Thennig, a suburb of Linz, 100 miles west of Vienna. Linz was the capital of Upper Austria. It was quoted by Hitler as the most German city in Austria, and his 'home'.

The 'Party' was well represented there and Eduard decided to join the N.S.D.A.P.

He had won his spurs during the anti-Jewish disturbances of 1925 and he may have been caught up in all the rhetoric. At the time, there had been no general support in the country for the Nazis, but their following grew rapidly in the subsequent years.

He was employed first at the 'Institute of Technic' and lived in Vienna between 1931 and 1933.

According to the N.S.D.A.P. district records, he was placed in the custody of district Leader of Party, Brigade Leader Geister. at I, Elisabethstrasse 9. Brigade Leader was a para-military rank used by the Nazi S.A. from 1920 onwards and the S.S. between 1932 and 1945 – equivalent to Brigadier General.

In a later statement held in the Bundersarchiv records, Eduard listed the Imperial Head of the Party, Rentmeister (Treasurer) Colonel Hans Geister and the S.S. Senior Troup Leader Harnish as witnesses to his party membership, which he said occurred on 9 May 1930.

Edi lived at 12 different addresses in Vienna over the following two years, sometimes with several spells at an address. Most were men's hostels, and he also used the Salvation Army hostel at III, Kolonitzgasse 2a on several occasions.

A later I.D. document from February 1933 rather strangely gives his occupation as a bookbinder.

In March 1933 Edi was sentenced to ten days' custody for causing bodily harm during a scuffle with a local security guard at the Vienna Town Hall. Brigade Leader Hans Geister then ordered him to Passau, on the Austrian/German border as a courier/messenger, presumably to keep him out of trouble. He served in this capacity for the Upper Austria brigade and Regional Office Upper Austria until November 1933. During this time, he again lived in hostels in Vienna.

Once again in later documents, Eduard stated that at times whilst a courier in Passau, he visited Dr Waechter in IV or VI district. Dr Waechter was a lawyer and Nazi activist in Vienna who later became a well know Nazi civil administrator. He was a very unsavoury character. He was deeply involved in the Nazi machine and narrowly escaped being implicated in the holocaust before seeking sanctuary with some monks, and dying in their care in 1949.

The last record of him in the Vienna Archives was on the 17 July 1933, when he was 'discharged' from the Salvation Army and listed as address unknown.

At the time in my research when I first saw these records, I knew nothing about his further life, and my assumption was that disappearing from a Salvation Army in 1933, in the cauldron that was Vienna, was bad news, and might have been the last I would hear of him.

Chapter 19
Beatrice Martha

1 September 1923

Beatrice's life had changed irrevocably. On the 1 September 1923 Bertie had ridden his motorcycle into a motor bus on the Brighton Road in Horley, and had died two days later.

She was in mourning but I suspect she was cursing him for the situation he had left her to cope with. Bertie had died two days before his 45th birthday. She was aged 46, widowed and had three young children to bring up on her own.

She was not in trouble financially, in fact she was reasonably comfortable, but the promised future of real wealth was gone. Her wayward husband, having compromised their finances by breaking into his Crofts Family Trust and covering a loan with the bequest, had lost it all because of his early death.

Her own mother, Caroline, had died the previous year in Tunbridge Wells after a stroke and she was probably still grieving for her. Her mother's estate was valued at just over £10,000, which would be equivalent to about £500,000 in today's value, so Beatrice's share after some other bequests, divided amongst the eight siblings, would only have been a modest sum, unless of course Bertie had managed to spend some or all of it already in the ensuing year.

There was Bertie's estate to add on, so Beatrice would have been able to rely on a small income from the capital.

Her father had died in 1905 and had left a considerable sum of money, some of which went to Beatrice, so she would have had some other money of her own. How much of this was left is not known, but as Bertie had raised other money to finance his business venture, probably not very much.

Because Bertie's indiscretion would have been discovered by his family following his death, his mother Bridget had subsequently left Beatrice out of her will.

However, Bridget, who eventually died in 1932, did make a settlement on Beatrice in 1931 to help her to manage. Despite the various bits and pieces of inheritance, Beatrice had become involved with moneylenders, and the settlement from her mother-in-law was needed to bail out her and the grandchildren.

The extended Humble-Crofts family were almost certainly hostile towards Beatrice; she was the daughter of a man involved in 'trade', and had run off with their favourite son Bertie. She may even have colluded in Bertie's embezzlement of the Trust. They had never thought her 'good enough' for Bertie.

So Beatrice was unlikely to get a lot of help there. However, she did manage in the end.

Beatrice moved from Horley soon after Bertie's death, and she and the three children lived between 1924 and 1932 at Barton, near Torquay in Devon. The reason for the choice of south Devon is not known. It was not an area familiar to her, though the Harrod family had lived in North Devon in her early twenties, and she and Bertie had spent some of the war years in Falmouth in Cornwall.

She had moved far away from both families, who were then based in Waldron in Sussex and south London, just when one would think she needed their help. Perhaps she wanted to get away to somewhere she was not known.

Much of what money she had was spent on schooling for the children. The two girls, Bridget and Margaret Beatrice, the latter known as Babs, went to a finishing school locally, and Michael went away in 1926 to Prepatory School in Bletchley, when aged seven.

In 1932 or 1933, soon after her mother-in-law dies, Beatrice and the family moved nearer to Michael's school, and lived in Littlewick Green, Maidenhead Thicket, in Berkshire. Littlewick Green was then an idyllic village on the Bath Road out of Maidenhead, with a cricket club on the green and charming cottages. Ivor Novello lived there. The phone books of the time tell us that they lived there until 1939.

The three children of Bertie and Bea's marriage were:

- Bridget Joan, the first daughter, was born in 1912 at Little Dumpton in Broadstairs. She had been conceived in India, almost immediately after her parent's wedding.

Bridget's words on her floral tribute for her father's funeral were those of a loving 11-year-old daughter. In 1936, Bridget, then aged 24, and her mother took a month's trip together to Madeira, boarding at Plymouth and travelling 1st class! Not an indication of a tight budget.

During WWII, Bridget worked with the A.T.A., Air Transport Auxiliary, probably in an administrative role. The Air Transport Auxiliary was a civilian organisation that ferried new, repaired and damaged military aircraft of all sorts between UK factories, assembly plants, transatlantic delivery points, maintenance units, scrap yards, and active service squadrons and airfields – but not to aircraft carriers. It also flew service personnel on urgent duty from one place to another and performed air ambulance work. Many of them were involved in the preparation, paperwork and maintenance for the flights, that was probably Bridget's role.

They took the place of men who were then free for combat. The A.T.A. did invaluable work.

By the end of the war, they had delivered 309,011 aircraft of more than 200 types including Swordfish, Albacore, Sea Otter, Walrus, Spitfires, Flying Fortresses and Lancasters.

The A.T.A. lost 174 people in the war, among them the famous aviator Amy Johnson C.B.E. She died in early 1941 when the Oxford aircraft she was ferrying crashed in the Thames Estuary.

After the war, Bridget went to work with what was then B.E.A., or British European Airways.

She worked in the administrative side of the ground staff, as a Special Facilities Officer at Heathrow Airport. Towards the end of her career, she dealt with all the V.I.P.s arriving at the airport.

Bridget was apparently an absolute dragon at work. You did not put a foot wrong with her!

In 1968, during her time with B.E.A., she was living in St. John's Wood, London, and in that year, she was awarded the M.B.E. for her services to the company.

After leaving B.E.A., Bridget had been head-hunted for a job at Claridges; her reputation for efficiency preceded her.

Bridget and Margaret Beatrice's niece described her thus:

'Aunt Bridget was a perfectionist – terribly smart and well dressed. When she came down to stay with us in the country, she could never get out of her high heels, and was never known to wear wellington boots. She was a city girl through and through. She was Special Facilities Officer with B.E.A. at Heathrow Airport, and only dealt with the rich and famous... I remember she was reported to have a man friend – Mr Danny, who I was told owned Brands Hatch (but that is very hazy).

She then retired and went to be Head Housekeeper at Claridges Hotel. She had a lovely apartment right at the top of the hotel, with one of those old sofas with drop sides which were tied up at the top. Both my brother, and cousin Jane and I were invited for supper from time to time, but always separately it seemed. I remember feeling very grand going in through the front entrance of Claridges to be greeted by the Manager ... and then getting the lift upstairs. Aunt Bridget used to tell us stories about the guests – one of whom, called Mrs D..., used to regularly have accidents in the lift which had to be cleaned up. But apparently, she was such a nice lady that everyone forgave her. Also I remember when Henry Kissinger came to stay, took over a whole floor and had to have telephones connected up all over the place.

Jane was always Aunt Bridget's favourite! When Bridget died, (of a brain haemorrhage) – she just fell down in one of the corridors one day – Mum, Jane and I went to sort out her belongings in her flat. We opened cupboards and found stacks of Hermes scarves, mountains of silk stockings and masses of expensive perfumes – all presents from grateful guests. They were all stacked in immaculate piles! We divided them out between us all, and I still have one or two pairs of the stockings and a couple of Hermes scarves. All the clothes went to friends or charity because she was a couple of sizes larger than any of us. Mum kept the Queens dress, which was a beautiful black and white real chiffon dress, with a rose at the waist, which Aunt Bridget had bought when she was presented to the Queen at Claridges.'

Bridget remained single and died at work from a brain haemorrhage early in 1976, aged 64.

- Margaret Beatrice, known as Babsie or Babs, was the second child of the marriage and was born in 1913, 13 months after her sister, whilst her parents were living in Athelington, Suffolk.

She married Ronald Herbertson at the end of 1940, in the Wokingham area in Berkshire.

Ronald, known as Sam, was born in 1918, in Dunbartonshire. In 1950, at the time when their daughter was born, he was a 'Rayon Manufacturer', and they lived in the small town of Ffynnongroyw, on the north-east coast of Flintshire, in North Wales. He later became a Director of what was then called Rank, Hovis, MacDougall.

Going back to her niece,

'Aunt Babs was married to Sam ... He was quite a jolly man I remember, and memories of Babs were that she always wore very red lipstick and her hair always looked perfect. They had the one daughter Jane. I used to spend time with them in school holidays, when my parents took themselves off for a holiday on their own.

I remember them living near Oxted, Surrey. Aunt Babs had a miniature dachshund called Teddy, who was known to urinate on the legs of the sofa, and had a disconcerting habit of rodgering everybody's legs! The only other thing I remember vividly was that Aunt Babs was a perfectionist, and would always plump up the cushions on the sofa immediately someone had got up! ...'

Sam, died on a golf course in Surrey at the back end of 1966, when he would have been 48 years old. Babs died of cancer in 1973. Her 1971 will left detailed instructions, including the bequest of a Wig Chest and Dining Room Chairs to Dr Lord, a man mentioned in an earlier chapter.

It was very difficult to find out about Beatrice Martha's life as a widow, especially once the children had grown up. Sources of first-hand information were scarce.

Her daughters had already died by the time my research started in 1988.

Her son Michael was very helpful with information once I found him, but was diffident when talking about his mother, with whom he had had a difficult relationship. He knew almost nothing about his father who had died when he was aged four.

Michael's wife, Anna, was very helpful and was able to fill in some of the gaps, and their daughter has added some personal information.

The telephone books show that by 1943 Beatrice was living at 'Virginia', St. Ives Road, Maidenhead. This was a large house in which she had an apartment. It is no longer in existence, but was right in the centre of Maidenhead, on the same road as the present Town Hall.

Michael remembered that his mother had a great deal of her possessions destroyed during the war, when a warehouse where they were stored was hit by a bomb. This might explain the paucity of photographs and memories that have passed through the family.

After the end of the war, she lived in private hotels in London, mostly in West London.

Beatrice was not popular with her grandchildren or her siblings. She was viewed as aloof and detached. One Harrod descendant told me, *'We were never good enough for her.'*

What did she do with herself? Did she have friends, did she ever visit relatives, or did they visit her? There is no information and this suggests to me that she was isolated and lonely.

Both the Harrods and the Humble-Crofts families thought her marriage had not been a good idea, so she was probably frozen out by both sides and then chose to keep to herself.

Beatrice was obviously delighted with son Michael's role with the Royal Family during the war. She was at one 'Morris' family christening and was said to have been invited to dine at the Palace during the war, with her son and the Royals, though Michael denied this. She was certainly at Michael's investiture. The rest of the family felt she became very snobbish about the 'Royal' connection.

In the late 1940s, she managed to upset the whole Conder side of the Harrod family, the family of Beatrice's eldest sister, Fanny. She did not respond to a request for help needed when Fanny was poorly and in a Nursing Home. To quote from a letter from a Conder descendant in about 1989.

'I remembered when Granny and Grandpa were very old and Granny in a Nursing Home, I asked whether they had heard from Bea, who was 22 years younger than Granny.' (she was actually 12 years younger). *'Grandpa said they never heard from any of the 'Harrods' and were somewhat upset about Bea as she had run away from home and stayed with them whilst they were a married couple. One thinks that perhaps this was when she got pregnant.'* I had told their family by this time the story of Dad's illegitimate birth, so I am unsure whether this statement was from her own memory, an adopted memory after hearing my story, or just my conjecture.

Beatrice was certainly branded as a 'difficult woman'. Anna stated: *'I got on well with Una Humble-Crofts and Maud Innes, both of whom were Michael's Aunts – I also learned a lot about Beatrice Harrod from them, and I regret to have to tell you that Maud did not care for her at all and certainly did not want her to join the Humble-Crofts family. I know that a lot of it was class consciousness which was very much to the fore in those days and I had it in my own family and grew up with it.'*

She continued: '...*even Michael did not care for his own mother – she blamed me for not always seeing enough of him after we were married and he used to come back on leave at intervals from North Africa to see me – If she but knew, he would never had visited her at all if I had not made him do so. Give her, her due, it must have been rather a shock to her, when, having met me in Algiers, Michael wrote and asked her to break off his engagement to a girl called Pam whom I suspect Beatrice had arranged, as she had masses of money! That was naughty of Michael, but I have to say he was very frightened of his mother, although she absolutely adored him, but she really was a very dominating character – I have always thought that when she heard I was a widow, she must have thought I was much older than him, and although I had breeding, I had no money!*

I cannot tell you how terrified I was when I had to meet her, by myself, when I came back to the U.K. on leave – Bridget was with her and that was my saving grace as I did like her very much – (Bridget, I mean!). I only knew my mother-in-law as Beatrice (no shortening of the name or nicknames) and Bertie was her husband, (Michael's father) as you know – my children really did not know her very well – they were very young when we emigrated to Australia. Just before we emigrated, Michael had left the XII Royal Lancers then and was farming in partnership with the husband of a friend of mine who had been in the W.R.N.S. with me – she blamed me for that, as she felt farming was below him after having been in the XII Royal Lancers!'

In the same year that Fanny Conder died, 1949, Beatrice met other members of the family at the 'Harrods' Centenary celebration lunch, which involved daughter Bridget, and other cousins. It was held in the Georgian Restaurant at the store.

The Evening Standard reported the event, mentioning Beatrice. The piece was entitled:

LADY IN GREY GOES TO THE ONE-FIRM SHOW

'*Standing quietly in the background of Harrods centenary celebrations in London today was a woman in grey. For her, the celebrations had a particular interest. But she was there almost by accident.*

The woman, Mrs Beatrice Humble-Crofts, was the only direct descendant present of Charles Digby Harrod, who bought his father's business in 1864 and sold it to Harrods Ltd. in 1889 for £120,000.' (This was not strictly true, as Beatrice's sister Eva and daughter Bridget were also present.)

'*It was as a customer that Mrs Humble-Crofts was invited to apply for a centenary book. Then Harrods did not know she was so closely related with the name of Harrod.*

So she told them and received an invitation to be present today.

150

Air hostess daughter

With Mrs Humble-Crofts was her daughter Bridget, tall, attractive, British European Airways hostess at Northolt...'

Photograph 8: Beatrice Martha, aged 72, and daughter Bridget, at 1949 Harrods celebrations (By kind permission of Harrods Ltd)

Various sources have revealed addresses for Beatrice during these years. Between 1945 and 1948, she lived at the Ashley Court Hotel, in Queensgate, a hotel with 67 residents. These establishments were not truly hotels in the modern sense, more like serviced apartments with long term residents.

In 1949, she was living at the Alwin Court Hotel, and for the years to 1953 she was at 55 Queens Gate, Gloucester Road, living with her daughter Bridget. There were 29 other residents.

By 1958, she was at the Nurray Guest House, 58, Frant Road, Tunbridge Wells.

In the late 1950s, Beatrice became increasingly difficult and aggressive due to her dementia and was latterly admitted to the Nursing Home in Roehampton.

Anna Humble-Crofts said: *'I was not popular with Beatrice... consequently, for several years after we were married, and she had met me at the wedding, although I tried my very best to get on with her, and be a good daughter-in-law, it just did not work and she blamed me for the whole affair. When Michael and I emigrated to Australia, 1951/52, after he had left the 12th Royal Lancers, (I was also blamed for that episode), she ignored me completely, and when she wrote to Michael, she did not mention me at all. It was not until we came back to the*

151

U.K. after about 2 years that we met up once more, as I felt it was most important that she should meet her grandchildren and get to know them. Michael's two aunts, Una and Maud, did not like Beatrice and were aghast that she had managed to marry Bertie, their very much-loved brother.

Beatrice had gradually become a bitter and twisted lady. She may have been always like this, but she had had a very difficult period of her life which may have been to blame. She had to give away her two illegitimate children, and had then lost her husband just when it might have felt that life had at last become normal. It must have taken a toll.

She had dominated her son and was probably influential in driving him to make the decision to move abroad to New Zealand, where he had originally intended to settle. Beatrice became more isolated as she became older and more infirm.

It is not known how much her daughters were involved in her last days. She died at The Priory Hospital aged 81, and her daughter Bridget reported the death.

Beatrice Martha's will was made just three months before her death. She must have been a bit confused by that stage and her signature does look shaky. She appointed her daughter Bridget and son Michael as Executors and Trustees.

Regarding the settlement made by her mother-in-law, Bridget Humble-Crofts in 1931, Beatrice left the capital and income from this; four sixths to son Michael, and one sixth each to daughters Bridget and Margaret. (Michael thinks he got about £10,000, so about £170,000, today.)

She gave all her jewellery and personal effects to her unmarried daughter Bridget. The rest of the estate was also left absolutely to Bridget.

Other parts of Beatrice's life after 1936 are tied to that of her son, Michael, and will be covered later.

Chapter 20
Stanley Harrod

1924

Dad 'escaped' from Leonard John Sergeant in 1924. It must have been an enormous relief to be able at last to get away. He was grateful for the rest of his life to his friend Alf Bielby and his family for giving him the opportunity to make a fresh start.

To go back to Dad's own story:

'According to my birth certificate, perhaps the most important document I possess – I was born at 22, Cheniston Gardens, Kensington, London, on September 21, 1906.

My mother's name is given as Beatrice Martha Harrod, and my father's name space is conspicuous by its blankness.

Therefore at whatever stage I became first named Stanley Taylor, I was certainly born and christened (Church of England), John Stanley Taylor. The existence of the prefixed Christian name John and the surname Harrod was not known to me until I was in my teens.'

He had spent his life before his teens as Stanley Taylor and later Stanley Sergeant. He assumed he had been born and christened as 'Taylor' whereas we now know it was as 'Harrod'. It must have been even more distressing to have thought that he had been abandoned in Liverpool by his real parents rather than by adopting parents.

The information carried by Dad from his childhood, taken as he left Sergeant is pretty sparse, but interesting.

The documents must have been quite a revelation to him. His birth certificate proved of particular interest.

He had always been known as Stanley and this remained his name of choice throughout his life.

The birth certificate was a copy of the original produced on the 23 November, 1910, that is around the time that his story with the Taylors begins. Dad was just over four years old at the time. The certificate told him that his birth was registered in Kensington with the name John Stanley Harrod and that his mother was called Beatrice Martha Harrod. The empty space for his father's name must have been a shock, but would have confirmed to him the reason for his adoption.

Why had the copy been ordered at this time? Was this when the Taylors adopted him, or was this when they made a decision to emigrate to Australia?

No information has been found to fill in the gap between his baptism in Frampton Cotterell 1906 and his appearance in Manchester in 1910.

We do not know how long he remained living with the Bielbys after his escape from Sergeant, but at some stage he was able to afford to move to lodgings, where he stayed for some years until he married.

Dad was obviously popular and hard-working, and got on well with his employer Benn Franks and the staff. His six-year optical apprenticeship finished in the winter of 1927, when he was just 21 years old.

At this point Benn Franks wrote a letter for him, a reference. It read:

'To whom it may concern.'
'This is to certify that Mr John Stanley Harrod has been in our employ since leaving school and entered into an Agreement with us on November 14, 1921 for six years.

During this time, he has been most willing, conscientious and attentive to duty.

He leaves entirely of his own accord and we can recommend him to anyone as being thoroughly honest and a good-living man.

We wish him every success.'

Dad left to earn better wages and opportunities elsewhere. As Dad had been such a good worker, Mr Franks waived his contractual two-year restriction to working locally, and soon afterwards Dad joined Prout Brothers, Opticians, at 38, Brook Street, Hull, where he was to work for the next 22 years.

Prouts was run by brothers James and Thomas. Their shop had been at Brook Street since at least 1911, but the business was established some years earlier, perhaps in about 1901.

By the time Dad started at Prouts, the brothers would already have been 64 and 51 years of age.

Dad became very popular with the staff and patients. He was competent, thorough and friendly. Mum described him later as 'the star turn' at the place. As the years passed and the brothers aged, Dad gradually took on more responsibility.

The brothers retired after some years and Dad became a Director of the Company. He had some vivid memories of his time there.

Prouts, like many opticians at that time, used to fit and maintain the false eyes for patients who had lost an eye after injury or operation, a situation much commoner then, following the Great War. This practice continued in the hands of opticians into the 1950s.

The shop had a glass cabinet with trays of glass, crescent shaped eyes, in different sizes and different colours. Dad remembered that Mr Prout used to lubricate and warm the glass eye in his mouth, before fitting it directly into the patient's empty eye socket, pre-warmed. How thoughtful!

Photograph 9: John Stanley about 1929, age 24

His work at Prouts, and his association with the Congregational Church filled much of Dad's life, but fortunately for me, not all of it.

Dad first met Mum, then Miss Nalda Stanley, when she was working as a receptionist at Prouts. She was told by Mr Prout that *'you are my smartest girl.'* The conjunction of the smartest girl and the star turn was inevitable.

Miss Stanley was seven years younger than Dad, and was born in Hull in 1913. They probably first met in about 1930 when Dad would have been about 23 years old and Mum was then 16. They got engaged in January 1935.

Mum came from a family steeped in the deep-sea fishing industry, as were most of the residents of West Hull at that time. The North Sea trawler fleet was enormous and Mum's father was a trawler skipper.

Little 'Miss Stanley' was a good catch for Dad, and vice versa. Little she certainly was. Her own mother was small and wiry, with a dark complexion, and Mum was the same height, 4 feet 11 inches.

They decided to get married in 1936 and were able to put down a deposit on a small house soon after.

Moving into their family home was a great event, especially for Dad, as he had not had a proper home since he was aged six years old in Manchester. They were destined to have a happy home and family for many years to come.

As Dad took on more responsibility at Prouts', they moved up in the world. Eventually, in 1949, with the help and backing of a London Optical Manufacturer and close friend, Dad decided to set up practice on his own in Hull.

'Harrods Opticians' was born and became both popular and fruitful.

His involvement with Albion Congregational Church continued and increased in the 1930s. He became a lay preacher and a staunch supporter and activist. Albion Church was an impressive large building. The front was a massive stone Doric portico of six fluted columns, approached by a broad flight of steps. The interior was in keeping with the grandiose exterior. There was seating for 1,642 and under the Chapel were schoolrooms and burial vaults.

The Church was almost totally destroyed by bombing in the war, and worship post-war took place in a more recently constructed ancillary building to the side of the original site.

Mum and Dad had three sons. My two older brothers also became opticians. We have all had our own successful careers and families. Dad was proud of us. Probably as a result of his upbringing, and having to forge his own pathway from almost nothing, he judged success by results and could never understand why anyone would not take full opportunity of what was available in life.

He must have felt that having produced a happy family of his own made up in part for his awful childhood and lack of family.

I was the last to leave home for college in 1963. That year, Dad and Mum went on holiday to Ireland.

With time on his hands after a partial retirement, during the following year, Dad decided during to write down the story of his early life. He was unable to complete the job, not because of lack of time, but almost certainly because of the hurt it caused.

He retired completely due to illness later in the 1960s after Mum and Dad had moved to Scarborough.

Photograph 10: John Stanley 1965, age 59

His health gradually deteriorated and he became increasingly frail. The last time I saw him was in April 1971, when Mum and Dad travelled to Chester, where I was working at the time, for the christening of our eldest daughter.

Dad looked ill. He died in Scarborough a month later. He was never one to give in.

Chapter 21
Eduard Oswald Maria Harrod

1933 – 1945

1933 was a momentous year for Edward Oswald Maria Harrod.

In August 1933, he was stuck in Passau, a lovely ancient town in Bavaria, in the southeast of Germany. Passau is located on the Austrian/German border, and sits on the confluence of the rivers Danube, Inn and Ilz, so is known as "The Three Rivers City".

He was being interviewed by the 'Secret Police'; soon afterwards to be re-branded as the Gestapo. They had confiscated his papers and he never got them back.

In that same year, Adolf Eichmann had started his training with the Austrian Legion in Passau.

Despite being the historical seat of the Institute for Catholic Studies, the town had a darker side in the 1930s decade leading up to the war, a side exposed after the war by the brave German author, Anna Rosmus. Despite an enormous post-war cover up, the city elders were found to have been active Nazis and the town turned out to have been home to no less than eight concentration camps, slave labour camps, and prisoner of war camps.

Many of its citizens were involved in the Nazi Party, and with the persecution of Jews long before other parts of the German Reich.

Everything had not gone well for Eduard in Vienna, where he had lived previously.

He was 23 years old and had been living in men's' hostels since he was 14, almost nine years.

He had moved around hostels in various districts of the city and spent time in homes and Police Youth Centres.

Eduard had joined the 'Party' in 1930.

On the 30 January 1933, German National Socialist leader Adolf Hitler became Chancellor of Germany and the fascist Austrian National Socialists were gaining support and were not far behind.

Later that same year, Engelbert Dollfuss and his Patriotic Front seized power in Austria and governed as an Austro-fascist dictatorship modelled on Italy and guaranteed by Mussolini. Though Civil War followed in 1934, the party remained in power until unification with Germany in 1938.

Having been ordered to Passau by his Brigade Leader Herr Geister, Eduard worked as a courier with the Upper Austria Brigade of the Party in 1933. It was during this time that he had his papers confiscated, probably the result of his earlier scuffle and sentence.

Administrative duties took him to Hanover in Germany at the end of 1933 and he was to make his future life there. Some forms completed by Eduard in later life show that sometime after 1933 he also worked as a bookbinder and a salesman for various companies.

But trouble was to follow him to Hanover.

As I completed the review of this chapter after some new research, I tried in desperation yet another search for more information about Eduard Harrod on the Ancestry website.

A tiny family tree was found, giving the name of Eduard Oswald Maria Harrod, who was listed as born in Vienna in 1912, and died in Germany in 1964. Could this be the same person? How could it not be the same person?

A frantic series of e mails followed with the owner of this site, Inge, in Houston, Texas, culminating in a long telephone call at 4 a.m. her time. She proved to be Eduard's daughter. She admitted she had entered the wrong date of birth on the website and it should have been 1909.

As a result of our discussions, there could be no doubt that we shared the same Eduard Harrod in our family. It was inherently unlikely that more than one Eduard Harrod could have been born at the same address in Vienna on the same day in 1909.

Her information was limited, but matched ours exactly. More information became available later after the sudden death of her widowed half-sister, Edith, at her home near Munich in Germany in November, 2013, Edith was the keeper of some of Eduard's papers, and her son allowed us to see some of what she had kept.

What follows is what was known by his family at that time, most of which must have come originally from the Countess, and then from Eduard himself to his family.

Eduard Oswald Maria Harrod was born on the 12 December 1909, in Vienna. It looks as though the name Maria, not uncommon as a middle name for a boy in Germany, was added sometime after his birth. The name Oswald was a later addition.

He was illegitimate and his father's name was not known to his descendants. A family rumour said that Eduard's father was titled, some sort of aristocrat. There were a lot around in the Europe of that time. Eduard had told his daughter Edith some particular details, but made her promise not to tell anybody else. Sadly, she died with many of her secrets intact. This meant we had to rely on what the rest of the family had heard, the papers left behind, and our research.

Eduard told Inge's brother-in-law that during her pregnancy, his mother, Beatrice, had lived on a ship with the first officer, who was her lover, and that the ship sailed in the Mediterranean. He said that she had had an affair whilst travelling in Europe. My first thought was that perhaps this was the same Merchant Sea Captain implicated in my father's birth, Bertie.

Eduard told his family that his mother's name was Beatrix, (German for Beatrice) and was a 'Harrod', connected to Harrods in London.

His family told me that Edi was placed at some stage with foster parents in Thun, Switzerland where he was looked after by a baker's family called Waeckerle, Waekerli, or similar. There must have been money available from somewhere, as he was said to have gone to an expensive boarding school and then on to University. This did not fit in with the known gaps I had found in Eduard's early life, between birth and three years, four and nine years, and then 20 and 23 years.

Inge remembered that when she herself was about five years old, so around 1946, she was taken by her family carer of the time to meet her father's foster mother in Switzerland. This would have been the first chance they would have had to travel there since the end of the war. They were given a cardboard box of treasures to take home to her father. She delivered this to her father but, tantalisingly, she never saw inside that box.

Eduard met his first wife, Dorothea Battermann, in the south of France, near Marseilles, sometime in early 1935. What they were both doing there is not known.

Eduard followed Dorothea back to Hanover where her family lived, and married her there in December 1935. He then lived in Germany for the rest of his life.

They had their first child in January 1937, a son, Hans, but he died in 1939, when just two years old.

A daughter, Ursula Dorothea, was born in January 1940. She still lives in Germany.

Inge was born in April 1941, in Hanover, like her siblings.

The family think that at some stage before the war, Edi had served for about a year in the Foreign Legion, and then during the war that Edi had served in the German Army. Ursula believes he was in Norway for part of the war and she told me he was captured by the British towards the end of the war.

He told his family he was treated very well and that he acted as an interpreter for his captors. He was fluent in English and also spoke French.

Inge has a photograph of herself when a child, with her father in uniform. It was said to have been taken near the Polish border at the railway station in Zippnow, now Sypniewo in Poland. She looks about age ¾ years, so this cannot have been 1941 as Inge suggests, but nearer the end of the war.

As far as I could make out, he was a Corporal in standard Wehrmacht uniform. It was a relief to find it was not S.S. uniform. I suspect it actually shows Eduard saying goodbye on the way to Pommern.

Inge's mother Dorothea died in Hanover on the 4 February, 1945, aged 34, when Inge was four years old. She died of a clot on the lung. Two months later, in April 1945, the U.S. 84th Infantry Division, who were advancing through that part of Germany, captured the city.

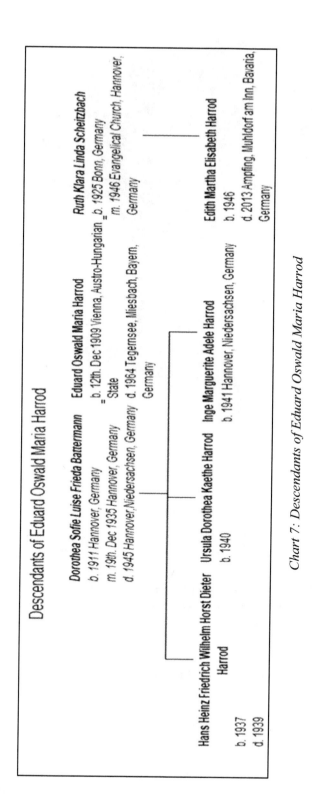

Descendants of Eduard Oswald Maria Harrod

Dorothea Sofie Luise Frieda Battermann
b. 1911 Hannover, Germany
m. 19th. Dec 1935 Hannover, Germany
d. 1945 Hannover, Niedersachsen, Germany

Eduard Oswald Maria Harrod
b. 12th. Dec 1909 Vienna, Austro-Hungarian
State
d. 1964 Tegernsee, Miesbach, Bayern,
Germany

=

Ruth Klara Linda Scheitzbach
b. 1925 Bonn, Germany
m. 1946 Evangelical Church, Hannover,
Germany

Hans Heinz Friedrich Wilhelm Horst Dieter Harrod
b. 1937
d. 1939

Ursula Dorothea Kaethe Harrod
b. 1940

Inge Marguerite Adele Harrod
b. 1941 Hannover, Niedersachsen, Germany

Edith Martha Elisabeth Harrod
b. 1946
d. 2013 Ampfing, Muhldorf am Inn, Bavaria,
Germany

Chart 7: Descendants of Eduard Oswald Maria Harrod

Photograph 11: Eduard in uniform, saying goodbye in Zippnow, Pommern,
1941, age 31

After her mother's death in 1945, Inge and her sister were sent to live for some time with her mother's brother and his wife, Wilhelm and Kaethe Battermann.

Eduard met his second wife, Ruth, on a train whilst returning from his prisoner of war camp. Eduard was looking for someone to help him with his two remaining girls. She had become pregnant and they married in Hanover on the 25 January, 1946.

Ruth is still alive, aged over 90, living in a Nursing Home in Munich, Germany. She is very bitter about Eduard as he was a womaniser and let her down, and she is not willing to talk about him.

Ruth and Eduard had a daughter, Edith, who was born in August 1946. Edith married twice and had two sons. Edith died during my research in November 2013.

The two girls from Eduard's first marriage lived with the Battermanns for some years. During her stay, Inge was sent to Switzerland by the Red Cross when she was aged seven or eight, so in 1948/49. Conditions were very difficult in

Germany in the post-war years and needy or undernourished children were sent for a holiday. She stayed some months with a sponsoring family called Bürn, in a small village called Cortaillod, near Neufchatel. It was a rural area with a local weaving mill and small-scale grape and fruit production. The family stayed in touch after she returned to Germany.

Inge went back there during a summer school holiday in either 1953 or 1954, when was aged about 12 or 13. During her stay, she travelled with her 'Aunt' Frau Bürn by train to Thun, a short ride away, to meet the baker's wife, Frau Waeckerle. She told Inge that her father had stayed with her and her husband for a short while when he was little. They stayed there for a couple of hours, and during this time, Frau Waeckerle took a box from under a cabinet, and retrieved a few papers and letters. These were put in a small box, which she took back to Germany for her father. As a well-behaved child, she did not ask all the questions she wanted to ask, nor open the box. The box was handed over to her father, and Inge never found out what were the contents.

Inge thinks her father visited England sometime after that and she wondered if something in the box had prompted him to find out more about his roots.

After the war, Eduard became a successful businessman, living in Hamburg and later Munich.

He became ill whilst on a skiing trip in northern Italy in 1964, when he was aged 54. He was thought to have a lung infection, but when he was admitted to hospital, kidney cancer was discovered.

Much of the family's story about their father was impossible to prove but was likely to be true.

However, some of the history was passed to Eduard from the Countess, so may not have been the complete story, and Eduard may have embellished the rest himself.

By pure chance, just before further Vienna details of the story had been discovered, I had organised a New Year trip to Prague, Vienna and Budapest as a surprise birthday treat for my wife's significant birthday, so I was in a position to check out some of the details.

In January 2014, I spent a day in Vienna looking at all the addresses we had gathered so far; especially that for the building where Beatrice gave birth to Edi, and seven other addresses where the Countess had lived during her recorded stay in Vienna between 1912 and her death in 1926. All but one was in the VIII district, within a half mile radius of each other. Where the old buildings still existed, they were part of tall terraced houses split into small apartments. It proved quite an emotional event wandering the same streets where Edi had run and played, most of them little changed.

Photograph 12: Eduard about 1960, age 50

I managed to talk to an elderly resident of the Floriangasse address where the Countess lived for four years, and got inside the hall to have a look around, though I could not get into the apartment itself.

Since this initial information that I obtained from the family, a lot of hard work has discovered more information about the Countess, her family, and Beatrice and Edi. This has come from both the local Vienna Archive records, from the Bundesarchiv, or German Federal Archives, old German newspapers and from the German Military Archives.

This is the sum of my present knowledge about the 'Austria story'.

Maria, later to be Irma, Countess Marie Grotta zu Grottenegg was born in Yverdon, Switzerland on the 20 February, 1862 or 1864, depending on which record is believed. She gave her name upon marriage to the Count as Maria de Joly. She was a Protestant. Yverdon is a French speaking area.

The local Yverdon archives have no record of a Marie de Joly born on that date, either in 1862 or 1864. There are some people named Joly in the area.

Maria married Count Eduard Grotta zu Grottenegg, as his second wife, almost certainly in 1892 and they had no children together. No marriage records have been found, but it looks as though they it might have been a 'deathbed marriage', literally as the Count died in June 1893, aged 65, at his estate in Siebenbürgen, which was then part of Transylvania and is now in Romania. Marie would have been 30 years old. The records of the Count's death in Transylvania stated that the Count died 'in the second year of his second marriage'.

The Count was born in 1828 in Klagenfurt, then in Slovenia, now in Southern Austria. He was Catholic. He married his first wife, Louise, in 1856, and they had two sons, Friederich and Josef. Louise died in about 1890.

Count Eduard lived at various addresses in Vienna between 1879 and 1893. This information comes from Lehmann's Directory of Vienna which sadly only lists the principal resident at each address.

Quite how Marie came into his life is not known for certain but she may have been involved initially as a nurse. The newspapers of the day record court cases involving financial irregularities just before the Count died.

This information given earlier about the Countess and Edi in Vienna was mostly obtained from the Vienna archives which cover the period from 1909 onwards, but also records in the Bundersarchiv which cover the period from 1933 onwards.

In these latter records, there are a series of letters between Eduard and various offices of 'The Führer for the N.S.D.A.P. in Austria'. There are 78 pages and some are from the 'Imperial Office' of the Party. They were written between 1936 and 1939, and cover events between 1930 and 1939. The headings of the letters are graphic lettering with an illustration of an eagle atop the swastika, and usually ending with *'Heil Hitler'* before the signature, with an addendum that *'Polite forms of greeting are omitted for all official party correspondence'*.

The letters referred to Eduard as *'the member of the German nation Eduard Harrod'*.

Some of the letters from Edi were in his own handwriting with his signature. He was always addressed as Eduard Harrod with the correct date and place of birth. From 1938 onwards, he signed several of the letters and some forms he completed, with the name 'Eduard Oswald Harrod', and the authorities then wrote back using this name. (See Document 1, an example of the letters written)

The letters are in essence a dialogue between Eduard in Hanover and the authorities, and also amongst different branches of the authorities, following the confiscation of Eduard's papers by the Secret Police in 1933. He had approached them in an attempt to get re-instated into the Party and get new papers. Eduard eventually gives up in 1939 having been blacklisted by the Nazi party.

The American website, www.scrapbookpages.com, which shows photographs and gives the history of the concentration camps in Germany, describes the Germany of 1936. Though dissidents and criminals were being held in camps, and many Jews were being persecuted and incarcerated, there was as yet no mass extermination taking place at that time. Germany held an International Chess tournament in Munich and the Olympic Games in Berlin in that year.

Nationalsozialistische Deutsche Arbeiterpartei

Reichsleitung

K 10.36

München, Briennerstraße 45
Briefanschrift: München 43, Briesfach 80
Telefon-Nummern: 54901, 58344 u. 50081
Postscheckkonto München 23319

Zentralorgan der Partei:
„Völkischer Beobachter"
Verlag: München, Thierschstr. 11, F 22131
Berlin, Zimmerstr. 88, F R 1 Jäger 0022
Schriftleitung: München, Schellingstr. 39, F 20801
Berlin, Zimmerstr. 88, F R 1 Jäger 0022

Reichsschatzmeister.
BoK IIIa/Hä/Hai/Lo.9.36.

Ihr Zeichen:

Gegenstand:

München, den 25. Sept.1936
Karolinenplatz 3
Tel.54633 u.59556.

An das Hauptamt V

Amt für Mitgliedschaftswesen - Karteiabteilung -

im H a u s e .

Betreff: Unterschlagung durch Vg. Eduard H a r r o d , Hannover,
geb. am 12.12.1909 zu Wien.

Mit Schreiben vom 29. v. Mts. gibt der Gau-
schatzmeister der Gauleitung Süd-Hannover-Braunschweig be-
kannt, dass der Obengenannte in seiner Eigenschaft als Orts-
gruppenkassenwalter der DAF-Ortswaltung Hannover-Welfenplatz
RM 90.--

zum Schaden der DAF unterschlagen hat.

Ich gebe Ihnen hiervon Kenntnis zwecks Vor-
merkung in der dortigen Warnkartei.

Heil Hitler.
i.A.

'In the summer of 1936, Nazi Germany was the envy of the Western world. From the depths of the Great Depression in 1932, Hitler had achieved an "economic miracle" in Germany in less than three years. As yet, there was no sign of Nazi aggression, nor any attempt at world domination by Germany. Gertrude Stein, the famous Jewish writer who was a mentor to Ernest Hemingway, even suggested in 1937 that Hitler should be awarded the Nobel Peace Prize.

Because of the Nazi program of nationalism, the German people had regained their self-respect after the humiliating Treaty of Versailles, which Germany was forced to sign at the end of World War I. They now had great pride in their ethnicity and their country. No people in the world were more patriotic than the Germans in 1936 and no other world leader had the total dedication to his country that Adolph Hitler had.

The ordinary Germans were satisfied with their lives and had no reason to fear the concentration camps or the Gestapo. Hitler was a hero to the 127 million ethnic Germans throughout Europe, whom he wanted to unite into the Greater German Empire, a dream that had been discussed in his native Austria for over 50 years.

The workers in Nazi Germany enjoyed unprecedented social benefits such as paid vacations under the Strength Through Joy program (Kraft durch Freude). Factory workers listened to classical music as they worked, and took showers before going home. In order to demonstrate their importance to the country, workers were allowed to march in Nazi parades, carrying shovels on their shoulders just like the soldiers who marched with their rifles.

While America and the rest of Europe were still in the depths of the depression caused by the stock market crash in October 1929, Germany had stabilized its economy and had virtually eliminated unemployment. Unlike the other countries in Europe in 1936, Nazi Germany was doing well, thanks in part to American investment capital.

Everything in Nazi Germany was clean and orderly; there were no slums; the trains ran on time. By 1938, the crime rate was at an all-time low because repeat offenders were being sent to a concentration camp after they had completed their second sentence.

A healthy lifestyle was encouraged by the Nazis and group calisthenics for young people were compulsory. Family values were the order of the day: abortion was banned; homosexuals and prostitutes were imprisoned; women were encouraged to be homemakers, and mothers with four or more children would shortly be awarded military style medals for serving their country.

It was safe to walk the city streets in Germany at night; no bars were needed on the windows of German homes to keep the criminal element out; all the social misfits were being sent away to the concentration camps; bums and vagrants were no longer allowed to beg on the streets. Money that had formerly been spent to care for institutionalized persons with mental and physical disabilities was now being used for other purposes as the mentally ill and the severely disabled were being put to death in gas chambers.'

One can see why Eduard might have wanted to join the organisation again.

However, under this veneer of efficiency and progress, the discrimination and persecution of anything and anybody 'un-German' was well underway. In May 1933, soon after Hitler became the Chancellor of Germany, the ritual of burning of books climaxed in Berlin, destroying any books, especially those by Jewish authors, deemed to be subversive or contrary to Nazi ideology.

What these letters revealed was as follows.

In early 1934, Eduard Harrod had been given leave by Colonel Hans Geister, his Vienna Brigade Leader, and he was sent to Hanover in Germany.

He had been working in Passau during 1932 and 1933, where Edi had joined the NSDAP and obtained his Membership Card three years earlier.

He had travelled back and forth to Vienna during 1933 where he continued to live in men's hostels.

Whilst back in Vienna in March of that year, he was convicted of causing bodily harm during a scuffle with a security guard at the Vienna Town Hall. He had been sentenced to ten days' detention. The details of the offence are not known but this may have prompted his transfer.

Crossing over the border at Passau for what proved to be the last time, in August 1933, his Membership Card was confiscated by the Secret Police.

This loss of his card was to be the cause of the endless problems for Eduard in the years to come.

From 1934 until June 1936, Eduard worked in the District Administration of the D.A.F. District, South-Hanover-Brunswick. The D.A.F., or Deutsche Arbeitsfront, was the National Socialist trade union organisation which replaced the various trade unions previously in existence.

Eduard settled down at last in 1935. He met Dorothea Battermann, his future wife, in Hanover where she had been born in 1911, and they married there in December, 1935.

Whilst employed at the District Office in Hanover he blotted his copybook again. He was dismissed without notice from the D.A.F. when he was found to have embezzled some funds, in total the sum of 90.00 Reichsmark. This was also to haunt him. It is very difficult to estimate the value of this today. From 1939 onwards and during the war there was a fixed rate which meant that 90 Reichsmark would have been worth about £8. In today's value that would be a little under £400.

From July 1936 onwards he worked at the Imperial Accident Insurance Office in Hanover.

Once settled, he tried very hard to re-establish his Party membership.

In order to gain entry back into the Party, Eduard had to prove the validity of his previous membership in Austria. He told them that his documents had been taken by the Gestapo in Passau, and many of the letters concerned the attempt to retrieve his documents or furnish proof of his membership.

Despite Eduard's best endeavours, evidence for the existence of his documents was not found by the Gestapo at the border office in Passau, the Hanover District Office or the Regional Office in Austria. The authorities began to question whether they had ever existed, especially after he gave two different numbers for his registration document.

They asked him to complete a questionnaire, under oath, and provide witnesses to his previous membership. The copy of the questionnaire which I obtained provided much of the information here.

Eduard suggested that they contact Herr Geister, now listed as Assault Storm Leader Geister, and he also offered other Party members he knew as witnesses, some of who sent references for him.

These included S.S. Obergruppenführer (or Senior Troup Leader) Harnish.

The rank Obergruppenführer was adopted by the Nazi Party in 1932 and was a very senior rank, secondary only to Himmler. There was also a Dr Wachter. This may have been Baron Otto Gustav von Wächter, a doctor and lawyer born in Vienna in 1901. He became a Nazi politician and administrative officer. During World War II he was head of the Civil Administration in the Kraków and Galicia districts of occupied Poland, before being appointed as head of the German Military Administration in Fascist Italy. He finished his career with the honorary rank of an SS-Gruppenführer (lieutenant general). His duties were said to have been confined to an administrative role, and after the war he claimed he was never part of the SS and Police forces in any of the occupied territories. He was accused by some of involvement in the Holocaust, though he claimed he was just a senior ranking official who was later influential in the Nazi Party.

Quoting these big names did not seem to have had much influence on Eduard's application.

He even mentioned his arrest in Vienna in 1925 during the Zionist Conference when requested for information of his 'activities for the N.S.D.A.P.'

His persistence in the application suggests that the benefits of membership were considerable.

The loss of his documents, even some doubt about their existence, and suggestions of forgery were used by the Party as reasons not to issue a further card. Just at the point when they might have relented and were about to issue a new card, evidence of his previous embezzlement came to light.

In August 1936 the Treasurer of the District Office South-Hanover-Brunswick notified the authorities that Eduard, in his capacity as district group treasurer of the local D.A.F., had embezzled money.

This led to an order that a warning card would be issued to all parts of the organisation, which was done by December 1936. Effectively this would *'make future inclusion in the Party impossible'*.

The authorities eventually found evidence of some of his documents in February 1937, including a temporary card issued in Vienna in February 1933, but forgery of part of the document was suggested. By this time, it was already too late, the warning card had been issued and this prevented his registration.

During Eduard's attempts to get back into the Party, family life went on as normal during this period. He was working in the Insurance office and busy with the letters to and from the authorities. In official documents he classed himself as a 'businessman' or 'administrative official'.

In 1937, Eduard and Dorothea's first child, a boy, was born. Their son Hans only survived until 1939, and died soon after his second birthday from some sort of brain tumour.

His final letter of refusal regarding his application arrived at the time of his son's death. Despite the effect this must have had on them both, he still wrote back suggesting an error had been made in the decision. Eduard continued to try very hard to get the authorities to change their minds, but at this stage he had not been told about the issue of a warning card.

A last desperate application by Eduard in September 1938 for a temporary membership card included the following standard declaration: '*I hereby make an application for the issue of a temporary membership card for the National Socialist German Workers' Party. I am of German descent and free of Jewish or coloured racial elements, do not belong to any secret association nor any other forbidden association or federation and will not join the latter during my membership of the National Socialist German Workers' Party. I promise to fully obey the Führer and promote the party with all my strength as a loyal follower of the Führer. I undertake to pay the fixed administrative fee and the monthly membership contribution, which is payable in advance, which arises for me from the contribution regulations of the National Socialist German Workers' Party. In addition, I am prepared to pay a one-off voluntary advertising contribution of ... Reichsmark.*'

It came to nothing despite his subsequent threats to take it to a higher level. He had tried extremely hard to become and remain a Party member. Being refused may in the long run have been his saviour.

Events in Europe were now moving rapidly towards war.

In 1938, Hitler annexed and occupied Austria. This upset Mussolini, who had been sponsoring the regime there, but he could do nothing about it. Hitler invaded Czechoslovakia in March 1939 and Poland in September 1939; the latter event being the straw which broke the camel's back and was the catalyst for the start of World War II.

An undated document, almost certainly a copy of his birth details completed in order to join the German Army, gives several details. It lists Eduard's date and place of birth correctly. As related in an earlier chapter, strangely it gave his mother's name as Pauline, and listed her 27 years old at his birth.

According to documents obtained from Deutsche Dienststelle, a records office for those who served in the Wehrmacht, or regular armed forces, Eduard was conscripted in April 1940. I suspect if he had been a party member, he would have joined the Waffen SS instead.

His personal records were sadly destroyed in the war, but some basic details remain in other records.

He joined the Infantry, and was assigned to the Nachrichten (or radio news and signals) regiment based in Hanover. Later in 1940 he was deployed with a Signals Regiment to Army group A in the west which invaded Belgium and also France through the Ardennes. It is interesting to speculate if he and Michael Humble-Crofts, his half-brother, and youngest son of Beatrice also involved in that part of the war theatre, might have been near to each other, on opposite sides, at some stage during the fight.

In 1941 he was in Poland, a Radio Operator, 1ˢᵗ class. Inge has a photograph of herself as a little girl, holding some flowers and saying goodbye to her father at a railway station at Zippnow. It is a long way from Hanover. He was probably on his way to Poland, but what was Inge doing there?

Later in 1941, and during 1942, he was back in Hanover, in a Signals Reserve Battalion. By late 1942 he had been promoted to 'Unteroffizier' or Sergeant. He may have been ill or injured as he seems to have spent about a month or more in the Clemintenhaus Hospital in Hanover in 1942.

He returned to action, *'fit for service'*, after three months and in 1943/44 was with an antitank Company, deployed in June 1943 in Molde, Norway, a coastal city north of Oslo. By this time he was a 'Feldwebel' or Sergeant Major.

In 1944 and 1945 he was deployed in the field at Arnhem, Aachen and Jülich, all sites of battles during the Allied invasion of the Rhineland. It is not clear if he was in the areas during the battles, but he was subsequently taken prisoner in April by the Americans on the Rhine.

No information about his time after capture is given, though I attempted to get any available records from America. I was told they no longer existed. Eduard's war was over.

Chapter 22
Michael John Muschamps

1935

In 1935 Michael John Muschamps Humble-Crofts, aged 16, left Pangbourne College in Berkshire after being a pupil there for four years.

Though the school was founded by Sir Thomas Lane Devitt in 1917 as The Nautical College, with the purpose of training boys to become Merchant Navy officers, and despite his father Bertie's career at sea, Michael then entered the Royal Military College, Sandhurst.

His mother Beatrice might have hoped he would follow in his father's footsteps, but he was destined to stick to dry land in the Army.

Michael had been Captain of Fencing at Pangbourne and played Rugby for the school.

He was Bertie and Bea's 3rd child of the marriage and the 1st son. He was born in 1918 in Falmouth, just nine days before the Armistice was signed at the end of the First war.

He was in truth her 3rd son, and the 2nd that she had named John. Michael was christened in Truro Cathedral a fortnight later. Sadly two days later, his Uncle Arthur, having survived the war, died of influenza in a Military Hospital in Dover, the day after his 35th birthday.

Muschamps might initially seem an odd choice for one of Michael's Christian names, but it originated in the family line five generations back. John Dodds had married Anne Muschamps in the early 1700s. Anne was Michael's great, great, great, grandmother.

Michael can never have really known his father who was killed in the road accident a little before his fifth birthday. In the following year, 1924, the family had moved away from Horley to South Devon and two years later, aged seven, Michael went to Prepatory School at Swanborne House, Bletchley, in Buckinghamshire.

In 1931 the family moved to Maidenhead, Berkshire, and that same year, Michael left Swanborne and went to the College at Pangbourne.

During his military training at Sandhurst, he had a six week stay in Gibraltar in 1937 when he would have been aged 18, an early introduction to serving abroad.

Michael had a liking for fast cars. In 1936, then 17, Michael is shown in a black and white photograph standing next to an Alfa Romeo racing car at the famous Brooklands race track. It was labelled, *'Michael with Alfa Monoposta of Arthur Dobson, Brooklands 1936'*. The label may be incorrect.

Photograph 13: Michael with Alfa Monoposta of Arthur Dobson, Brooklands 1936

It was a beautiful car and would, of course, have been painted bright red. Arthur Dobson was one of two car racing brothers, Arthur and Austin Dobson, who both participated in the Grand Prix circuit.

The Alfa Romeo Monoposta was the Italian racing car of the early 1930s. It gradually became under-powered compared to the 'Silver Arrows' of Germany, the Mercedes-Benz and Auto-Union cars, sponsored by the Nazi regime, who were winning most of the races.

Enzo Ferrari, chief of the Alfa team at that time, had to find an answer. Enter the amazing Alfa 'Bimotore', which had two straight eight engines, mounted one in front of the driver, and the other behind, somehow shoehorned into a special beefed-up chassis. It sounds lethal.

Not surprisingly, the Bimotore, later billed as the first 'Ferrari', had stunning top-end performance. Its two 3.2L engines produced a total of 540hp and propelled it through the rear wheels at 200 m.p.h. Despite the power, the added weight, fuel consumption and the rear tyre wear of the car meant it was never competitive. The distinctive side-panel extra fuel tanks of the Bimotore, evident in the photograph with Michael, confirm the car at Brooklands was actually a Bimotore, not the Monoposta as labelled.

The only two Bimotore cars built were dismantled into parts when Arthur Dobson arrived at the Scuderia Ferrari workshops, wanting to buy one. Some reports say this was 1937. A sale was a sale and that meant cash-in-hand, so Ferrari ordered that one car be re-built and Dobson took it home, racing it with some success before selling it in 1938.

During Michael's late teens, war was brewing, the fun was over and his role was sealed.

In 1938 he was commissioned into the XII Royal Lancers, Prince of Wales's, a very prestigious cavalry regiment with a splendid history.

In 1751 the regiment was officially styled the 12th Dragoons and in 1768 King George III bestowed the title of The 12th Prince of Wales's Regiment of Light Dragoons, and the regiment was given the badge of three ostrich feathers, and the motto "Ich Dien".

They were armed with lances in 1816 after Napoleon's cavalry had shown their effectiveness, but lances were removed from their weaponry in 1903 until an influential lobby secured their reinstatement in 1909. The Regiment served on the Western Front throughout World War I – mostly, but not entirely without their lances!

In the more mobile opening months of the war, cavalry played a vital role. Amazingly, in a war dominated by artillery and tanks and trenches, in 1914, C Squadron of the 12th Lancers made a successful charge against a dismounted squadron of Prussian Dragoons. They celebrate Mons/Moy Day annually, which commemorates the last occasions on which the regiment charged with lances.

Following the war, in 1928, the XII Lancers finally gave up their horses and were equipped with armoured cars.

At the start of the second war in 1939, Michael soon saw action. He was sent to Belgium as a 2nd. Lieutenant with the doomed British Expeditionary Force, and campaigned in France and Flanders. Beaten back in 1940, the Lancers played a large part in shielding the retreat to Dunkirk from where Michael was evacuated. The regiment re-grouped back in England.

Michael was however retained in England, and between 1940 and 1942 he served in the 'Morris Detachment', guarding the Royal Family. This group of about 40 men, under Major Timothy Morris, worked in armoured cars shadowing the King and Queen and the two Royal Princesses between London and Windsor. At a time of anxiety about a German invasion, their duty was to act as a personal bodyguard to their Majesties. They were stationed at Wellington Barracks when the King was at Buckingham Palace, and Combermere Barracks when he moved to Windsor.

They rehearsed the role of a mobile column, getting into buses, fighting from them, and getting out again, and their secondary role of dealing with parachutists in the Elstree neighbourhood. There were several false alarms.

The Detachment served as part of the Coats Mission, led by Major J.S. Coats. They had the job of transporting the Royal family to any one of four houses, in different parts of the country, in the case of a German invasion.

Michael had a number of photographs showing the Detachment, with their vehicles and the Royal car in front of Windsor Castle; and the Officers with the Royal Family on a snowy day.

Photograph 14: Michael (4th from R) with officers of the Morris Detachment with King George, Queen Elizabeth and the two Princesses. 1940

Michael had several invitations to balls at the Palace and met the family and children on many occasions. As a consequence of his service, Michael was awarded the M. V. O. 5th Class in 1942.

The Victorian Order is awarded for service to the Royal Family. His mother Beatrice and sister Bridget accompanied him for lunch at Windsor after the private investiture.

Following his service in London, he re-joined his Regiment abroad and fought in North Africa. He was with the 1st Armoured Division at the Battle of El Alamein on the 23 October 1942 and served in the Western Desert in 1942 and 1943. The XII fought in armoured cars acting as reconnaissance.

It was during his time there that Michael became engaged to Pamela, who came from Marlow. It was announced in 'The Times' in late 1943. She was the same age as Michael, 25, and was apparently his mother's choice!

Whilst engaged to Pamela, and still in Tangiers, Michael met Anna Roach, nee Stuart MacLaren. She was a 23-year-old widow serving with the Wrens in North Africa. She had been widowed in 1940 after just six weeks of marriage, a not uncommon wartime occurrence. Her husband, Flying Officer Frank. A.

Roach, was with 224 Squadron, and had been killed in action in a bomber flying a patrol into Norwegian territory.

Anna was a free spirit and good looking, and she certainly turned Michael's head; she told me herself that she was very good at it! She had a self-confessed reputation as a man chaser. The result was almost inevitable. Michael wrote home to his mother asking her to call off the engagement, something he should have done himself.

The announcement of Michael's second engagement was also made in The Times, in early January 1945, when he was a Captain. Michael was given leave to the U.K. in order to marry Anna, which he did in August 1945, at Rusthall Church, Tunbridge Wells. Anna's girlfriends did not think she would be capable of settling down – but she did.

His mother Beatrice, having chosen the first girl herself, was opposed to the marriage. Nevertheless, she attended the wedding, but a lifelong dislike between Beatrice and Anna was the result.

Apart from Michael's mother, no other Harrods attended the ceremony.

Lillian Anna Stuart MacLaren was born in 1920, in Bayswater, London. She was the daughter of Squadron Leader Archibald Stuart Charles Stuart MacLaren – yes, this is not a misprint, there are two Stuarts in the name.

Archie MacLaren's life story is interesting. A very short version follows here, but a fuller account is easily accessed on line and has been written up by his granddaughter, Vanessa.

Archie went to school at Charterhouse. Soon after he left school, he fell in love with a young actress, and in order to end this relationship, he was sent by his mother to Canada with £5 to 'make good'.

He returned home in 1911, then aged 19. He was a dashing and handsome young man.

He married in 1915, and in the same year gained his Flying Certificate as a 2nd. Air Mechanic in the Royal Flying Corps. Flying became his life, and he rose to Squadron Leader. He had a distinguished war in bombers flying into Europe and the Middle East.

He was involved in several unique flights.

In July 1918, he captained the maiden flight between England and Egypt in a Handley Page O/400 bomber. He developed a taste for long distance flying.

Just after the war, on 13 December 1918, with Stuart-MacLaren as Captain, and with two other officers, and three sergeants, they took off from Martlesham Heath, in Suffolk, bound for India, in a Handley Page V/1500 heavy bomber.

The route was via Rome, Malta, Cairo, Baghdad and finally Karachi. They arrived on 15 January 1919, having covered 5,560 miles at an average speed of 77 m.p.h., to join in the Third Afghan War.

The bomber was an open three bay biplane with four engines and could carry a heavy bomb load.

Three months later, one of the other officers flew 'Old Carthusian' as she was known, through the Khyber Pass in pre-dawn darkness. She was fully loaded with bombs and the target was the royal palace of Amanullah Khan in Kabul.

The bombs did little damage, but with the resulting panic, the Khan surrendered. The single bombing raid is credited with ending the war.

Stuart-MacLaren was one of several flyers from the era who after the war made extravagant journeys in their pursuit of records and continuing excitement.

He became famous as the leader of a valiant but failed attempt at a Round the World Flight, flying in an open cockpit, in a single-engine biplane with a crew of three. Madness really.

They set off from Britain in March 1924. After several near disasters, two changes of engine and a replacement plane, the journey eventually ended in August of that year, when the plane was forced by thick fog to land on water off Bering Island, in the northern waters between Russia, Japan and the U.S.A. They had flown 13,100 miles up to this point. They were badly damaged but managed to taxi northwards with a crewman balancing on what remained of each lower wing to stabilise the floatless plane and prevent it capsizing. Three exhausting hours later they reached shore. Disappointed, he eventually travelled home by boat. He died in Madeira in 1943.

Michael's war continued during and after his engagement to Anna.

In 1943, at the end of the Desert War in North Africa, the XII Lancers served as a corps-level reconnaissance asset in the Italian Campaign. Michael joined the 1st Armoured Division as Staff Officer Operations later in 1943.

Italy was a difficult theatre of war for both the British and the Americans. In 1944, at Salerno, where landings took place, the 1st Armoured Division was badly smashed up. Afterwards, Michael joined 8th Army H.Q.as Staff Officer, Operations. In 1945 the XII were initially used as infantry at the battle of Cassino and in 1945 men of the XII Lancers were the first Allied troops to enter Venice.

Soon after his wedding at the tail end of the war in 1945, Michael returned to Italy as 2nd-in-Command of the Derbyshire Yeomanry, and was promoted to Major. He was moved to Austria and was serving again with the Derbyshire Yeomanry later that same year.

He had had a tough and busy war; Dunkirk, El-Alamein and then Salerno, with a spell at Buckingham Palace in between!

In 1946 he was again given leave to travel back to the U.K., this time to witness the results of his previous leave, the birth of his first child in Hastings.

Michael obviously enjoyed army life. He remained in the army for some time after the war. Again in 1946 he was posted to Barce, Bengazi, in Libya, where he was joined by Anna and their four-month-old son.

In 1948 he re-joined the Regiment at Barnard Castle, near Darlington and just when he was due to be posted to Malaysia, he decided to retire. He left with the rank of Major.

Like a lot of men who served in the war, especially those with no other occupation before the war, he found it difficult to settle back into civilian life. This is reflected in his multiple changes of jobs and homes over the next few years.

For a while he farmed at Eastwrey Barton, near Lustleigh, in South Devon. This is now a luxury guesthouse in the lovely Wray valley, in the middle of the

Dartmoor National Park scenery. He farmed in partnership with the husband of a friend of Anna's from her W.R.N.S. days.

Anna told me that Beatrice thought farming was below him after he had been an officer in the XIIth Lancers! Beatrice had become something of a snob since the family dalliance with the Royals.

Michael and Anna's second child, a girl, was born in Devon in 1948.

Michael farmed in Lustleigh until 1951 and then decided to make a move abroad. For a while, before they set off, Michael, Anna and family lived temporarily in Tunbridge Wells, not far from his mother.

Anna wrote her memory of this time and her mother-in-law:

'Just before we emigrated, we had bought a house in Lustleigh, due to my grandmother having died and left me some money, I asked her (mother-in-law Beatrice) to come and stay so that she could see something of her grandchildren, aged just over two, and a few months old at the time. She had been with us for a few days and I always took her breakfast up to her, to have in her bedroom, when one morning after our usual greeting she pointed her finger at me, looked like thunder and said to me – "May God forgive you." I was staggered and said, "What for," and her answer was "For taking my son's love away from me". I was terribly upset and told Michael when he came home at lunchtime. He stormed up to her and told her to apologise to me, which naturally she would not do, so he said "in that case I am taking you to the station, to go back to London", and I never spoke to her again, nor her to me, until we came back from Australia. I took my hat off to Michael knowing how scared he was of her. She and Michael kept in touch with the odd letter when we were in Australia but I was never mentioned and she asked me to give back a ring which she had given me.'

Having managed to alienate herself from the Humble-Crofts for marrying Bertie, and the Harrods for being a snob, she had now distanced herself from her son and daughter-in-law.

In 1951, the family sailed to New Zealand intending to continue to farm there. Fate played a hand here. The ship travelled via Sydney in Australia, but it never sailed on to New Zealand due to a strike whilst it was docked in Australia.

Left high and dry in Australia for some months, they had to make some money, so moved to Melbourne, where a job had been found for Michael by an acquaintance who lived in Perth. They never travelled on to New Zealand, and stayed in Melbourne for a year, but things did not work out.

Anna said of their stay in Australia: *'Michael and I lived in Melbourne whilst in Australia. He worked in a factory which made melamite. We were introduced to the man who owned the factory when on board ship emigrating to New Zealand. That was where we intended to go, not Australia, as that was the last place I wished to settle in. Regrettably, the boat strikes were on when we arrived in Sydney, which lasted 6 months, and as we had all our belongings in trunks and suitcases with us, we were unable to afford to fly with all that baggage to New Zealand, so had to stay in Sydney.*

Michael was lucky to be offered a job by this man. I disliked Australia intensely, a man's country, no culture in those days and as he had been offered a job on a fruit farm in Kent before emigrating, and having 2 small children, we decided to come back to the U.K. and take the job, so that is what we did.

If we had got to New Zealand, I think we would have settled there.'

They arrived back in England in 1952 and stayed for a while with Michael's old friend from the War, Major Morris, who lived near Heathfield. Michael took a job as manager of Mascall Pound Fruit and Hop Farm near Paddock Wood in Kent, and he worked there from 1953 onwards for about ten years, until the farm was sold. Remarkably, Anna and Beatrice at some stage started talking to each other again.

During Michael's stay in Kent, Beatrice became ill, and died in 1958. This was covered in an earlier chapter.

After his mother's death, life must have become a bit easier for Michael without the added worry and responsibility. Michael was aged 39 and the children were then twelve and nine years old.

The loss of his job at the Fruit and Hop farm in 1962 turned out to be an opportunity for Michael. They had moved about quite a bit before this job, but when he left Kent after 10 years, Michael and Anna moved even more frequently, every two years or so as his job required.

Michael joined Bayer U.K. Ltd., a pharmaceutical company, in Herefordshire, as a Regional Manager and they moved to live in Ross on Wye. He was to stay with the company for 18 years.

By the following year they had moved to Chardstock, in Devon and Michael was transferred to the S.W. Region in 1964. In 1966, he was moved to the S.E. Region and they lived first at Tunbridge Wells, then Benenden in Kent and later Beckley in Kent.

After a short spell in Tayside, Michael decided in 1980 that after 18 years with Bayer, he would retire. Ill health was given as the reason though the details are not known. He would have been 62 years old. They moved back to Kent.

Further moves began in earnest, looking for the idyllic cottage with roses round the door that Anna had dreamt about. In 1985 they moved to Suffolk, and in 1986 to Sidmouth in Devon, where I met Michael for the first time.

Soon after our first meeting, in one of his early letters to me, after looking at photographs of my father, he wrote:

'It is just beyond me to think that I had a brother and all those years that we missed seeing one another, and it is inevitable that I am your Uncle Michael, but don't you dare call me that.'

Little did he know that he had a third brother.

Photograph 15: Michael 1988, age 70

By 2000, Michael and Anna were living in Topsham, on the Exe estuary south of Exeter. Here they stayed; this was their last move together. Their daughter moved in next door a short while later and still lives there, having combined and adapted the two cottages.

Whilst living in Topsham, Michael became increasingly frail and Anna could no longer cope. He was admitted to a nearby home which made him very miserable. I saw him last when he came out for lunch with us when my wife and I were visiting.

Michael died in 2003, two weeks after his 85th birthday. He had had an eventful life.

Anna continued living for a while in Topsham and then rather surprisingly decided in 2006 to go to live with a friend in Madeira. Almost inevitably, this did not work out and she soon came back to Topsham. When she needed more help, she moved into delightful sheltered housing locally. She celebrated her 90th birthday there, but later, in 2010, when her memory and mobility problems worsened, her admission to a home in Exmouth became necessary. She died in August 2013, aged 93.

She was the last of a generation who were actually involved in some of the events in this story.

Chapter 23
Eduard Harrod – The Puzzle

It may have already struck the reader that there are some gaps, and several discrepancies in Eduard's story. I am hamstrung by the situation in which many of his personal details and history that I have obtained were already second or third hand information.

Eduard only learned of his past from the Countess. I think I have got to know enough about her to mistrust her accuracy. Eduard's family were given information solely from Eduard himself, who was also not a reliable witness. There are almost no documents passed down in the family to confirm much of what was said. The box given to Inge by Eduard's foster parents in Switzerland is not available to me and the two family members with probably the most verbal information are Eduard's second wife Ruth, who is unwilling to talk, and their daughter Edith, who died in 2013.

The only absolute facts I have are those from the documents and records retrieved from various archives. Even some of these rely upon Eduard's evidence given at the time.

I think that Eduard Harrod was born in Vienna on the 12 December 1909, in an apartment used by the Countess Marie Grotta zu Grottenegg. I am sure the Pauline Harrod listed as his mother on his birth documents is a false trail laid by the Countess. Beatrice's signature could be misread as Pauline, but this would not explain the different age quoted.

Who was his father?

The answers to this question depend upon the answers to many other questions about the relationship between Beatrice and the Countess.

There must have been some sort of link between the two women. Why did Beatrice choose Vienna and that apartment to have her baby unless there was already a link? Beatrice travelled from and back to Paris for her stay in Vienna. What was she doing in Paris?

Finding out more about the Countess would help. So far, the records in Switzerland have not been found. There does not appear to have been a Marie de Joly born there around the dates given.

Marie could have lied about any or all of her details, her maiden name, place or date of birth.

It is certainly possible that she added the 'de' to impress the aristocracy she was joining, and there are Jolys in the records in Yverdon.

There was a Marie Louise Joly born and baptised in Yverdon in March 1858, to a single mother Jeanne Louise. Of all the fibs a woman might tell, I suppose her age is the most likely, so perhaps she altered her date of birth later to make herself younger. She would then have been 35 when she married the Count rather than the disclosed 29.

In newspaper reports about the Count in the last few weeks before his death, there are details of several financial irregularities involving him and a woman called Marie Missar. Just in case this was the real maiden name, I looked for her name in the Yverdon records, but in vain. How did the Countess meet the Count? She was apparently single when she married him in 1893, so aged 30ish. Could she have been married before, and de Joly was her married name, not her maiden name? All of this is possible but I have no access to records which might clarify the situation.

I think it is likely that during Beatrice's time in Europe with her Harrod family in 1901, or at a later date during further travel, she may then have made the acquaintance of the future father of Eduard and the Countess, perhaps together. Josef, the Count's remaining son, was by then the holder of the title and may well have still been in touch with his stepmother. It is easy to visualise 24-year-old Beatrice meeting Josef at a Viennese Ball in 1901, and dancing with the handsome 41-year-old man. This theory would of course require them to have kept in touch for several years afterwards.

If Josef were the father of Eduard, it would back up Eduard's family idea that the father was an aristocrat and that they met on a European trip, but would not explain the idea that she spent part of her pregnancy on board a ship in the Mediterranean. The family myth that he was a Merchant Captain raised the attractive idea that Bertie had fathered everyone! There are several reasons discussed earlier that make this idea untenable.

The father could of course have been from England.

Beatrice states in her correspondence with the F.O. that she had been in contact with the father regarding the demands of the Countess for money, but that he refused to help, and that she was told that she could not force him through the law courts. This would suggest an English father, but does not rule out Josef. Either way, she still had the means in 1916 to contact the father of the child conceived in 1909.

The idea of Josef being the father would explain why Beatrice decided to use of the Countess and Vienna for the place of birth, and the Countess's willingness initially to look after the child with no payment.

So, if you are reading this and you are a descendant of Josef or his family, I would love to check your DNA against that of Eduard's descendants.

The biggest puzzle of all is about Eduard himself.

The records available and the gaps in the records do not match the story told to the family by Eduard.

There seem to be two Eduards.

There is the Eduard who stayed with foster parents in Switzerland, went to an expensive boarding school and then university, and spoke three languages.

There is the other Eduard who was missing after birth for two years, stayed with the Countess for about a year, then went missing for a further five years, between the age of three years and eight years old. He then lived in homes for delinquents and hostels for the next nine years, getting into trouble with the police on several occasions, and being imprisoned for two short periods. During this time, the Countess died and may have been ill for a while, which would have added to Eduard's problems.

From 1930 onwards his records are continuous. He was then aged 19. He joined the N.S.A.D.P. and then worked for them whilst apparently working for short periods as a salesman, a bookbinder and a courier for the Brigade, until 1933 when aged 32, he moved to Hanover, Germany.

Somewhere during this time, according to his submissions to the Nazi authorities, he went to elementary school, secondary school and college. He didn't mention to them any trips to Switzerland. According to the story he told his relatives, he also joined the Foreign Legion for a year or so.

There is very little evidence to back up the Switzerland story, apart from Inge's memories.

There are no records of a baker and his family in Thun named Waeckerle or anything similar.

I have contacted all the universities in Switzerland in existence before the war. Not all have records for the period, but those that did have no records of Eduard Harrod or Eduard Waeckerle, (just in case he took their name during his stay).

However, Eduard's daughter, Inge, did remember being taken to Thun, in around 1953 or 1954, when she was 12 or 13 years old, to collect a box containing what were presumably Eduard's paperwork and memorabilia. I wondered why Eduard did not make this trip himself or accompany them.

There are no long enough or suitably timed gaps in the records of Eduard in Vienna to for him to have gone to Switzerland to a boarding school and then university. And yet, there were Eduard Harrod memories in the box his daughter collected. Frau Waeckerle said Eduard only stayed a short time when he was little, so is it possible this took place during the gap between 1915 and 1918.

Perhaps Eduard went there for a short period but the school and university story was a fib.

I began to wonder if there were two Eduard Harrods. The later one obtained the records from Thun to back up his story later in life, but could not go himself for fear of not being recognised.

I had begun to formulate a conspiracy theory that at the time seemed far-fetched.

There is no evidence to back up the Foreign Legion story.

I contacted the Foreign Legion and there are various Legion records on line. None contained an Eduard Harrod, though Legionnaires sometimes used false names. During the pre-war period there were several Legions, not just French but German as well. The German Foreign Legion took part in the Spanish Civil War when they formed the Condor Legion, which was involved in the infamous bombing of Guernica. The only time when there was a gap in his records was between 1927 and 1930, when he was between 16 and 19 years old, so it might have been possible then.

Addressing my theory, it is inconceivable that two Eduard Harrods were born on the same day at the same place in Vienna. So the inevitable conclusion is that there were two Eduards at some stage, one the real Eduard, born on the 12 December 1909 in Lazarettegasse, Vienna and the other an imposter, added or substituted at some stage.

I discussed this theory with Inge, Eduard's daughter in Houston. Eduard's photographs in later life were not unlike my father and his brother Michael, but were not as striking in their similarity as between my father and Michael.

The clincher for this imposter theory came with the decision we made that Inge; her sister and I should compare DNA results. On Family DNA, a comparison of matches called Family Finder can be used to determine the closeness of relationships between subscribers.

Inge, her sister and I should have shared a close relationship via our common grandmother, Beatrice, two of whose sons were our respective fathers. Family Finder showed no relationship between me and Inge and her sister, though their close relationship together was confirmed.

So we did not share the same grandmother, as we had thought.

Something had happened to the Eduard born in 1909 leaving the later Eduard to take over his name and history. When did this happen?

There is a continuous record of Eduard Harrod from 1930 onwards, and Inge can confirm that Eduard's signature in the letters of 1936-1939 were those of her father, who subsequently fathered Inge and her sister from 1939 onwards. So it was before 1930.

Together with the question of when the substitution happened, there is the question why?

There was no point in a substitution unless the original was 'lost'.

The Countess may have given the young baby Eduard away soon after Beatrice's departure back to Paris in 1910, and then needed a substitute to substantiate her claim for money in 1912 after Beatrice married. This theory is given some credence by the Swiss story, as Eduard might have been sent to Thun when a baby, and then the paperwork associated with this original was obtained by the second Eduard after the war. When the Countess wanted to get the money from Beatrice after her 1911 marriage, she found a child from the numerous orphanages in Vienna in 1912, had him baptised with the correct details in April 1912, and then obtained a copy of the birth records from the Magistrates in 1913.

As pointed out earlier, there is no record in Vienna of Eduard between his birth and 1912.

Soon afterwards, in 1915, Eduard disappears from the records again until 1918.

Is this just a lack of records, or did the Countess once again dispose of a child and get yet another in 1918 to back up further claims.

I wondered for some time about Eduard's gradually increasing Christian names over the years.

He was recorded at birth as Eduard Harrod. Could this have been the Countess's choice as she was going to take the baby, and she called him after her later husband, the Count?

He was baptised as Eduard Maria Harrod in 1912, by the Countess. I am not sure why she would want to muddy the water regarding his name. It may just have been personal vanity.

Then in 1938/38 Eduard himself added the name Oswald to his name, and this was copied by the German authorities. There were no Oswalds in the family, so why? Could it be that during the first Eduard's stay in Switzerland, he was renamed Oswald Waeckerli and he was adding the name to cover any further investigation of his history by the Nazis?

At his marriage in 1935 to Dorothea, he was entered on the record just as Eduard Maria.

His daughter Inge had no recollection of her father using the name Oswald during her life.

A further question of course then arises. What happened to the original Eduard Harrod?

There are no on-line searchable deaths of an Eduard Harrod in Switzerland or Austria.

There are records in Germany for an Edward Werkele who married Maria Elizabetha Volhard in Baden in 1947 and had three children. There are others with similar names but at the wrong time or the wrong place.

There is one Oswaldj Waikerli in the Slovakian records, with a wife Ursula and children Matthias and Tobias, but with no dates given.

Yet, if the second Eduard was able to get the documents in the box released by the baker's wife, she must have lost track of his whereabouts and been persuaded that her Eduard was asking for them.

I am not sure I will ever know the answer to this conundrum. Once again, DNA could answer this question if a descendant of the original Eduard, assuming he had some, turned up and put their DNA on line so that a match was found.

I can only live in hope. But somewhere I have lost an Uncle, and gained cousins that are not truly my cousins.

This all seems very far-fetched and rather like the 'Prince and the Pauper' story, but I can find no other logical explanation.

Part 2

Part 3

Chapter 24
The Author

2013

2013 saw the death of the final character in Beatrice Martha's story. Anyone who had known her personally had gone when Anna Humble-Crofts died.

I had started writing up my family history findings some years earlier. I had been researching since 1986 and had accumulated an enormous quantity of facts and figures, paper records, electronic records, reminiscences and photographs.

I knew no one but me would be able to sort it out, so I needed to write it all down for posterity. I was working full time as a G.P. so I had limited time to spend on a book and kept putting off the day when I could start. I was also still actively researching and learning new facets to the story, so in any case I did not know how and when to start.

By chance I found a workshop at Cheltenham Literary Festival, and the subject was – 'Writing up Your Family History'. Perfect. I made time for it.

I took away two important tips.

- There is no good time to start. Start writing now.
- Avoid using any adjectives unless necessary.

I followed the first, and tried to follow the second, but was not (very – sic) successful.

The document I produced was enormous. 1500 pages and over 1000 photographs! It filled a CD.

This was not a book to read, but I felt that there was a readable story within it.

Try as I might, I was unable to let go of all the facts and figures, so my first efforts at writing the story made torrid reading.

I was also a little diffident about writing about characters that were involved closely in the story but were still alive. So in 2013, I set about a re-write in earnest.

In my first effort, I used my father as the leading character of the story. This was a sentimental decision prompted by my sympathy for his tough start in life and my love and respect for his gritty, never-say-die attitude. The story did not work and though it was praised by several publishers, it was not felt to be a potential commercial candidate.

I was given some advice about books to read and styles to consider, and this proved helpful.

As the reader will have observed, I still haven't shaken off facts and figures.

It gradually became obvious to me that Beatrice Martha was the natural focal point of the story.

She was certainly a complex lady. She was part villain and part heroine.

Whereas others who know the story have felt she was a foolish and unpleasant character, though I never met her, I have come to feel very sorry for her.

She had so many setbacks and disappointments in her life it was no wonder she became a bitter and twisted woman. The Humble-Crofts family felt she was not worthy of their boy Bertie, and by the time she was middle-aged, she was pretty well universally disliked because her aloof attitude and insularity.

She made a lot of mistakes. She was a determined woman and was a risk-taker. She seems to have picked men who were charismatic but flawed. However, without her mistakes, there would have been no Calcutta, no Vienna and no Countess in the story.

She died a lonely and confused lady.

There have been several versions of the book written in the ensuing years, all done to try to make the story more 'commercial', a phrase repeated to me by publishers. I hope I have been successful.

This second part of the book will look at many of the characters and their families in more detail.

Chapter 25
What Happened to the Taylors?

The Taylors, Percival Joseph and Emily Ann, were the first known couple to 'adopt' my father, and for many years were viewed by my father as his parents.

Detailed information about them was quite difficult to find.

The information obtained latterly about the Taylors in Australia, (Chapter 2), proved very interesting, and helped formulate a further theory about the events surrounding my father's adoption and subsequent abandonment.

Everything found out about them in the Australian records, such as their respective parents, and the place and date of their marriage, matched exactly the facts I had discovered in England.

Though they travelled separately, the Taylors both arrived in Australia in 1913. No definite individual boat or port of disembarkation has been found for either of them. The 1913 arrival of Emily suggests a later departure for her than I had estimated, perhaps then in November 1912.

They lived in the suburbs of North Sydney for the rest of their lives and had no children of their own, nor did they adopt any more.

Percy Joseph Taylor took up his original occupation as a Jobbing Printer. He died in 1928 from nephritis, aged 60. Nephritis is a kidney problem sometimes leading to kidney failure. He was listed as a Roman Catholic, died in a Catholic hospital and was buried in a Catholic cemetery! This was a bit of surprise considering all the references to the Church of England in the story and that the Taylors had married in a Church of England church.

The informant of the death was a friend and neighbour called Mr Wardle.

Emily Ann Taylor was recorded as an invalid pensioner. She died at her home in 1933, from Heart Disease, aged 63, and was buried in a Church of England cemetery. Another member of the same Wardle family was the informant.

There was no sign of any other Taylor family members in the area in the newspaper death notices. If they had any relatives in Australia, they must have lived some distance away or been unable to attend the funeral.

More research in Australia was needed and the results, though not solving the riddle of Dad's abandonment in Liverpool, did throw more light on the Taylors.

Lorraine and Cherie, my Australian researchers, commented after reading my father's story that, *'he would have made a great Australian'.* Quite a compliment! How interesting to speculate what would have become of his life if he had travelled with his 'father' to Australia.

Having proved for certain that both Mr and Mrs Taylor did go to Australia focused my mind on what might have happened in Liverpool.

Repeated searches in Liverpool, including correspondence with local historians and a lot of time spent on line, have failed to show any further substantive information about Dad's stay in the 'Hostel of Hope' during 1912/13. Dad's letters provide most of the information.

When I re-read a sentence from Dad's account of this time, regarding his arrival in Liverpool, it suddenly struck me that it was of particular importance.

'...and I was left at a children's adoption home run by a spinster lady in Colebrook Road, Liverpool.'

The Hostel of Hope was in Bedford Street, Liverpool; and the original children's branch, Sunny Bank, was in Arnside in Cumbria. The latter apparently closed in 1909 before Dad's arrival in Liverpool.

Searches of the internet give very few hits for the 'Hostel of Hope', and just a few threads were found in family history forums. In one thread, in a Liverpool genealogy discussion forum, I found another man searching for details of the Hostel. His grandfather, the son of a local woman, had been adopted from the Hostel in the same year as Dad, 1912. Perhaps they even knew each other! Neither of us made any progress with further research for some long time. Another forum listed a little girl, adopted at the age of five weeks in 1905.

A breakthrough came in 2012 when I re-discovered a website showing some of the regional newspapers of the era. Searching for combinations of all the place names and people involved revealed a number of advertisements offering children for adoption. Almost all of them emanated from Miss Whishaw at Arnside.

The adverts all appeared between 1903 and 1920, though the vast majority were in the period 1903 to 1910, and there were none between 1912 and 1917. Overall, there were 330 adverts, but many were repeats in sequential editions advertising the same child or children. I calculated that altogether the adverts represented about 150 children. Most of the children were billed as a few weeks or a few months old, though there were a few older children, the oldest being an eight-year-old, advertised in the Hull Daily Mail in late 1911. Close, but not the right age.

The majority of adverts, especially in the earlier years, were in in the Manchester Courier and Lancashire General Advertiser and a Derby newspaper. Altogether, they had used 25 different newspapers, predominantly in the Midlands and North of England, but there were a few adverts in Surrey and Essex. Significantly, there were several in the Hull Daily Mail and Yorkshire Evening Post.

All the adverts before the end of 1909 gave the Arnside address, whereas all those from early 1910 onwards gave the Liverpool address. This matches the closure date for Arnside.

In the years when Dad was involved, 1912 and 1913, there were just two adverts, neither of which seemed to fit his specifications. One of the earlier adverts read:

'ADOPTION HOMES WANTED for Baby Boy, 16 months old, and for Baby Girl, 10 months old; both children bright and healthy; no premium nor payment, references given and required. – Whishaw, Sunnybank Orphanage, Arnside, Carnforth.'

From 1906 onwards, all the adverts also included the words – *'complete surrender'*. I have taken this to mean that there would be no connection maintained once the child was taken and that no 'returns' would be allowed.

The Children's Branch of the Hostel was not a large venture, even in its heyday.

As suggested by the number of newspaper adverts and repeats, the actual number of children passing through Sunnybank during the most active years was perhaps about 20 each year. Comparable figures from the Liverpool Seaman's Orphanage reports show that in 1909 alone that organisation dealt with 1,278 children!

It was difficult to speculate about the origin of the children. The majority being a few weeks or months old suggests that perhaps they came from a local home for unmarried mothers, but the spread of ages must mean that either they kept some children for some time or had another source for unwanted children.

It would not have been that unusual in this era for a child to be given away or abandoned by a single or widowed, or poverty-stricken parent.

I decided to chase the characters involved with the Hostel to see if this provided more information or any connection with other parts of the story.

Constance Mary Whishaw was born in Chipping Norton, Oxfordshire in about 1858. She was obviously the source of the finance and nominally the Head of the enterprise.

Her father, the Reverend Alexander Whishaw had been born in St. Petersburg, Russia in 1823, and was educated at Oxford University. He married three times and had several years as Vicar at Chipping Norton, Gloucestershire, with his 2nd. wife Agnes Louisa, where Constance was born in 1858.

Constance Whishaw never married. The 1901 census shows she was the Head of the Home at Sunny Bank, Arnside, looking after four 'inmates', all girls aged 13 or 14. They were all from the Liverpool area apart from one who was from the Forest of Dean. These inmates did not fit the age profile of the children later offered for adoption.

In 1911 there were similarly four female inmates at the Liverpool Hostel of Hope, aged between 14 and 42, but no young children.

By 1911, Constance had moved and was living in Clevedon, Somerset, so she was obviously no longer hands-on with the charity, though her name still appeared on the paperwork until about 1912.

Miss Whishaw wrote books, mostly of a religious nature. Her most successful book was published in 1897 – *'Being and Doing'*; a selection of helpful thoughts from various authors, *'arranged for daily reading'*. It was full of homely and sensible Christian advice.

Constance Whishaw had obviously devoted her life to 'good works'.

The information about Constance Whishaw confirmed she was no longer in Liverpool during Dad's stay in 1912 or 1913.

As would have been expected from the adverts and telephone directory findings, there was no sign of Sunnybank in Arnside in the 1911 census. Constance's brother, Alexander, was living in Arnside in 1911, but in a different house.

Other records show that during the early 20th century there were numerous small homes set up by wealthy do-gooders in the larger cities of Britain, often catering for 'fallen women'. Most did not last very long. The Hostel of Hope may have fallen into that category.

Elizabeth Ellen Martin, the secretary of the Hostel of Hope, was a single lady who had been born in Sale, Cheshire in 1862. After working with her mother as a dressmaker for many years, she moved to a seven-roomed house in Colebrooke Road in Liverpool sometime between 1901 and 1911. In 1911 she was living there with her widowed mother, three sisters, and a brother and sister-in-law. As the correspondence showed, she worked from home and by 1912 was the principal administrator. By 1927 she was the Matron of the Hostel of Hope. She died in 1935, at another address in Liverpool.

What does all this information tell us about Dad's temporary placement in Liverpool?

Miss Whishaw was the money and brains behind the Hostel of Hope, which ran for about 20 years as a home for young women who had fallen on hard times.

She was involved in the children's branch at Arnside. In 1901 the children were all teenaged girls, then between 1903 and 1909 it ran as an orphanage for much younger children. It closed in 1909 and by 1911 Miss Whishaw was not actively involved in the organisation. She was no longer living either in Arnside or Liverpool.

There is no sign of any younger children in the 1901 or 1911 censuses of the Hostel of Hope in Liverpool, so despite the headed notepaper used in 1912 and 1913, if there was still a children's branch after 1909, it was certainly not at Arnside or at the Hostel of Hope in Bedford Street.

None of this helps us to understand how and why Dad was taken in and later placed by them in 1912. The circumstances of his involvement must have been on an individual basis. Why was that?

Dad remembers travelling to Liverpool, and travelling from Liverpool to Hull, so my conclusion is that he was housed somewhere in Liverpool for the duration of his stay. This is where we return to the sentence from Dad's story that I mentioned earlier. He stated he was *'left with a spinster lady in Colebrook(e) Road'*. There were only two spinster ladies in the set-up, Constance Whishaw and Elizabeth Martin. Miss Whishaw was living elsewhere in 1912. Miss Martin was the secretary and in 1911 was living at Colebrook Road with her family. So it looks as though Dad was housed with Miss Martin in 1912.

Adoption was, until 1926, a completely unofficial affair, with no obligatory investigations needed, or official records kept, making it extremely unlikely that any further documentation will ever come to light to completely explain the developments.

It was a mystery why Dad was left in Liverpool in 1912 with a small set-up like the 'Hostel of Hope'. It had stopped dealing with children at their Arnside branch some years before and had pretty much stopped advertising further children anywhere. It was a minor organisation in an out-of-the–way location in Liverpool. The Hostel of Hope was about three miles on foot to the north of the city centre and railway station, and Colebrooke Road was nearly three miles to the south.

How on earth would Joseph Taylor have come across it? Why not use one of the many large children's homes in the city, many closer to the railway station?

An intriguing theory was prompted by my re-investigation of both Miss Perks at the Nursing Home in Kensington where Dad was born, and the Hostel of Hope in Liverpool. No evidence has been found that would help to identify when Dad was first adopted by the Taylors, and my assumption has been that this was soon after his birth registration in Kensington and baptism in Frampton Cotterell.

By the end of 1906 he had already moved out of London. Hence, when his story starts in Manchester aged four, he may already have been part of a loving family for some time.

I have tried looking for connections between the Harrod family, Frampton Cotterell, Miss Perks and her Nursing Home, the Hostel of Hope, Miss Whishaw and the Taylors, without success.

Several pieces of circumstantial evidence have however made me wonder if Dad's initial adoption by the Taylors might have been via the Sunnybank Orphanage in Arnside.

Firstly, the Nursing Home in Cheniston Gardens where Dad was born appears only to have been in existence between 1904 and 1909. The Sunnybank Orphanage in Arnside was in existence between 1903 and 1909.

Secondly, in the letter to Sargent from the Hostel of Hope dated February 13, 1913, Miss Martin states that Dad's father was a Merchant Captain. How did she know that, when in theory Dad had been dumped at the Hostel by Mr Taylor, unless she had been involved in the original adoption?

Thirdly, it is a mystery why Dad seemed to have been a special case, being offered for adoption in 1912/1913, several years after the Children's Branch of the Hostel of Hope seems to have ceased functioning.

Lastly, and most convincingly, how and why did Joseph Taylor choose to leave Dad with Miss Martin at Colebrooke Road in Liverpool unless he already knew the organisation and their rather obscure address? It would have been much more likely, assuming he was not familiar with Liverpool, that he would leave Dad with one of the larger and better-known children's orphanages in the centre of the city, especially when Sunny bank was no longer functioning as an orphanage in 1912. The Hostel of Hope did not seem to advertise in the area and would have been difficult to find.

The possible explanation, the only one I can find, is that the nursing home and the orphanage were connected. Perhaps Miss Perk's establishment in London was a source of children for Miss Whishaw's orphanage in Arnside. Dad would then have been taken in by Miss Whishaw in 1906/1907 and so was already known to the orphanage in 1912. The Taylors had acquired Dad after they had answered an advert placed by Miss Whishaw for Dad in 1906, and so the Sunny Bank name was already known to Joseph Taylor in 1912.

As it happens, having looked at all the adverts from Arnside during 1906, some of them stand out as possible adverts for Dad. One in particular, dated the 28 September 1906, in the Lichfield Mercury, a week after Dad was born, lists 'a superior boy, a few weeks old'. Were this truly to be an advert for Dad, it would of course require that the advert was placed whilst Dad was still in London, as his birth was not registered by Beatrice Martha Harrod until the 10 October.

If my theory is possible, then Joseph Taylor, finding he was forced to leave Dad behind in Liverpool, would make a beeline for the Hostel in Liverpool who had arranged the original adoption. The address on the paperwork held by Mr Taylor would fortunately have been Colebrooke Road.

What was Mr Taylor to do otherwise? His wife was already in Australia. He had to find someone who could take Dad and find a new home for him. The sequence of events might have been as follows.

Joseph heads to Bedford Street only to discover that the Hostel no longer deals with children and that they are actively involved only with women in distress. He recalls the Colebrooke Road address and finds that Elizabeth Martin is still living there. Fortunately, Miss Martin, despite the 'complete surrender' phrase used in the adverts in 1906, recognises the problem and might have felt sympathetic or duty bound to take Dad back in the circumstances, and try to place him again. There being no Sunnybank in Arnside available, he was lodged with Miss Martin in Colebrooke Road.

Miss Martin takes Dad back and uses the same method of advertising as used some years previously to find a new home for Dad. She would have looked for a rapid disposal for the child and may not have been as choosy as they might have been a few years earlier.

This was successful, but it was a flawed system from Dad's point of view, as the vetting system for the adopters was almost non-existent.

The question is whether this theory can ever be proven. The simple answer is no, the evidence is circumstantial. I have yet to find any evidence of a connection between Miss Perks and Miss Whishaw, but I will keep looking.

However, the theory certainly would explain some of the remaining questions regarding Dad's time in Liverpool.

I promised to return to the further findings about the Taylors in Australia.

Having discovered that the Taylors did reach Australia and lived out their lives in New South Wales, I decided to see if I could find out anything else through any living relatives of the Wardle family who were their friends and neighbours and were the informants at their respective deaths.

The Wardle family proved to be more complex than I had bargained for, so get ready to be muddled.

Mary Ann Wardle, (1860-1934), was the informant for Mr Taylor's death in 1928, and her son, Walter Junior, (1886-1977) for Mrs Taylor in 1933.

I found a descendant, Penelope Wardle, who is the great-granddaughter of Mary Ann.

Penelope's father was another Walter, who was born in Australia in 1920 and was still alive at the time of contact, then aged 92. He has a reasonably clear memory, but had only a vague recollection of the Taylors.

The Wardles were all living in South Manchester before 1910, half a mile from the Taylors.

My research and Walter's reminiscences revealed that Mary Ann's husband was also a Walter, (1859-1932). They had married in 1882 and had four sons, Harry, Walter, John and Arthur.

Somewhere between the birth of Arthur in 1895 and 1905, Walter Senior and Mary Ann parted company.

Walter Senior (1859-1932) had a daughter in 1905, with another woman, Ellen Jane.

Mary Ann emigrated to New South Wales, Australia, with her eldest son Harry and his wife in July 1910.

Soon after, in October 1911, Walter Senior married his partner Ellen Jane, and between 1911 and 1913, they emigrated to New South Wales with their daughter, and Walter changed his name to Bertram Ward. They had a son born in 1913.

Walter Junior ran the family electrical company in the city with brother Arthur.

Walter Junior married Mary Ethel Osborne in November 1911, she was the adopted daughter of Walter Senior and Mary Ann.

Walter Junior emigrated to New South Wales in February 1912 with his new wife Mary, and his brother Arthur.

So, by 1913, all the Wardles were in New South Wales, albeit in different areas.

Had any of them arranged to travel with Emily Ann Taylor? The travel dates do not coincide, but one family may have encouraged the other to follow.

I did find one living descendant of the Manchester Wardles who lives in Scotland. Unfortunately, he knew nothing about the Taylors. There were also some Wardles in Macclesfield in the early 20th century, but none had a fish and chip shop, and none seemed to be linked to the Taylors.

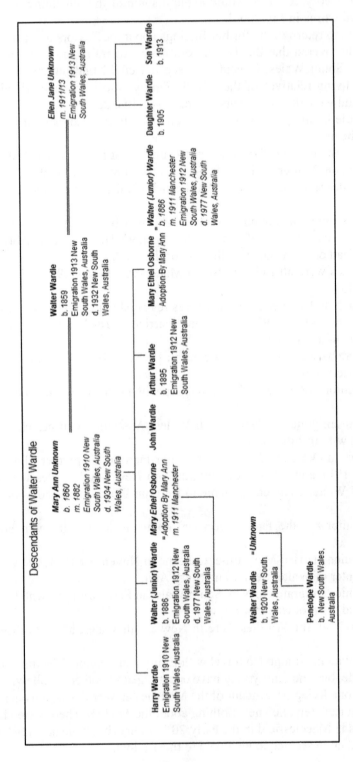

Chart 8: Descendants of Walter Wardle

I went back to check the most likely boats used by Percy Joseph Taylor and his wife Emily Ann on their separate voyages to Australia.

Emily Ann probably travelled on the 'Zealandic' from London to Sydney on the 3 October, 1912; so no match there, although there was another Walter Wardle on the same boat, seemingly unrelated, and the wrong age.

Percy Joseph may have travelled on the 'Pakeha' from Liverpool to Sydney on the 4 February, 1913, this had yet another unrelated Mrs and Miss Wardle on board. All these unrelated Wardles did however live in South Manchester in 1911, but sadly, none could be linked to our Wardles.

The youngest Walter Wardle still living in Australia did eventually talk more to his daughter, and remembered something about the Taylors! He believes that his parents and the Taylors knew each other in Manchester for some time before they departed from the UK. There were photographs of these together, though sadly none of them had survived!

So the records indicate the Taylors and the Wardles arrived in Australia a year or so apart, but were in touch before and after arrival. It certainly might explain why Mrs Taylor was brave enough to set off by herself before her husband; she had her friends waiting for her.

The living Walter Wardle then gave me some more information. He remembered Emily Ann Taylor was a 'renowned' ballet dancer, a new revelation to me. Extensive research on the internet has revealed nothing about this. At the age of about 42 when she arrived in Australia, she must have long ago given up dancing, other than perhaps teaching. Her husband Percy Joseph went back to his occupation as a printer when in Australia, the job he had before starting the gramophone shop. Walter recalls that he had a printing press in the front room of his house at Leichhardt.

By the time Walter knew him, Percy Joseph was a sick man and was living alone, and his wife Emily was in a *'very large nursing home'* in Leichhardt, following an attack of polio.

Walter recalls that Joseph in later life also had a great deal of difficulty walking and getting around in general. Walter and his parents often visited his house; if he was running short of food, they would go to a nearby grocery store, *'just down the street'*, to buy supplies. This was the main source of Joseph's food as it was too much for him to go the short distance to the shop.

Walter and his parents visited Emily Ann in hospital as well. He recalls that she used an *'old fashioned wheelchair'*, it had a wheel with a handle about shoulder height that was attached to a chain on the large wheel below. She was able to turn the handle to move the chair. Her legs were paralysed and she couldn't walk, but she still had use of her arms.

Percy died in 1928 in hospital, suffering from nephritis. Walter remembered that his scant possessions were passed on to Mary Ann Wardle.

Emily Ann died five years later of heart disease in her nursing home.

Unfortunately, Walter was not aware of any other Taylor family or children, nor had he ever heard mention of a 'son' left in England. I guess the Taylors would not have wanted to mention that.

So, interesting information, but no confirmation of what had happened in Liverpool.

The likely story remains unconfirmed but unchallenged. The sequence is as follows:

Emily Taylor travelled to Australia ahead of her husband Joseph, whilst he was winding up affairs in Manchester.

She joined up with old friends, the Wardles in New South Wales.

Dad was 'parked' temporarily with friends in Macclesfield during this time. Perhaps Joseph was waiting for clearance papers for Dad to travel.

Joseph Taylor later picked Dad up and they travelled to Liverpool, intending to board a boat to take them to Australia to join Mrs Taylor.

Once in Liverpool, Joseph finds that Dad's papers, including his birth certificate, a copy, are not enough to allow his emigration. One can imagine Joseph's panic as he tries desperately to persuade the authorities to change their minds before the boat leaves. Almost certainly, he will miss it.

Faced with the reality that he cannot take his son with him; he must find some way to find a safe future for him. He is in a large city and knows nobody else who might help apart from the same charitable organisation who originally offered Dad for adoption. He manages to find them and they agree to take him back.

Joseph Taylor is able to re-book his passage to join his wife in Australia, probably distraught but reassured by the knowledge that Dad is in good hands and will probably find another loving family to care for him. Well, that is what he thought.

Joseph sets off knowing that he has an awful task ahead of him, to explain to his wife what has happened. She is excitedly waiting to greet her husband and son in Sydney, unaware of the drama of Liverpool. Did the events sour their relationship or bind them together in adversity? I will never know.

It does not sound as though their life in Australia was very successful.

Chapter 26
What Happened to Sergeant?

After having earlier read the happy part of Dad's story, it may be a good time to complete the story of the man who dominated the darkest part of Dad's life, Leonard John Sergeant.

After 1933, 10 years after Dad 'escaped', Leonard Sergeant moved from Kingston Terrace to 74 Naylors Row, which was quite close by. He is in the 1939 census living alone in Naylors Row, then aged 65 and still working. He died, very close to that address, in 1941.

Hull was extensively bombed during the Second World War. It was a major strategic target for the German Luftwaffe, targeting the docks, the fishing industry, shipbuilding and other food related industries. It was also within range of German bombers. Hull was pasted. It has been estimated that 92% of houses in Hull were damaged by bombing during the war.

On the night of the 8 May, 1941, Hull suffered the heaviest bombing raid of the whole war. Well over 400 people died that night, a quarter of the total toll of civilians killed in Hull throughout the war. Hundreds were injured and 40,000 people were made homeless in the one raid.

Half of the 400 dead were buried at a mass funeral as they could not be identified.

On that night, Leonard Sergeant responded to the sirens warning of the raid and went to the shelter which was close to his home, the Naylors Row Bomb Shelter. Much of the surrounding area was flattened and there was a direct hit on the shelter.

He was the only person inside to die. He was aged 67 years.

I have often wondered if Dad had kept an eye on Sergeant over the 20 years after leaving him, or had he, as I suspect, put him to the back of his mind and hoped they would never meet again?

I then wondered if he might have learnt about his death and what his reaction would have been.

Dad worked throughout the war as a fire watcher, as he had had been turned down for service in the forces on medical grounds. The firewatchers worked on the roof of prominent buildings throughout the city. They were often in danger and featured in the casualties as they were concentrated in the areas most likely to be targeted.

The records show that on the nights of the 7 and 8 May 1941, when the seriousness of the raids was realised, every man and woman in the Civil Defence

Service, on or off duty, and despite the difficulties of travel, reported for duty. During the raids, schoolchildren acted as messengers, as most normal means of communication were either destroyed or partly out of action. It sounds as though it was 'all hands-on deck'.

That night Dad would have taken his turn on fire watch duty on the rooftops of the city centre of Hull. By the time the all-clear was sounded, he would have known the location of all the bombs and fires.

It is possible that like many people, he checked the posted lists of casualties the next day at the Central Library.

I suspect that though present members of my family, including me, and perhaps others reading this story, might let out a silent whoop of vengeance on hearing the news about Sergeant, my knowledge of Dad leads me to think that he would have just confined himself to a certain grunt of grim satisfaction.

Leonard John Sergeant's death certificate confirms the date and place of his death. The certificate was issued *'under Defence Regulations'*, after an Inquiry held on the 27 June that year by Mr A. C. Minn, Deputy Coroner for Hull. The cause of death was given as, *'Due to war operations'*.

One interesting, and rather gruesome footnote to Sergeant's life emerged from relatives who were called upon to try to try to identify his body after the bombing. As mentioned earlier, there were more than 400 deaths that night, and many were laid out in temporary morgues for relatives to try to identify them. Many of the bodies were badly disfigured and sadly beyond recognition.

These casualties were buried in mass graves.

Many of them had their head or limbs blown off and an attempt was made to fit the parts to bodies for identification. Sergeant apparently had long, dark, curly hair.

When eventually identified his separated head had been put on a female body!

Chapter 27
More About the Harrods

Research into the Harrod family revealed that my ancestors were a resourceful and dogged lot.

I was able to pick up a trail of the family in the late 18th century and the early 19th century.

Like many working folks of that era, they managed through hard work and education to pull themselves gradually up the social ladder to a more comfortable middle-class existence.

Despite that, even at the height of their fame and fortune, in the eyes of those with had inherited money and breeding, the Harrods would have remained 'trade'.

The oldest direct Harrod ancestors found so far are William and Tamah Harrod. They were the parents of Charles Henry Harrod, the founder of the Harrods shop. They were both born in the second half of the 18th century. William Harrod, born in 1767, was my great, great, great grandfather.

I have been able to trace pretty well all of their descendants, but none of their ancestors.

Many other Harrod families, here and abroad, have made contact over the years of my research, often with family trees stretching back well beyond the time of our earliest ancestors. They usually sought to find a connection to 'Harrods' the store, but so far none have been found that can be linked at this time to our branch. I have no doubt that when I eventually discover the origins of William Harrod and his ancestors, I shall find connections to many of them.

Contact with other researchers was made mostly using genealogical websites, where your family tree can be made available to others if you wish. On some occasions contact was through the archivist at Harrods store, who gets a lot of letters from Harrod family 'wanabees'. Over the years I have developed a relationship with several of the successive archivists, and they often forward letters to me to try sort out and answer.

William worked with the Excise for 20 years, five years in Suffolk from 1792 to 1798, and 15 years in Essex from 1798 to 1812, the year in which he died.

There were initially some reasons to believe that he may have his origins in London or close by, and only moved to Suffolk and Essex for his work. Despite extensive research in Suffolk, Essex and Southwark, and more recently in Lincolnshire and Ireland, no definite record of his birth or baptism has been found, so no more distant ancestors have been discovered.

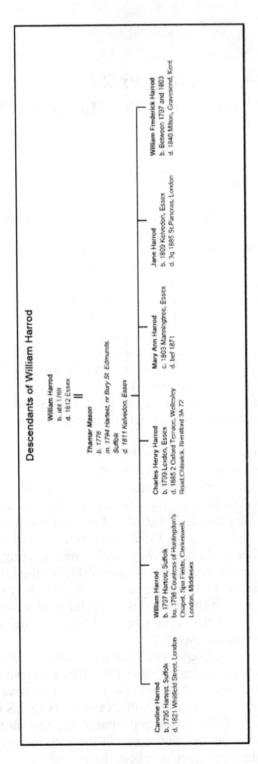

Descendants of William Harrod

William Harrod
b. abt 1769
d. 1812 Essex

=

Thamar Mason
b. 1776
m. 1794 Hartest, nr Bury St. Edmunds,
Suffolk
d. 1811 Kelvedon, Essex

Caroline Harrod
b. 1795 Hartest, Suffolk
d. 1821 Whitfield Street, London

William Harrod
b. 1797 Hartest, Suffolk
bu. 1798 Countess of Huntington's
Chapel, Spa Fields, Clerkenwell,
London, Middlesex

Charles Henry Harrod
b. 1799 Lexden, Essex
d. 1885 2 Oxford Terrace, Wellesley
Road,Chiswick, Brentford 3A 72

Mary Ann Harrod
c. 1803 Manningtree, Essex
d. bef 1871

Jane Harrod
b. 1809 Kelvedon, Essex
d. 3q 1885 St Pancras, London

William Frederick Harrod
b. Between 1737 and 1803
d. 1840 Milton, Gravesend, Kent

Chart 9: Descendants of William Harrod

The villages in North-East Suffolk, just south of Lowestoft, still seem the most likely bet for his birthplace at the present stage. There is a clutch of Harrods in the area of Thetford, Wangford and Blything in that part of Suffolk, and others at Henstead, and the surrounding villages of Barsham and Benacre. The National Gravestones index records Harrods in the nearby villages of Kirkly, Rushmere and Worlingham. The area is full of them.

William Harrod married Tamah Mason in Hartest, a village in the triangle of Clare, Long Melford and Bury St. Edmunds in Suffolk in 1794. He was 27 years old and she 18. He was working in that area at this time. Both were listed in the Hartest Parish Records as 'of this Parish'.

There are several different spellings of her name. She signed the register of marriage as Tamah; she was recorded as Thamar on the baptism entry for one of her children and Tamar on the baptism entries for the rest of her children and in the register of her burial in Kelvedon, Essex.

Her own signature as Tamah seems likely to be the most accurate spelling.

It looks, from their marriage and children's baptism records, as though William and Tamah were non-conformists, despite the entries in the local parish records.

At the time of their marriage in Hartest, William had been working with the nearby 'Clare Ride' in south-west Suffolk for 18 months. Long enough, one presumes, to meet a local girl. Prior to this, as his first posting with the Excise, he was on the 'Saxmundham Ride' about 30 miles away to the north-east, as a Supernumerary. Saxmundham is about 20 miles south of Lowestoft and is not too far away from those Suffolk villages mentioned earlier as centres of Harrod population, but just far enough perhaps so that he was not well known there.

The Minute Books of the Excise Board, retained at the National Archives, show that like other excisemen, William changed posts every few years, possibly to reduce the risk of corruption. He rose from being a 'Supernumerary' in Saxmundham to an Officer on the Colchester Ride.

Hartest is a delightful Suffolk village, with a large triangular village green, a lovely simple church, and a pub which, prior to the 1830s, was a small Manor House. The village is about six miles north of Clare, which is just on the Suffolk side of the Essex/Suffolk border. Clare had been a prosperous town since the middle ages and was heavily involved in the local wool and cloth trade, being especially renowned for its broad cloth until the 1600s. By the following century the cloth trade was declining and agriculture came to be the principle local occupation. The prosperity continued until the decline of agriculture nationwide in the mid-1850s, at which time the whole area declined in both wealth and population.

We must assume that William met Tamah during his time working there and that she was local to the area, despite the lack of any other evidence of her family.

The Kelvedon records reveal that Tamah Harrod died in June 1811; her age is given as 35. William died the year after Tamah, in April 1812. His age is given as 43. Their non-conformist status is suggested by the appearance of their burial records as required in the Parish records, though there were no graves to be found in the churchyard. Their deaths within ten months of each other raises the possibility of some sort of epidemic, but no definite information is available to confirm this. There were documented epidemics of measles in the area in both 1811 and 1812.

Their last child had been born in 1809 so I wondered if Tamah died during or soon after the birth of another child. However, I could find no trace in the records of a Harrod baby born in or near Kelvedon in the period before her death.

The last entry in the Excise Board records reports William's death, suggesting he might have died at work, though there is no evidence for this. Death whist working for the Excise was not a rare event.

Though initially it looked as though William and Tamah had only two children, trawling the Parish Registers for Essex at the County Records Office in Chelmsford and for Suffolk at Bury St. Edmunds for the places where William was stationed, showed that in fact that they definitely had five children, and possibly six.

Of the five, Charles Henry, the third child born in 1799 in Lexden, Essex, was to become the founder of Harrods. The others were:

Caroline, who was born in 1795, died unmarried aged 26.

Mary Ann, born in 1803, and Jane, born in 1809, both married and had families and lives of their own in London.

William Frederick was reputedly born in 1803, so unless he was a twin to Mary Ann this date could be incorrect. He married and had three children. He became a Jeweller in Southwark and took over Charles Henry's Cable Street shop whilst Charles was' missing' in 1836. There is a second William in the records who was born in 1797 and died in 1798, and he was also buried in a non-conformist cemetery. He may have been another child of William and Tamah. Parents commonly called a later child the same name if they had lost one in infancy or childhood.

Following the death of their parents William and Tamah in 1811 and 1812, the children would have been respectively sixteen, nearly thirteen, about eleven, eight and two and a half years old. Was the eldest living child, Caroline, old enough to look after the others? It is likely that the family were not left well off and I suspect, though have found no proof, that one or other of the grandparents looked after the children. It is most likely that after their parents' deaths, the children might have gone back to Tamah's family in Hartest, just 20 miles away across the Suffolk border, rather than William's family, wherever they were.

Charles Henry Harrod maintained a connection throughout his life with the area where he met his wife, a member of the Digby family, who lived near Birch in Essex, just south-west of Colchester. This is not far from Kelvedon where his parents died, so I think they remained in the Essex/Suffolk area at least for a few years, and then moved to London.

Many historians have stated that Charles Henry started his working life as a Miller in nearby Clacton. Though this is possible as he was certainly in the area, and his wife's family were mostly millers, I have not been able to find any evidence to confirm this story. He must have started work sometime early in the

1810s, probably between the ages of 14 and 16, and joining a local family business would have seemed the obvious thing to do.

Nothing is known about what actually happened to the children between 1812 and the early 1820s, when the records show that Caroline died in 1821 in Camden, and William Frederick married in 1822 in Holborn; followed by the first re-appearance of Charles Henry in 1824 in Southwark.

In 1824, 12 years after his father's death, Charles Henry opened his draper's shop in Southwark, when he was 25 years old, and some years before the 'official' start of his retail career in the 1830s in the East End of London.

In his books about Harrods, Tim Dale reported the claims that Harrods was the only large London store not to have started life as a draper's, but as a grocer's shop. British History on Line states,

'Harrods is untypical of the great London department stores in having risen not from a drapery or general goods business but from a grocer's shop.'

Sadly, he did start life as a draper.

In 1930, he married Elizabeth Digby in the Parish Church of Birch. A Special Licence was required from Lambeth Palace as Elizabeth was under 21 years old, in fact she was probably 17. In the Banns, Charles is recorded as still resident in Southwark at that date. A Mason relative was one of the witnesses at the wedding.

Throughout their lives, both Charles Henry and his son Charles Digby retained a link with the Birch area of Essex. Both appeared to own land and property in the area and Charles Digby later became the Lord of the Manor of Layer Breton, the parish next door to Birch.

The London Directories of the time show that Charles Henry had a shop at both 228, Borough High Street and a storehouse in the adjacent Maidstone Buildings. They are beautifully illustrated in Tallis's maps of the actual facades of the buildings in London streets from 1838 to 1840. Oddly, though next door to each other, the two premises were in different Southwark Parishes.

Charles Henry was in a transient partnership with a William Wicking whilst in Southwark, but that was dissolved in 1926. What a relief! 'Harrod and Wickings' of Knightsbridge just does not sound as good as 'Harrods'.

Rather confusingly at the time, I unearthed several other Charles Henry Harrods in Southwark, three in fact, all in the same family. They belonged to a family who originated in Lincolnshire. To date, no connection to our family has been found, but the proximity of this family in Southwark to our family might suggest they were connected by as yet unknown ancestors of William Harrod.

I have not been able to prove why Charles Henry left Southwark in 1831/32 and subsequently started up in business as a Grocery and Tea Dealer in Cable St., near Well Close Square, Stepney, in East London in 1834.

It has been attributed to money received from his wife's family, the Digbys, as in 1834 Elizabeth Digby's father James died, leaving her £300, probably worth about £15,000 today.

Further research showed that Charles Henry's business south of the Thames got into financial trouble, and it could be that the Digby money came just at the right time to be able to make a new start.

Charles Henry may have correctly decided that there was more money to be made in tea. The East India Company Charter Act of 1833, which amongst other things abolished their tea monopoly, opened up free trade in tea and so encouraged many people to become tea dealers and grocers at this time.

The country was mad about tea.

Elizabeth Digby, known as Eliza, was born around 1810, and was the eldest daughter of James Digby Senior, a successful pork butcher and miller from Essex. The huge Digby family were butchers, millers, farmers or agricultural workers in and around Birch. For a few decades they were quite affluent and owned land locally.

The Digby family proved very confusing when researched. The many branches of the family each had large families; they were all born and lived in close proximity to each other; and the names of the children were duplicated in almost all the families. Even in the direct line of Digbys with which the Harrods were involved, there were eight generations of 'James' in a row as the name of the first-born son. It took me several years to sort them out.

The Digbys were also non-Conformists, and were involved in Harrod family life for three generations.

After he was widowed, Charles Henry had successive Digby nieces as housekeepers whilst living in Kensington in retirement. Several Digbys, together with a son of Charles Henry set off together in 1863 to find a new life in New Zealand.

After Charles Henry's Southwark business ceased trading in 1831, he subsequently started up in some premises in 1832 in Upper Whitecross Street, just north of the Barbican area of London, probably just trading as a wholesale grocer.

The Cable Street shop in East London opened in 1834 whilst Charles Henry and his family were living just down the road in Rosemary Lane.

The area was quite cosmopolitan at the time and for several decades was home to waves of different immigrants. It was renowned as an area for dissenters and non-conformists. It was home to several German-owned Sugar Refineries and Warehouses, and one of the surrounding districts was known as Rag Fair, a district for the sale of second-hand clothes.

The Harrod Grocery business in Cable Street continued for over 20 years following its start in 1834, probably until 1856. Charles additionally ran other premises in the City area north of the Thames; in 1849 at 41, St. Mary at Hill as 'Harrod Charles, Colonial Produce Dealer'; and in 1850 at 38, Eastcheap as 'Harrod Charles Henry, Wholesale Grocer'. The latter business ran on well into the 1860s and probably beyond.

Charles Henry and Elizabeth had six children, five of whom were definitely born in Cable Street, and all of them were given her maiden name, Digby, as their middle name. Early in my research, I had only found four children, starting with my great-grandfather, Charles Digby, born in 1841.

The first born was missing from the records and unknown to me until some documents were discovered which covered a spell Charles Henry had in jail. They revealed the existence of this other child, who was born in 1832 and died in early 1837 during Charles's time in custody.

The second child, Elizabeth Digby, was born in 1835 and died in Cable Street in 1839 after measles, then often a fatal disease. She was buried at St. Mary's Church in Whitechapel. Charles and Elizabeth had lost their first two children in the course of two years, not such an unusual occurrence in the day.

Charles Digby, my great grandfather, was their third child, born in 1841.

His brothers, William Digby and Henry Digby were born in 1842 and 1845 respectively, and both survived.

The youngest child, Joseph Digby, was born in 1847 died in 1854, following scarlet fever. He is buried with his father in Brompton Cemetery.

The unusual pattern of the children's birth dates caught my attention when I first found them.

Charles and Eliza married in 1830, yet no children were apparently born before 1835, unusual in those days of limited or no contraception. Then after the child in 1835, there was a six-year gap.

I wondered perhaps if they must have lost children in earlier pregnancies. After 1841 children followed with the regularity normally expected. New findings showed the reasons. There had been a child prior to 1835, and Charles then went missing after 1835 for a while.

In the early years of the 21st century the Ancestry website added a search facility for the England and Wales Criminal Registers including also details of Proceedings of the Old Bailey between 1674 and 1913. A search for 'Harrod' threw up several results. There were a few reports of theft from Harrods Stores, but two other cases where a Charles Harrod or Charles Henry Harrod was the defendant. That got my instant attention.

A 'Charles Henry Harrod' was accused in 1888 of Breaking the Peace, and Libel, and appeared at the Old Bailey on the 30 July of that year. He pleaded guilty to *unlawfully publishing certain libels of and concerning Sir Reginald Hanson.* This one proved to be one of the other Charles Henrys living in Southwark.

The more interesting trial proved to be that of my Charles Harrod, held at the Old Bailey on the 9 May 1836 before the Recorder, T. Clarkson Esq.

The Proceedings contained the following case.

RICHARD MORAN was 'indicted for stealing, on the 2nd of April 1836, 112lbs. weight of currants, value £3 5s; and 1 bag, value 6d; the goods of John Healey Booth and others, his masters; and CHARLES HARROD for feloniously receiving the same, well knowing them to be stolen; against the statute.'

Could this be the previously squeaky-clean Charles Harrod, founder of the prestigious store?

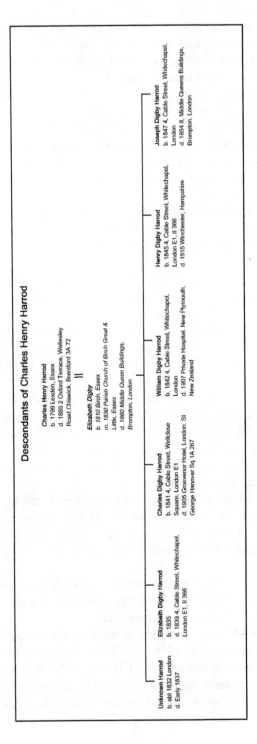

Descendants of Charles Henry Harrod

Charles Henry Harrod
b. 1799 Lexden, Essex
d. 1885 2 Oxford Terrace, Wellesley
Road, Chiswick. Brentford 3A 72

=

Elizabeth Digby
b. 1810 Birch, Essex
m. 1830 Parish Church of Birch Great &
Little, Essex
d. 1860 Middle Queen Buildings,
Brompton, London

Unknown Harrod
b. abt 1832 London
d. Early 1837

Elizabeth Digby Harrod
b. 1835
d. 1839 4, Cable Street, Whitechapel,
London E1, II 366

Charles Digby Harrod
b. 1841 4, Cable Street, Wellclose
Square, London E1
d. 1905 Grosvenor Hotel, London. St
George Hanover Sq 1A 267

William Digby Harrod
b. 1842 4, Cable Street, Whitechapel,
London
d. 1907 Private Hospital, New Plymouth,
New Zealand

Henry Digby Harrod
b. 1845 4, Cable Street, Whitechapel,
London E1, II 366
d. 1915 Winchester, Hampshire

Joseph Digby Harrod
b. 1847 4, Cable Street, Whitechapel,
London
d. 1854 8, Middle Queens Buildings,
Brompton. London

Chart 10: Descendants of Charles Henry Harrod

Richard Moran, a year older than Charles Henry, was a Porter at Messrs. Booth, Ingkedew & Co., who were wholesale grocers at 68, Upper Thames Street. From the evidence presented, it was likely that Harrod had been accepting stolen goods for some time and that the Police had been watching him, and persuaded the carman involved (the cart driver, John Warner), to turn Queen's evidence. That this was our Charles Harrod was confirmed by mention of his house in Rosemary Lane and the grocer's shop.

Charles Harrod made matters worse by trying to bribe the policeman, and pleading for his wife and family when confronted with the evidence. He was quoted as saying to the policeman, *'Oh, consider my wife and family, what am I to do?'*

At the end of the transcript, at the time just before sentencing, there is a long list of people who gave 'the prisoner Harrod' a good character. They included a local surgeon, a draper, a silk merchant, a tea dealer, a chemist and numerous other loyal friends who were mostly in business locally.

The Times newspaper of the 18 May 1836 reported that the Recorder summed up by observing that if the jury were satisfied that the evidence of the accomplice was confirmed by the other witnesses for the prosecution, that there could be little doubt of the guilt of both prisoners.

Despite the pleas and the character witnesses, both Harrod and Moran were found guilty and sentenced to seven years transportation. Charles was taken to Newgate Prison after the trial and remained there for three weeks, awaiting a move to a holding ship prior to transportation.

This sentence did not seem to fit in with my known facts as Charles Henry appeared five years later in the 1841 census, and, accepting that he was the father of Charles Digby, born in January 1841, it looks as though he was around in the spring of 1840, four years after his sentence.

So, did Charles Henry ever serve his sentence? Very few prisoners came back from transportation.

Most died or stayed there voluntarily after their sentence was completed.

In addition to the revelation about Charles Henry's criminal record, the documents revealed new information about the family. During the taking of evidence and cross-examination, it became apparent that Charles Henry had a brother called William Frederick Harrod, a man unknown to me at that time. In the transcription of the trial, one of the witnesses stated, *'Harrod's brother was with me at the time'*, and *'I know Harrod's brother, but not the prisoner'*, and later, William Frederick Harrod spoke on his brother's behalf.

'I am the prisoner's brother, and am a working jeweller, living at No. 129, Tooley Street. Mr Selwood and I have been intimate some time – I was with him at the Thames police-office, on Saturday, the 7th of May, when my brother was there, under charge – I heard Fogg say…'

James Fogg, the police officer, was later re-examined and gave evidence that, *'the witness Harrod asked me to be as lenient with his brother as I could and asked me to take something to drink...'*

Frederick William was subsequently found listed in the 1839 Pigot's Directory at Cable Street as a Grocer, standing in during Charles' absence. William had married in 1822 a local girl, Nancy Brant, and they had three children. Frederick was widowed in 1829 and had also lost one of his children, so would have been in a position to take over Charles' business and look after his wife and family during his absence.

The Prison Hulk Registers and Letter Books for 1836, also now available on line, show that after sentencing, Charles Henry Harrod was taken to the Prison Ship 'Leviathan', moored in Portsmouth, and arrived there on the 30 May, 1836. This is confirmed by the Newgate Prison records held at Kew, which showed that he was in the prison between the 7 May, (the day of his arrest and two days before his trial), until the 30 May.

Prison hulks served as holding stations for prisoners prior to transfer to other ships for the transportation to Australia. Most of them were literally hulks, usually old warships that were no longer sea worthy.

The 'Leviathan' was a third-rate ship of the line and in her prime was armed with 74 guns. She was built in 1790, based on a French design, and served at the Battle of Trafalgar. After active service, she was de-masted and laid up in Portsmouth as a Prison Hulk. She was later broken up in 1848.

Between 1788, when the first penal colonies were established, and 1868, over 160,000 prisoners were transported from England. The conditions on board were horrendous. In an account by John Frederick Mortlock in his 'Experiences of a Convict', he describes his experience in Leviathan in 1843:

'...they conveyed me (chained hand and foot to a man now driving a cab in Tasmania) by railroad to the hulk Leviathan at Portsmouth;' (The first railway route from London to Portsmouth was via Eastleigh, Fareham and Gosport. The station at Gosport was opened on 29 November 1841 and passengers had to use the ferry to get to Portsmouth. Charles Henry must therefore have travelled by road in 1836; though the dates above suggest he arrived in Portsmouth on the same day he left Newgate – quite a feat in 1836.)

Mortlock continues: *'and quickly transmogrified me into a strange-looking object, whom no one could recognize... At any rate I was no longer shut up in gaol, to me the most dreadful of punishments, now, I hoped, done with for ever. This, however, as will be seen, turned out to be a mistaken expectation. The hulk, an old (Trafalgar) ninety-gun ship, being very full, contained more than six hundred convicts (from starvation and discipline, tame as rabbits), housed on the three decks, which were divided into compartments, separated from each other by bulkheads, and from the gangway down the centre, by iron bars, giving the appearance of a menagerie. Owing to the height of the wharf, alongside of which she lay, the larboard row of cells, on the lower deck, was nearly in darkness, and insufficiently ventilated. "New chums," therefore, in their location down below, breathed very foul air... A pernicious habit also existed of sluicing out all the decks every morning, with salt water... The chilly dampness arising from this, proved a fertile source of sickness.*

...As a reward for three months of good behaviour, a light ring (called a basil) above the ankle, scarcely to be felt, succeeded the irons, Upon losing the weightier decorations, my foot in walking used to fly up in an odd manner for some time afterwards, till the muscles grew accustomed to their lighter load... I found the carrying of timber and other hard work very irksome at first, although labour is not severe punishment to a strong man well fed; but we suffered from a lack of sufficient food... Hence the mortality was great, it being whispered that the head doctor at the hospital ship, enjoyed a contract for supplying surgeons in town with bodies for dissection at six guineas a piece.'

The records confirm that most of the convicts on board when Charles Henry joined them were actually transported later, there being an annotation in the 'how disposed of' column in the records, with what looks like the initials of the transport ship and the date. A few died, and a very few were pardoned.

In that column opposite Charles Henry's name, there is the annotation 'Penit..y', with the date 1 July, 1836. I learnt that this meant 'penitentiary', and that he was sent on to prison.

So he was lucky, but why?

Richard Moran, his co-defendant, also held on 'Leviathan', was sent off in the transport ship 'Sarah' later in 1836 and arrived in Van Diemen's Land, or Tasmania four months later, with 253 other convicts. After six years he was pardoned and he was declared free in 1842. No further information about him is available, so presumably he remained in Tasmania.

Perhaps Charles was too ill to transport? In most cases, convict ships were privately owned merchant ships that were chartered by the British Government for one or more voyages to the Australian colonies. It is known that the Captains of these transport ships were very reluctant to take on board prisoners who were ill, as there was an enormous amount of paperwork involved if any prisoner died during the voyage. Following serious outbreaks of disease with heavy loss of life on board some early convict ship voyages, later voyages were strictly regulated in terms of provisions and medical support, as a result of which deaths on board ship during these long passages were generally lower than on assisted immigrant ships on similar voyages, and many convicts actually arrived in a better state of health than they had enjoyed before leaving!

Clarification of the reprieve was found with a further discovery early in 2013 of documents on line relating to a 'Memorial' or appeal for Charles Henry Harrod in 1836. This consisted of 13 original documents together with the original folder and list of contents.

Each document consisted of several pages of hand-written letters and reports. I have transcribed them and unravelled the story of Charles Henry's partial reprieve.

In summary, a Petition was presented by George Grote, Esquire, a Liberal M.P., of 62, Threadneedle Street. It listed the dates and sentence of Charles's conviction, with a summary of his social status. It states that a Surgeon, Mr Capper, had been asked for a medical report and had said he *'is rather a weakly and debilitated subject, altho' not labouring under any specific Disease.*

The Police were asked to enquire as to his character. Their report from a Superintendent at Whitechapel 1st Division was a rather mixed report, though on balance probably supportive. He stated, *'I should say he was irreproachable; a Mr Hewit who is a respectable Chymist living near his (Harrod's) late residence, assured me he would readily become security for him, to the amount of One Thousand Pounds and several others seem to have equal confidence in his honesty.*

A person named Habgood, an Oilman and a Mrs Henshaw, grocer, insinuate they had heard he was a receiver of stolen goods, but can prove nothing, and I fear they speak interestedly being in the same trade and it is evidence to me that there is a jealousy.'

In Charles' own statement, he accepts the verdict and asks for clemency. He claims the stolen property received was the only article he had received.

He states that he was ruined by the mercantile *'Panic of 1825'* from having been a *'respectable and responsible tradesman'*. Charles then pleads regarding his wife and two young children, one three and a half years old and the other one year old, both in delicate health. Thus he reveals the existence of their first child, born in about 1832, and also pleads about his own poor health, stating *'that a transportation for that period would find its termination only in the grave.'*

The banking panic of 1825 in London has been called the first modern financial crisis, the first Latin American crisis, and the first emerging market crisis. And while the panic displayed many of the key elements of past crises in our era – fluctuations in money growth, an investment bubble, a stock market crash, and bank runs – this crisis had its own twists, including a Bank of England that hesitated before stepping in as lender of last resort. It is best known for an infamous bond market swindle surrounding an entirely made-up Central American principality, the mythical nation of Poyais. There were even engravings produced of the mythical capital, 'Port of Black River', of this mythical state. Charles may have lost a lot of capital in the bank collapses.

His appeal against his sentence by George Grote was backed by the statements from Charles Henry himself, with the Medical and Police reports, and no less than 190 of his friends and colleagues who signed the Petition.

There was an individual appeal for mitigation from William Mason, a Glover of 8, Fore Street in the City. He wrote:

'Feeling strongly for him and his family, having known him during a period of Five and Twenty Years, and being convinced that up to the time of this most unfortunate transaction, he had maintained an unblemished and irreproachable

Character, I respectfully beg to offer my humble Testimonial in his favour. Allow me earnestly to solicit your Lordship's attention to the fact that he was originally a Linen Draper, but unsuccessful in Business, and was unacquainted with the Trade which he has had for the last Two or Three Years pursued.'

A friendship of 25 years takes it back to 1811, just when Charles parents had died. William Mason could easily have been related to his mother's Mason family. He is listed in London directories as variously a Haberdasher or Linen Draper between 1829 and 1840.

There were several other individual appeals.

James Baker, a Surgeon who had known him for five years.

John Pollard Searle, a 23-year-old Tailor from Shoreditch stated he had known Charles for some years and said that *'he has always sustained the character of an honest and upright tradesman.'*

John Hewitt, Chemist and Druggist of Cable Street, who stated *'I beg further to inform your Lordship that from his heretofore sober and industrious habits and from his assiduity and perseverance in business which I have had daily opportunities of witnessing on account of his occupying the house adjoining mine, I should have no objection to become security for his future good conduct.'*

There must have been a further appeal from an Alderman Wood, as on the 24 June the records reveal a reply that was disappointing; *'...have considered the petition. I am directed to express to you his Lordship's deep regret that he cannot...'*

However, a reply to George Grote's Petition was given five days later, on the 29 June 1836, stating that in the circumstances, Charles is to be removed to a General Penitentiary instead of being transported.

So, after 32 days on the Leviathan, on the 1 July, he was sent to Millbank Prison.

In this bundle of documents, there was additionally an appeal from his wife Elizabeth, dated May 1837, written after he had been in prison for almost a year, which contained the following impassioned plea from her as the petitioner:

'That during the long confinement of nearly twelve months in the Penitentiary Mill Bank your Petitioner's husband has as your Petitioner is assured conducted himself with great propriety.

That your Petitioner is of a weakly constitution and incapable of supporting herself and Infant child.

That recently the Elder child of your Petitioner has been removed by death which has added to your Petitioners afflictions.

That your Petitioner's husband is subject to illness which confinement is calculated seriously to increase and to render fatal to him.

That should your Petitioner's husband remain in confinement much longer your Petitioner can have no hope of ever overcoming the consequences.

Your Petitioner therefore must earnestly pray your Lordship to save her and her husband and child from absolute and irreparable ruin and premature death, by mercifully remitting further confinement of your Petitioner's husband. And your Petitioner shall ever pray, Elizabeth Harrod.'

It must have been difficult to ignore this heartfelt plea, and the authorities obviously agreed that Charles had been punished enough. Though there is no official document to confirm this, I suspect he was freed soon afterwards. There is a scribbled and only partially decipherable note across the top of her letter, my best interpretation of which is, *'Rec'd from Mr Ald.n Wood, Can't hold ?incarcerated pardon when seen G.C ?ance.'*

He was a lucky man to survive this episode. He was obviously guilty.

London would certainly have been a different place if he had succumbed!

A couple of years after Charles was in prison, his brother William was himself on trial at the Central Criminal Court, in 1839, also charged with receiving stolen goods, three silver spoons. He was acquitted!

Charles Henry obviously learnt his lesson and throughout the rest of his life gained a deserved reputation for honest dealing.

It was probably providential that Charles was back in circulation, as his brother William Frederick died in Milton, Gravesend, Kent, in 1840, aged 43.

Charles settled back into family life and prospered. After 14 years of trading, by 1851, he had moved home from Cable Street to a more salubrious residence in Bethnal Green, about one mile north of the river. The 1851 census shows the three youngest children living at home, together with a servant.

Charles Digby, the eldest, was missing but was eventually found elsewhere in the census, recorded as Charles Harrud! He was listed as a schoolboy, aged 10, boarding at a private boarding school, Edwardstone School, in Suffolk, 70 miles to the north.

Charles Henry's increasing prosperity meant he was soon ready to make his next move away from the crime and filth of East London.

From 1854 onwards, Charles Henry and his family are to be found in West London in a small house and grocery facing the Brompton Road, then called 8, Middle Queen Buildings. The directory listing is: *'Grocers and Teadealers': Harrod, C.H.*

He had probably been involved in those premises since 1849. According to Tim Dale, Philip Burden, who was the previous owner of the shop, was already a wholesale customer of Charles Henry's and they may have become friends. Burden was reputed to have found himself in financial difficulty and the shop was becoming a problem for him. Charles Henry began to help him by paying the rent. Between 1849 and 1854 there was a gradual hand over of the shop, and in the meantime the Harrod family continued living in Bethnal Green.

The newspapers have reported that Charles Henry had needed capital of £500 to take over the shop, something like £50,000 today. This presumably came from the profits earned in Cable Street.

Unlike today, in the 1850s, and for some years afterwards, this part of the Brompton Road was not particularly salubrious. Queen's Gardens, a narrow lane two doors away from the shop, contained a few little cottages and a large woodyard, and North Street behind, was said to be *'a mass of filth from one end to the other'*. The shops on the Brompton Road were single-storey extensions tacked on to the fronts of the original houses of the 1780s. A rather sanitised artists' impression of the shop frontage in 1849, produced by Harrods in 1993 for publicity, painted a more refined picture, with clean streets and handsome carriages.

Charles Henry had the vision to see the potential of the site. The fashionable part of London was beginning to spread westwards and the Great Exhibition of 1851, held at the Crystal Palace in Hyde Park, drew crowds and their attention to the area.

In the decades prior to 1850, the road west from Hyde Park Corner lay through a then rather unsavoury Knightsbridge Village, possessing none of the fine buildings now present, and next on to rural Kensington. There was danger in the maze of dirty back streets along the route, and highway robberies in the district were common. The area was gradually changing from semi-rural hamlet to built-up suburb, initially by ribbon development and then later back filling. Hence in the early 1850s, Charles Henry's customers were a small and poor community of locals.

Charles Henry's eldest son, Charles Digby, would have been 13 years old when the family settled in Brompton Road in 1854. Tim Dale suggests he was sent to a Grocer's shop in the City at the age of 16 to learn the business, though no confirmation of this has been found. Perhaps he worked at his father's wholesale premises at 12, Eastcheap which were still in use in 1857. Certainly by the age of 20, he was working with his father in the Brompton Road shop.

The family would have been hit hard by the death of their mother, Elizabeth, in the winter of 1860, at home in Brompton. She died aged 50, from Capillary Bronchitis, a form of lung infection involving the smaller breathing tubes and causing bronchopneumonia.

The Harrod boys would have been aged 19, 17 and 15, so would been pretty independent.

According to the following year's census, five months later in spring 1861, Elizabeth's role in the house has been filled by Elizabeth Neville Digby, a 20-year-old niece from Birch.

Charles Digby is listed in the census as a 'Commercial Clerk' and brother Henry Digby as a 'Shopman'. William Digby has already left home and was working as a butcher in Munster Street, St. Pancras. He was living with and working for his distant cousin Alfred Tiffin, another Digby relative.

The nature of Brompton Road began to change with the first significant widening of the road in 1862. The main frontage ceased to be residentially desirable, although the property behind remained useable. Brompton Road became the official name of the road in 1863 and the old terrace names and numbers disappeared. Commercial activity gathered pace. Tattersalls, the racehorse auctioneers, moved in 1864 from Hyde Park Corner to a large site behind Nos. 38–58 Brompton Road, almost opposite Harrod's shop. It was the start of a friendship between the Tattersall and Harrod families.

From 1860 onwards, Charles Henry Harrod, and then more energetically his son, Charles Digby, began the process of transforming the small grocer's shop into the great department store.

As the Daily Mail of 1949 put it, in an article celebrating Harrods' centenary, '...the clarion call of opportunity was sounding, and by 1861, when a migration of 'gentry' to Knightsbridge had already begun, Henry's son, Charles Digby, heard the call so plainly that he persuaded his father to sell him the business.'

In 1854 the shop consisted of three rooms, and the frontage was between 30 and 40 feet wide.

Charles Henry employed two assistants and a messenger boy, and the shop sold mainly groceries and hardware goods, with a turnover of £20 a week. The family moved from Bethnal Green into the living accommodation behind the shop.

Having initially taken over the lease of the property in 1853, Charles Henry then acquired the shop outright, giving it his own name. He slowly began to expand the range of goods offered at the store.

The expansion took place in the late 1850s and early 1860s, when Charles Henry began the transfer of ownership of the store to his son, selling it to him in instalments.

By 1861, young Charles Digby, then 20 years old, enthusiastic, ambitious and hard-working, became the sole owner of the store. By 1864 he had made enough money to clear the debt he owed his father. Once this was done, he married Caroline Godsmark and his father moved out to live a short distance away in York Cottages, Thurloe Place. His brother William Digby had left for New Zealand in 1863, and Henry Digby, his youngest brother, moved out in 1866. Charles was the king of the castle.

Charles Henry lived in retirement for 20 years, and died aged 85, in 1885, at 2 Oxford Terrace, Chiswick, not far from his son Henry's residence.

William Digby Harrod emigrated with his Uncle John Digby and family, and his cousin Joseph Sampson Digby, to Christchurch, South Island, New Zealand. He was a Remittance Man in the ship 'David G. Fleming'. A remittance man is a term for an emigrant, usually from Britain to a colony, supported by regular payments from home, on the expectation that he stays away following problems at home. It has been suggested he fell out with his brother Charles, or that there was a young woman 'in the family way.' No evidence of a rift has been found but the timing of his move supports the idea.

After farming for a spell with his Uncle in Ashburton, William joined the Military Settlers scheme to fight against the indigenous Maoris. Service was rewarded by land on which to work and live and this must have seemed like an opportunity for William to lead his own life.

Only a few weeks after he had landed in New Zealand, William enlisted in the forces in Canterbury and was appointed a Private. He was transferred to Okato, to the 'Taranaki Military Settlers'.

Okato is a small coastal township in rural Taranaki, North Island. Today it is still a small town, with a population of about 520 people.

Many Maori died defending their land; others allied themselves with the colonists to settle old scores. In all, there were an estimated 3000 casualties, the majority of which were Maori. Making matters worse, land confiscation was the fate of many of the survivors. Inevitably, the might of the Empire prevailed.

During his service with the Military Settlers William was awarded the New Zealand Medal, which was presented by Governor George Gray in 1867.

Once settled on the land he had been awarded, William took a full part in the local life, though he was not universally liked. His best friends were his neighbours, the Corbett family.

William farmed in a small way. He was at one time County Clerk for the Okato County and in his later years was appointed a Justice of the Peace.

William never married, and the evidence suggests he lived alone all his life.

He died in the Private Hospital, in New Plymouth in 1907, aged 64 years. His death certificate states he had died of 'Hernia, Senile heart decay, Cardiac Failure – three days'.

He was buried in the Corbett Family plot, beneath the shadow of Mount Egmont at Okato Cemetery with an expensive looking grey marble stone. The Taranaki Herald report of the funeral stated, *'He was not much known to the outside world, being of a retiring disposition.'*

He left the majority of his £3,800 estate, (over £350,000 today), to his younger brother Henry Digby, then living in Winchester. It looks as though the Public Trustee took his land back into the public domain, the rationale of which was not explained.

Henry Digby Harrod was the youngest surviving son of Charles Henry and Elizabeth. Having worked for a while in the family shop, he branched off into his own grocery business in about 1866.

Over several years Henry ran a number of retail establishments, and many overlapped for some years. Henry Digby, in contrast to his brother Charles Digby, felt the route to success was with multiple small branches rather than one large shop.

He was successful in a modest fashion; in 1891 he was employing 9 men and 1 boy.

His first shop, 40, Old Compton Street, was in Soho, London and probably opened in 1865.

He lived there for about 13 years with his family, and the first five of his 12 children were born there.

He remained at the same address until at least 1886, possibly until 1893. During this period of apparent stability for Henry, Brompton Road had been transformed by his brother Charles from a small Grocery Shop into a Department Store.

The British holds a publicity leaflet from the shop in Old Crompton Street from 1885, together with a price list for teas and coffees.

It reads: *'H. D. Harrod (Grocery Stores) Best Grocery Stores, 40, Old Compton Street.*

Notice. The well-known Christmas Club; which always gives satisfaction to its supporters has commenced, and we invite all to join at once to secure the benefits. We present to every subscriber of 8/ – a bottle of Foreign Port or Sherry, and to every subscriber of 6/ – 1/4lb. of Black or Green tea... Sugars, Fruit, Sago, Tapioca, Rice...at smallest profit on cost and the best value in London...'

Henry married Caroline Wade, a 22-year-old, in Colchester, Essex in 1871, and they set up home in Old Compton Street. She was the fourth daughter of a Suffolk Ironmonger, who had worked initially in Clare in south Suffolk. This was the birthplace of Henry's grandmother Tamah, almost a hundred years earlier, and also where Henry's grandfather, William Harrod the Exciseman, had lived for a while 70 years earlier. When she married Henry, Caroline was working as a Milliner in London, less than half a mile from Old Compton Street. Had the two families known each other in Suffolk?

Henry and Caroline were prolific breeders and had 12 children altogether.

He was living in Chiswick at the time his father died in 1885, but he opened a shop in the High Street, Winchester sometime early in the 1890s, and the family then moved to the town. There were still descendants of Henry Harrod's family there in 1965.

A remarkable insight into Henry Digby's view of the Harrods shop and his relationship with his father and brother is revealed by a letter shown to me by Sebastian Wormell, Harrods' Archivist, in 2008. The letter is itself a copy, as hand-written at the top it states,

'Copy of letter, supplied by Mr (William) Kibble to Harrods Secretary in 1924.'

William Kibble was a relation by marriage of the Harrods, and worked for a long time in the store, having taken Henry's place when he left.

The letter is from Henry, presumably to William Kibble, and probably written during the last few years of his life. It sounds as though William Kibble had asked Henry for his recollections of the early days in the store. The letter reads:

'Ivy Dene, East Hill, Winchester.
Jany.27.
Dear Sir,
Yours to hand. I am glad to see you are still in the land of the living like myself and hope you will continue in good health and long life yet to come.
You ask me for facts which I can't give as I was a boy and therefore am not clear. But I will tell you all I know and as far as I can recollect my father took over the business from a Mr Burdin who went to some other country as near as I know 1853 or 1854 and carried it on in conjunction with his Wholesale Business which he had in Eastcheap at the time. We all moved into the house at

the back of the shop – I went to school close bye and helped in the shop on and off till about 1858 when I went away in the country to live' (He would have been about 13 years old then) 'My brother C. D. Harrod took it over in 1861 and my father went to live opposite the Museum. I returned home about 1863 and went and lived with my brother until as you know I went to Compton Limited and you came into my place. You would know the year; I think it was 1866. During my last term with my brother, we made the first move to improve the business by having a new front put in which you recollect, and it was that that drew the attention of the Public to our shop and I dare say the windows the first time. We steadily advanced especially in the Tea Trade and built up as very nice counter trade which you know was when I left it about 200 to 250 per week and very profitable. The rest you know as you were on the spot when he took up the store trading and succeeded.*

I have given you all I know except mere trifles. But if anything comes of it, I should like my Father's name to be much honoured before all other things as he was the person which was the principal factor in the making of success, for without his Father's help my brother could have done nothing.

My Father's name was Charles Digby Harrod so there can be no mistake.
With kind regards and well wishes,
I remain,

Yours faithfully, (signed) H. D. Harrod

Henry must have been getting forgetful when he wrote the letter, as in the last sentence, he really meant that *'My Father's name was Charles Henry Harrod so there can be no mistake.'*

He had been at pains to point out that he thought it was his father, not his brother who should take the main credit for the shop. It seems as though perhaps Charles had fallen out with Henry as well as William.

I have met and corresponded with many of Henry's descendants. Several relatives distinguished themselves. One of Henry's sons, Frank, was awarded the Military Cross and the Croix de Guerre in the Somme in 1916. After the war, Frank went into the administrative side of education, working in Local Government. By 1936 he was Director of Education in Coventry, a post he held during the Second World War, until 1945. He was awarded an O.B.E. in 1952, and advanced to C.B.E. later.

One of Frank's children, Lionel, born in 1924, also had an illustrious career in the Army with an impressive C.V. He served in the Grenadier Guards during W.W.II., and later saw service in Suez, Cyprus and Hong Kong, then moving to the Welsh Regiment. He served on the British Defence Staff Washington between 1969 and 1970, was Military Attaché in Baghdad in 1971 and was promoted to Major-General in 1976. He worked as Assistant Chief of Staff (Intelligence) to the Supreme Allied Commander Europe, (SHAPE), between 1976 and 1979.

His proudest moment was when he was appointed Colonel of the Royal Regiment of Wales between 1977 and 1982. Retiring from the Army in 1979, he became the Inspector of Recruiting until his final retirement in 1990. His motto was 'Soldiering must be fun.' During his career he was awarded O.B.E.

Henry Digby Harrod died in 1915 in Winchester, aged 69.

To return to Charles Digby in the 1860s. This was a time of change not just for Harrods but in London and England.

In 1861 Victoria's husband Prince Albert died, prompting the start of one of the longest bereavement periods in history. The first horse drawn trams started in London. The Metropolitan Railway, later the Metropolitan Line, was in the throes of construction linking the main line railway stations of London with underground tunnels. In 1868 it was extended to South Kensington. The Penny Post had been established in 1860, and remarkably, there were at least ten deliveries of letters daily. There were eight collections a day at the five green Iron Boxes, first erected in 1855, on the kerbstones of the leading thoroughfares. The nearest to Harrod was at Rutland Gate, on the south of Hyde Park, and about 300 yards away from the shop.

In the 30 years after taking over the shop, Charles Digby took the business into overdrive and changed the shop into a store. Charles had the personality, the energy, drive and the vision to make it happen, and was helped by often being in the right place at the right time.

He was brimming with new ideas and not afraid to try them out.

Though Charles Digby was a hard taskmaster, he never expected his employees to work harder or longer hours than he himself. He was an enthusiastic man, who managed to infect his staff with his enthusiasm and encourage them to follow his example.

He had an engaging personality and managed to retain the common touch with his customers, who vied to be served by Mr Harrod 'in person'.

Charles Digby married Caroline Godsmark, a grocer's daughter, on Thursday, the 31 March, 1864 at St. Mary's Church, West Brompton. They had met when they both attended Trinity Chapel, on the south side of Knightsbridge close to Albert Gate. Charles Digby was appointed Honorary Librarian of Trinity Chapel in 1861. Caroline Godsmark taught in the Sunday School and sang in the choir.

Charles Digby's character might explain why he chose to marry on a Thursday; it was the quietest trading day of the week!

I found out quite a lot of personal details about Charles in an unpublished book by Gilbert Frankau, which was commissioned by Harrods and is still in their archives. Gilbert Frankau was a World War I poet and later a novelist. He was invited by Harrods to write their story and was given access to Harrods' records.

I was allowed by Harrods to see much of his work, and have used some of the information in my story. Though quite detailed, it was not always totally accurate. Frankau was prone to flights of fancy and elaborate rhetoric, which may explain why the story was never published.

However, he was able to furnish some more personal details.

Charles Digby was punctual and punctilious. After regularly starting the day with bacon and eggs, he was the first into work and usually the last to leave.

He worked in his shirtsleeves most of the time and when out wore a bowler hat rather than the top hat of many of his contemporaries. One of his more well-known habits was the twirling of his keys on a chain when he was preoccupied. Charles Digby was a lifelong non-smoker and abstemious with alcohol. He disliked sealing a deal with a drink, a traditional method amongst the business community.

He was reputed to be very honest. His son, Henry Herbert Harrod, interviewed at the age of 70 about his father, said; *'Father couldn't have told a lie or done anything dishonest if he tried.'*

Very little detail is known about his home life, though Frankau records his love of cricket. Apparently, he often went to Lords and The Oval to watch Test matches and would undoubtedly have watched W.G. Grace in the 1880s. He is known to have frequented the London Theatres – he took his wife, Caroline, to watch the famous actor, Henry Irving, at the Lyceum Theatre.

Some details of his life came from a document left by one of his family.

'The Story of Mr C. D. Harrod', is the script of a talk given by Katherine Emily Conder, (1898 to 1989), to the Harrods staff in 1932. She was an unmarried granddaughter of his and was alive at the tail end of Charles Digby's life, being seven years old when her grandfather died. She worked in the store herself for some years later in her life. I think both Frankau and Tim Dale took some of the personal details of Charles Digby from this script.

Her account of the early days of Harrods differs from the accepted view, attributing little of the vision of the future shop to her great-grandfather, who she calls Henry Charles rather than Charles Henry Harrod. She wrote:

'The task of preparing the "Story of Mr C. D. Harrod" has been considerably more difficult than I anticipated when I cheerfully accepted Mr Lawe's invitation to come here and tell it. During his lifetime, and he died a little past middle age, the significance of his achievement had scarcely begun to be appreciated so that, while there are of course, records of the development of his work, there are but few records of the man himself. The two, naturally, are inseparably bound, and the best I have been able to do is to piece together the records of the development of Harrods Stores with personal reminiscences of those who had intimate personal contact with its founder and so to sketch a portrait that I hope is in due proportion and likeness to the original.

I must ask you throughout the narration to dissociate me as far as possible from the bias of personal relationship. My grandfather died when I was only a small child and I have but few, though very happy, memories of him. Ancestor worship forms but little part of the modern creed, and so I hope you will regard me as quite detachedly interested, as I feel myself to be.

At the same time, I must admit that I have been able to discover very few faults recorded against him. In his case it seems that the Shakespeare dictum has been reversed; the good that he did lives after him, the evil, if any, was interred with his bones.

The first Harrods shop in Brompton Road was founded by my great-grandfather, Henry Charles Harrod, in 1849, a small but "select" grocer's shop which he had thought little of extending. Charles Digby Harrod left school at about 16 years of age, and entered a wholesale grocery business in the city. He very soon began to dream dreams and see visions of the possibilities for the development of his father's business, but he was not then allowed to put them into practice. However, he cherished them secretly and used those years of minority to exercise his own powers of observation, to watch the ways and means of current trade and commerce and to think out schemes for making his visions into practical realities.

In 1861, Henry Charles Harrod withdrew from the business and Charles Digby, at the age of 23 reigned in his father's stead.' (He would in fact have been aged 20 when he took over in 1861).

'For five years longer he continued his observations, meanwhile consolidating the business as it stood, winning and extending the favour of his clientele with reliable goods, attractively displayed, and by unfailing personal attention to the personal requirements of his customers.

By 1866 his plan of attack was ready. He had observed that West End shops were charging exorbitant prices, mainly because they were forced, on the one hand to allow their customers two- or three-years' credit, and on the other to give large bribes to the servants in order to retain the patronage which their employers left to a great extent in their hands.'

There followed a detailed description of his early method of selling goods cheaply and quickly, allowing no credit. In 1866, he also installed the new fully glazed front shop window.

His business grew and he gradually imposed his not inconsiderable personality on the place.

She gave several insights into his character: *'C. D. Harrod made it his business to know each and the work of each, down to the youngest and humblest worker. In this way he was accorded a loyalty which was to stand him in good stead in the Crisis of the House of Harrod.'* She refers here to the fire of 1883, mentioned later.

Over the 20 years following Charles Digby's take-over, the shop grew in size and grandeur. He and his wife, together with his enlarging family, progressively filled the living quarters at the back of the Kensington shop where their first two daughters were born. The family moved to Hill Street, now called Trevor Place, in Knightsbridge in 1868. The house was a four/five storey high terraced house with stabling, and they stayed there for about six or seven years. The third daughter and their only son were born there. By this stage they were more prosperous as they now employed a cook, a housemaid and a general domestic servant in the house.

Before 1875 they had moved out into the 'countryside'. Their residence was in Ditton Marsh, Thames Ditton. Situated on the Thames, near the east border of the Parish of Esher, it was then sub-urban and featured nearby the newly opened Sandown Park Racecourse. It was convenient for Charles Digby with good road and rail access. Their fourth daughter was born there but they only stayed for two years, before moving to Sydenham.

Their new home, Armitage Lodge, Wells Road, Sydenham was one of two detached houses built in Wells Road in the early 1850s for Edward Saxton, a local Solicitor. The house no longer exists.

It sat on the upper slopes of Sydenham Hill facing south with superb views across the countryside below. They would have been able to see the famous Crystal Palace less than a mile away. This had been moved there from its original site in Hyde Park where it had been built for the Great Exhibition in 1851. Charles Digby would have seen it at both sites.

Sydenham Hill Station was opened in 1863 to cope with visitors to the Crystal Palace, but proved inconvenient for that attraction. At the time, it would have then been the nearest station to the Harrods. When Upper Sydenham Railway Station was opened in 1884 by the South Eastern and Chatham Railway it was much closer to the family, just below the house and across the Wells Road, with the rail tunnel running under the hill beneath their house. The trains ran into Victoria Station, a brisk walk away from the store!

Armitage Lodge was a grand 19th century villa, very modern for its day and with 16 main rooms.

It had airy nurseries, a bath with running hot water and ample stabling. It was a house to suit a man of ample means with a growing family. Their last three daughters were born there, starting with Beatrice Martha in 1877.

The years from 1870 onwards were particularly busy ones for Charles Digby, with multiple new building extensions at Harrods store, and then the Silver Jubilee of the shop in 1874.

Neighbouring properties were progressively acquired which allowed enlargement of the shop and the number of departments, so that what was once a grocery store gradually became a department store.

A seemingly catastrophic fire which engulfed the whole shop just before the Christmas rush of 1883, was turned by Charles Digby into a triumph, with a new and modern store arising like the proverbial phoenix out of the ashes, whilst business continued as normal from temporary premises.

A painting of Charles Digby, the original of which is held by my cousin James Weightman, shows him in his pomp, and was probably painted at about the same time as the photograph taken of his wife, Caroline.

By 1891, then aged 50, Charles Digby decided he should retire. A mixture of poor health, exhaustion, and the lack of a male heir to take over the business persuaded him this was the right course of action.

He sold out to a Limited Company, but falling sales forced the new management to ask Charles Digby to come back for some months to settle things down, whilst they appointed a new General Manager.

Having finally retired some months later, he moved with his wife and unmarried daughters to North Devon. He bought the Manor House in Morebath, knocked it down, and built a splendid new residence he called Morebath Manor.

In preparation for his retirement, Charles also took over a town house close to Harrods, at 1, Evelyn Terrace, Cranley Gardens, in Kensington. After the move to Devon, it was used by the family when visiting London.

The story written by Miss Conder in 1932, partially reproduced earlier, continues with her account of her grandfather's life after retirement, with a glowing account of his achievements.

'After such a strenuous business life he withdrew into the heart of the country, living first at Morebath, on Exmoor, and later at Heathfield in Sussex. Here he devoted his energies to the welfare of the country folk, and manifested quite a different set of interests. He took up very keenly the question of adult education and the wise use of leisure. He founded and guided Village Institutes and Social Clubs. He took a keen interest in politics, and promoted Liberal Associations...He was fervent in support of anything that concerned the welfare of children and was a true fairy godfather to the village schools and to the children's section of the local Workhouse.'

The move to Morebath in 1891 was a great success for Charles Digby. Away from London, he forgot about the business and as Miss Conder said, devoted his life to the local community.

The house was, and still is, a spectacular home built with no expense spared.

Ten years on, his wife Caroline was missing city life, and the remaining four unmarried daughters, who included Beatrice Martha, were probably keen to be nearer to London.

Whilst a move to Culverwood House, near Heathfield, in Sussex was being arranged, Charles and Caroline took the family away. They are missing from the 1901 census and had applied for passports in late 1900. My guess is they all went to Europe and Beatrice may well have improved both her language skills and widened her contacts whilst away.

After settling at Culverwood, Charles Digby took up once again the life of the benevolent and active squire as he had in Devon. This was cut short by his sudden death in August 1905.

A few months later, after the Christmas that proved to be Beatrice's first misconception, his widow and remaining unattached children moved to Tunbridge Wells. Caroline died there in 1922.

Having mentioned Beatrice's siblings in passing, there follows a brief resume of their lives.

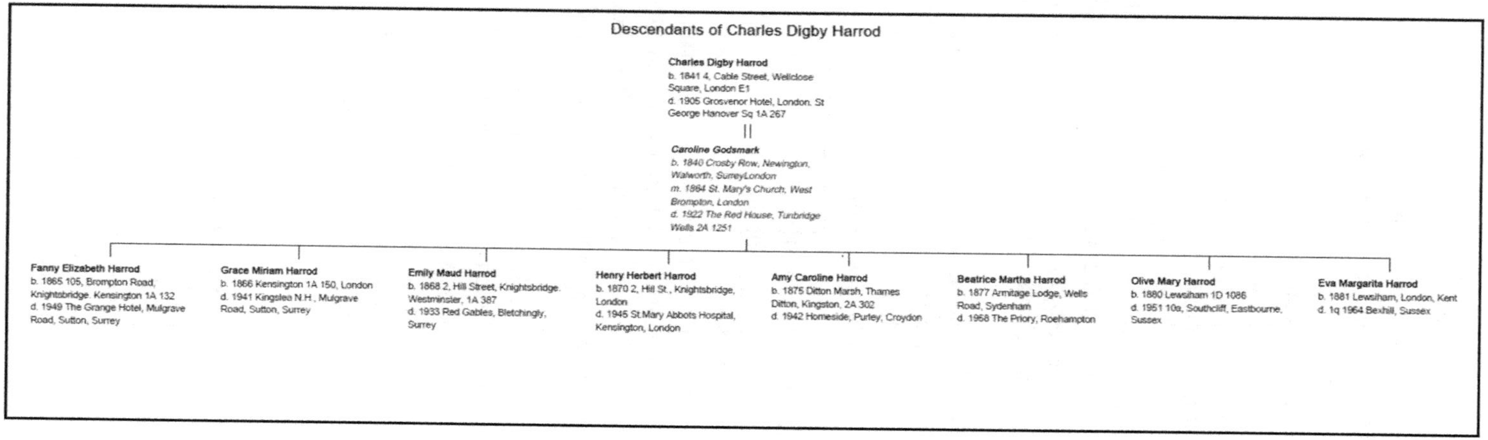

Descendants of Charles Digby Harrod

Charles Digby Harrod
b. 1841 4, Cable Street, Wellclose
Square, London E1
d. 1905 Grosvenor Hotel, London, St
George Hanover Sq 1A 267

=

Caroline Godsmark
b. 1840 Crosby Row, Newington,
Walworth, Surrey,London
m. 1864 St. Mary's Church, West
Brompton, London
d. 1922 The Red House, Tunbridge
Wells 2A 1251

Fanny Elizabeth Harrod
b. 1865 105, Brompton Road,
Knightsbridge Kensington 1A 132
d. 1949 The Grange Hotel, Mulgrave
Road, Sutton, Surrey

Grace Miriam Harrod
b. 1866 Kensington 1A 150, London
d. 1941 Kingsfee N.H. Mulgrave
Road, Sutton, Surrey

Emily Maud Harrod
b. 1868 2, Hill Street, Knightsbridge,
Westminster ,1A 387
d. 1933 Red Gables, Bletchingly,
Surrey

Henry Herbert Harrod
b. 1870 2, Hill St , Knightsbridge,
London
d. 1945 St Mary Abbotts Hospital,
Kensington, London

Amy Caroline Harrod
b. 1875 Ditton Marsh, Thames
Ditton, Kingston, 2A 302
d. 1942 Homeside, Purley, Croydon

Beatrice Martha Harrod
b. 1877 Armitage Lodge, Wells
Road, Sydenham
d. 1968 The Priory, Roehampton

Olive Mary Harrod
b. 1880 Lewisham 1D 1086
d. 1951 10a, Southcliff, Eastbourne,
Sussex

Eva Margaritta Harrod
b. 1881 Lewisham, London, Kent
d. 1q 1964 Bexhill, Sussex

Chart 11: Descendants of Charles Digby Harrod

-**Fanny Elizabeth** was the first child, born in 1865. She was known as Fanny by the family.

She married Eustace Reynolds Conder at the Congregational Church, Upper Norwood in 1887. She was 22 years old, and he 29. The marriage was celebrated by the Reverend George Martin, who was to become her sister Grace's father-in-law two years later. The Conder family lived in Forest Hill, about one mile away from Armitage Lodge as the crow flies.

The Conders are a family with many branches and with many gregarious ancestors. Amongst the more talented Conders are a number of non-conformist preachers, some of who contributed to the Leeds Congregational Hymn Book as writers; the bookseller, publisher and author Josiah Conder; the British/Australian artist Charles Conder; the explorer, mapmaker and Biblical and Altaic scholar Major Claude Reignier Conder; the Railway contractor Francis Roubiliac Conder; the Anglo-Japanese landscape architect Josiah Conder; and more recently Peter Conder the naturalist and Neville Conder the architect.

Fanny and Rennie had five children, three of who survived childhood.

Fanny probably helped Beatrice during one of her illegitimate pregnancies. When many years later Fanny and her husband were old and infirm, the family became quite bitter about Beatrice's lack of involvement in their care. She was never forgiven.

Fanny died in a home in Surrey in 1949, aged 84. Her husband Rennie outlived her by four years, dying in 1953, at the grand age of 95.

-**Grace Miriam** was born in 1866.

She got married in 1889, aged 22, to Herbert James Martin, a Solicitor. They married in the Kensington Congregational Chapel in Allen Street, just south of Kensington High Street. He was 26 years old and had been born in Deptford in 1862. The service was conducted by Herbert's father, the Reverend George Martin.

The Martin family are descended from Huguenots who lived in the Picardy region of France and came over to England to escape religious persecution, probably in the late 17th century. They were involved for many years in the silk trade in Spitalfields in East London.

Herbert James Martin acted as solicitor for much of the Harrod family's business. He is named as the Executor for several of his sisters-in-law, and their families.

There were three children. The eldest, a son, died on the Somme in WWI in 1916. The two daughters both lived long lives.

Grace died in a home in Cheam in 1941, aged 74, and Herbert died in 1953, aged 90.

-**Emily Maud** remained single and lived much of her life in Purley, close to her sister Fanny. She died in 1933, aged 64.

-**Henry Herbert** was born in 1870. As the only boy, he would no doubt have been spoilt, not only by his parents, but also by his sisters. This did however bring with its high expectations.

Much more is known about his life.

He was educated at Merchant Taylors School between 1883 and 1889 and then went up to Peterhouse College, Cambridge, gaining his B.A. in 1892. He qualified as a solicitor in 1897, but never practised.

He remained a single man throughout his life, and spent much of his time writing fairy stories and collecting pictures and books. Jean Pitt, his niece, remembers that he was: *'sweet but dreamy, a poet but no businessman, which was sad for Charles Digby Harrod as he could not pass Harrods on to him.'*

Henry Herbert's lifestyle certainly did not fulfil his father's expectations and must have been a disappointment to him. Charles Digby Harrod had spent his life working hard and developing Harrods, so having his only son and heir to the business decide to train as a solicitor, and then spend his life with fairy stories and books must have difficult to accept.

Henry lived much of his life in private hotels in West London in the area round the southern end of Earls Court Road. This was not an unusual style for young men of the day 'living on their own means'.

Henry Herbert published his first book of fairy stories, entitled, 'The Lord of the Deer, and other Fairy Tales' in 1907. The book's illustrations and his 'bookplate' were by Gilbert Ledward, a friend and a prolific and renowned sculptor of the early 20th century.

His second book was entitled 'Nine Little Fairy Tales', and was published in 1923. It was illustrated by Henry himself.

He was fascinated by book illustrators and their works, and by sketches by well-known and less well-known artists, some contemporaneous. He built up an enormous collection of over 20,000 pictures, paintings, prints and illustrations, which he bequeathed to the Victoria and Albert Museum.

After Henry's death in 1945, the V. & A. retained only those pictures which filled gaps in its collection, numbering about 1,600; the rest were auctioned to pay for death duties.

In 1958 The Times featured an article about the publishing by the V & A in 1948 of the catalogue of their acquisitions, delayed by the war until that date. Volume II for that year is remarkably devoted entirely to the bequest from Henry Harrod. The article stated,

'Mr Harrod...was a collector on an omnivorous scale.
The drawings in the Harrod bequest include a few by old masters, but the majority consists of English drawings, many of them sketches, mostly of the nineteenth century, though some are earlier, or later, and some are by Continental artists. Among them are examples of du Maurier, Keene, Leech, Linley Sambourne, Phil. May and other Punch Illustrators; of Cornelli and other designers of theatrical costumes; and of draughtsmen as variable as Blake, Sir Thomas Lawrence, G. Cruikshank, Burne-Jones, Wilkie, Beardsley and Rowlandson – to name only a few at random.
The value of this acquisition, which includes also examples of many minor draughtsmen, is clearly very great to an historical reference collection such as

*that of the Department of Engraving, Illustration and Design – and all the more
so since the accent is on the nineteenth century, which so far has not been
intensively cultivated by collectors.'*

I was able to view some of the illustrations and books left to the V & A on a
joint visit to the collection with Sebastian Wormell, Harrods Archivist, and
James Weightman, a Harrod cousin. The collection is not on show at present.

The collection encompasses a huge range of pictures including interestingly,
three Charles Edward Conder drawings, among which is his 'Imperia la Belle'
of 1906; and a 'View of Porlock and Porlock Bay' by Francis Towne, 1785,
probably acquired because of the family's interest in the area.

There are pictures from the 18th, 19th and 20th centuries. There are drawings
by Gustave Doré; Du Maurier drawings for Punch; 'pin-ups' by Coleman used
by De La Rue on cards; designs for theatre and Ballet costumes; and Max
Beerbohm's drawings of pre-W.W.I. celebrities.

As a writer of fairy stories and collector of pictures and books, it seemed
impossible that he might also have collected firearms! However, to my surprise,
I discovered an article from the Times of 1914 which gave the story of his
collection. It was so out of character that I thought for some time that it must
have been a different Henry Herbert Harrod.

The article stated that he had collected firearms for several years, and had a
remarkable collection dating from 1700, which with a total of about 800 pieces,
was believed to be the most representative collection in the country. Another
article in the Daily Express of 1935 was headed; *'ONE-MAN ARMS MUSEUM'*,
and sub-titled, *'£10,000 History of The World's Battles'*. It revealed that the
collection was housed in a room 14ft. x 20ft., on the top floor of Harrods
Furniture Depository. The collection was then valued at £10,000, a sum
equivalent to about £500,000 today. I suspect these rare collectibles would have
gained value more rapidly since then and would be worth considerably more
today.

The collection consisted of a mass of firearms of all ages, and included some
early hand grenades and bayonets. These had killed Frenchmen at Waterloo,
Englishmen at Blenheim and Cawnpore, Turks at Acre, Russians at Balaclava,
and Germans at Ypres. He had been collecting since 1906, and spent an average
of ten hours per week cleaning and caring for them.

The reporter quoted an enthusiastic Henry, *"This... belonged to George IV
when he was Prince of Wales, silver and gold mounted, and this, belonged to
Tippoo Sahib, last Sultan of Mysore. But it did not save his life at Seringapatam,
where he was killed in 1797."*

It is not entirely clear what happened to the collection. There is no mention
of it in his will, and it is said he offered the collection to the Nation but his offer
was rejected. Photographs of pieces that were once in his collection appear in
other treaties on the subject, and his collection formed the basis for some books
on the history of firearms. Whether an individual or an organisation took over
the collection before his death is not certain, but in 1974 and 1975 parts of the

collection were auctioned over three auctions by Wallis and Wallis, a specialist auctioneers in Lewes, Sussex.

An approach to Wallis and Wallis recently unearthed the catalogue of the auction from 1974 which proved fascinating and confirmed some of the story about Henry. One of the staff, Susan, actually remembered the sale and 'risked life and limb' climbing over old boxes of records to find it.

Henry Herbert led a pretty relaxed life. He remained single all his life. The family said that as well as writing fairy stories, he visited several children's hospitals in London, including Great Ormond Street, reading and telling stories to the sick children. He was much loved by his nephews and nieces for the same reason.

Henry Herbert Harrod died in 1945, aged 74, in St. Mary Abbots Hospital, Kensington, London.

-**Amy Caroline**, the fifth child, was born in 1875. At the age of 32 years, in 1907, Amy Caroline married Arthur James Weightman at St. Paul's Parish Church, in the village of Rusthall, near Tunbridge Wells.

Arthur Weightman was a 'Chemical Agent'. He had an office in the heart of the City of London, in St. Mary Axe, off Leadenhall Street. He spent his working life dealing in the trade, mostly with Europe.

I suspect he was instrumental in helping Beatrice with her transfer of money to the Countess in Vienna between 1911 and 1914.

Arthur and Amy had three children, all of them living into adulthood. Of their living grandchildren, James is the owner by inheritance of several Charles Digby Harrod treasures, including his portrait, his Bible and some presentation items from his time at Morebath. His sister Philippa has documented the Weightman ancestors and has produced a beautifully illustrated scroll to show this. Her family can be directly traced through 15 generations to around 1500. Other branches of the family go back to Richard de Rodvile, living in the time of William the Conqueror in the 11th century, more than 24 generations.

Arthur Weightman died in Purley, Surrey in 1925, aged 61 years, as the result of a Road Traffic Accident. Amy Caroline died 17 years later, in 1942, aged 67 years.

-**Beatrice Martha** was the sixth child, born in 1877. She was known by the family as Bea.

Because she was unknown to my family during her life, and not until well after her death, what has been learnt about her has been of necessity second or third hand, and has certainly not produced a favourable impression of her.

I found she was universally disliked by most of the living relatives who knew her.

On the Harrod side of the family, Natalie Oliver, a grand-niece, like the rest of her family, was not too fond of Aunt Bea – *'she seemed rather pompous towards my father's family.'* She never forgave Beatrice for the aloofness she displayed, which they put down to her 'Royal' connection, and for her lack of contact at the time of the illnesses and deaths of Natalie's grandparents', Rennie and Fanny Conder. She told me; *'Michael'* (Uncle Michael, Bea's son and Dad's brother) '*was invited at the beginning of 1939 to Windsor Castle as a young officer to mix with the two princesses and Aunt Bea was invited once to dinner there. But I really couldn't forgive her in totally ignoring Granny in her old age – no letters, or visits.'*

Many thought her 'snooty'. A grandson of her sister Fanny said, '*Bea and the two daughters were about the most toffee-nosed people I knew and certainly made me feel a poor relation.'*

The Humble-Crofts also disliked her and were opposed to her marriage to Bertie.

It is possible to understand why Beatrice may have been as described; reasons can be found in her story that would have made her bitter about how things turned out for her.

She had a privileged up-bringing and started life, like all her siblings, in a comfortable, loving and financially secure family. Were the problems part of her nature or did her circumstances cause them?

-Olive Mary was born in 1880. She was well liked by the nephews and nieces I have met. She remained single and died in 1951, aged 70 years, in Eastbourne.

-Eva Marguerita was the eighth and last child born in 1881. Her future husband Dr Frederick Millar Rodgers proposed to her on the steps of St. Paul's Cathedral, London and they married in 1912.

Fred was another son of a non-Conformist Minister. He became a doctor and specialised in mental health, eventually becoming Medical Superintendent at Winwick Hospital, Warrington, which was the County Lunatic Asylum for Lancashire. Their descendants have proved particularly interesting, with some exotic characters and interesting stories, best saved for another day.

Chapter 28
More About the Humble-Crofts

When I started my research, my known family was small in number, and I knew no family history.

The discovery of the 'Harrod' connection gave me a wider family group, some living relatives and a lot of history. The finding of the connection to the Humble-Crofts, Humbles, Crofts and Whites gave me, at a stroke, a huge family of ancestors with a decent family history going back several generations, and in some cases centuries, but very few living relatives.

At one point in the process, I had to change my focus. Having initially exclusively researched Harrod history, I found out that genetically I and my brothers were Humble-Crofts and historically we were Humbles. Bertie Humble-Crofts, my paternal grandfather, Beatrice's husband, had been born John Herbert Humble. The full explanation for this will become apparent later.

The Humbles have an extensive history and many known ancestors, but circumstances have contrived to produce a living family which is limited in number, and the Humble-Crofts family in particular have, at the time of writing, only three living representatives with that surname.

The main source of information about the family after contact with my uncle Michael Humble-Crofts was Maughan Innes, Michael's cousin, who had collected details about several branches of the female line, and spiced his information with a lot of gossip and humour. Later, Michael's daughter Vanessa became the main source of information as she accumulated the photographs and ephemera of the family and made them available to me.

The family had been researched to a degree by Michael, and even more extensively by his grandfather, Canon William Humble-Crofts, who had spent a considerable amount of time and money tracing his ancestors. A series of letters to the Canon have survived, from various contacts and relatives, many of whom had visited the ancestral Humble home in Bamburgh, Northumberland to report back. William visited the area himself in both 1899 and 1913.

The Humble family line has been traced back to the early 17th century. The earliest confirmed Humble found was John Humbell-Heppell, whose children were born in the mid-1600s.

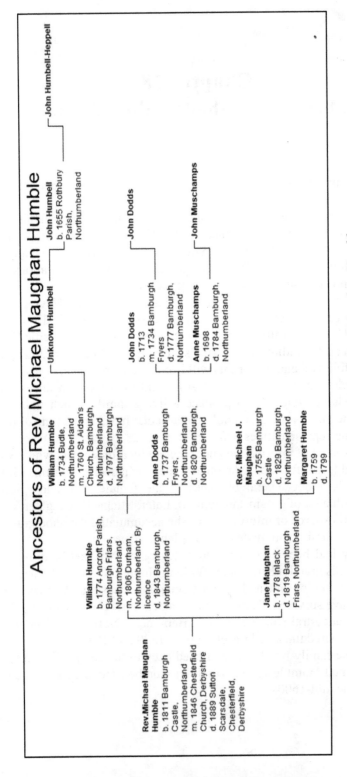

Ancestors of Rev.Michael Maughan Humble

Rev.Michael Maughan Humble
b. 1811 Bamburgh Castle, Northumberland
m. 1846 Chesterfield Church. Derbyshire
d. 1889 Sutton Scarsdale, Derbyshire

William Humble
b. 1774 Ancroft Parish, Bamburgh Friars, Northumberland
m. 1806 Durham, Northumberland. By licence
d. 1843 Bamburgh, Northumberland

Jane Maughan
b. 1778 Inlack
d. 1819 Bamburgh Friars, Northumberland

William Humble
b. 1734 Budle. Northumberland
m. 1760 St. Aidan's Church. Bamburgh, Northumberland
d. 1797 Bamburgh, Northumberland

Anne Dodds
b. 1737 Bamburgh Fryers. Northumberland
d. 1820 Bamburgh, Northumberland

Rev. Michael J. Maughan
b. 1755 Bamburgh Castle
d. 1829 Bamburgh, Northumberland

Margaret Humble
b. 1759
d. 1799

Unknown Humble

John Dodds
b. 1713
m. 1734 Bamburgh Fryers
d. 1777 Bamburgh, Northumberland

Anne Muschamps
b. 1698
d. 1784 Bamburgh, Northumberland

John Humbell
b. 1655 Rothbury Parish, Northumberland

John Dodds

John Muschamps

John Humbell-Heppell

Chart 12: Ancestors of Rev. Michael Maughan Humble

There are a number of John Humbles in the tree, and there is some confusion in the records, and amongst the Victorian Humbles who researched the history, about which John was which.

The family lived in Rothbury Parish, Northumberland, in the middle of the Rothbury Forest, about ten miles from the north-east coast, and midway between present-day Newcastle to the south and Berwick to the north. There were many Humbles in both Newcastle and Berwick.

William Humble, a descendant born in 1734, became a Farm Manager and wisely married the owner of the farm, Anne Dodds, in nearby Bamburgh. Her mother was Anne Muschamps, whose surname was used later in the family. The farm was situated at Windmill Hill, close to Ancroft, just inland from Holy Island. The base for the family for several generations after that then moves to Bamburgh, nearer the coast and famous for its connection with Bamburgh Castle and with the lifeboat heroine Grace Darling, who was born there in 1815. More recently 'Outred, son of Outred of Bamburgh' actually Outred the Bold, has made the place better known.

The Bamburgh Humbles went through a prosperous phase as owners of their own land, and the next William, born in 1774, studied at Cambridge before going back to the farm.

This William married Jane Maughan in 1806. Jane was born in 1778, the only child of the Reverend Michael J. Maughan of Bamburgh Castle, and his wife, Margaret Humble, a Humble cousin.

Michael Maughan was the first of several clergymen in the family. Maughan is another name which has been used by the family in the ensuing centuries.

Though the main line of Humbles had remained in the Bamburgh area, a side branch thrived in Abergavenny in Wales producing a long line of chemists.

William and Jane had four children, all apparently notably good looking. Their son, Michael Maughan Humble, was born in 1811 and continued the family line.

Michael Maughan Humble also went to Cambridge, to Emmanuel College, and became a priest. He was ordained at Durham in 1835 and started his working life as a Curate in Felton, south of Alnwick, and then at Bamburgh.

He was the first Humble in our line to make the move south from Northumberland on a permanent basis. By 1839, at the age of 28, he was the Rector in the Parish of Sutton Cum Duckmanton, Sutton Scarsdale, just south-east of Chesterfield in Derbyshire. He worked there for the rest of his life, for 50 years in fact, until 1889. He is recorded as a tall gentleman with an aristocratic bearing, and became a friend of the 'Spinning Jenny' Arkwright family.

He married Maria Anderson Terry in Chesterfield in 1846. Both families were comfortably off, and there was a Marriage Settlement set up by her family to pass much of their wealth to any grandchildren.

The Andersons and Terrys were from North Yorkshire and their family has been traced back to the 17th century. Another Anderson girl also married Michael's brother.

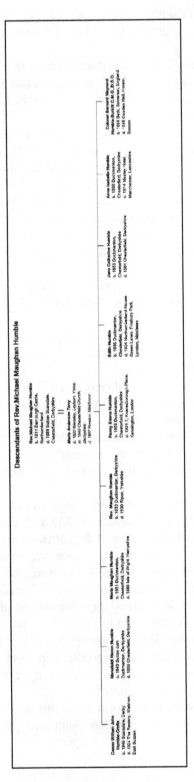

Descendants of Rev.Michael Maughan Humble

Rev. Michael Maughan Humble
b. 1811 Barnsburgh Castle,
Northumberland
d. 1889 Sutton Scarsdale,
Chesterfield, Derbyshire

＝

Maria Anderson Terry
b. 1820 Wensley, Leyburn, Yorks.
m. 1840 Chesterfield Church,
Derbyshire
d. 1897 Rowton, Middlemer

Marie Maughan Humble
b. 1851 Duckmanton,
Chesterfield, Derbyshire
d. 1966 Isle of Wight, Hampshire

Mansfield Heron Humble
b. 1849 Sutton cum
Duckmanton, Derbyshire
d. 1969 Chesterfield, Derbyshire

Canon William John
Humble-Crofts
b. 1846 Scarsdale, Derby
d. 1924 The Rectory, Waldron,
East Sussex

Rev. Maughan Humble
b. 1853 Duckmanton, Derbyshire
d. 1930 Ripon, Yorkshire

Fanny Starre Humble
b. 1855 Duckmanton,
Chesterfield, Derbyshire
d. 1931 7, Knaresborough Place,
Kensington, London

Edith Humble
b. 1856 Duckmanton,
Chesterfield, Derbyshire
d. 1924 Northumberland House,
Green Lanes, Finsbury Park,
London, Middlesex

Jane Catherine Humble
b. 1853 Duckmanton,
Chesterfield, Derbyshire
d. 1961 Chesterfield, Derbyshire

Anna Isabella Humble
b. 1860 Duckmanton,
Chesterfield, Derbyshire
d. 1914 Mosley Hotel,
Manchester, Lancashire

Colonel Barnard Maynard
Humble-Burdit C.M.G.,D.S.O.
b. 1864 Bath, Somerset, England
d. 1949 Coarden Hall, Horsen,
Sussex

Chart 13: Descendants of Rev. Michael Maughan Humble

Michael and Maria had nine children, born between 1846 and 1864; four sons and five daughters. All but the last one were born in the Parish.

That Michael and Maria were very much in love is demonstrated by a poem written 33 years later, with accompanying drawings, by Michael to Maria on the occasion of her next birthday after the birth of their first grandchild, my grandfather, John Herbert Humble in September 1878. It was dated January 3, 1879, her 59th birthday. The poem says:

'To my very dear Wife on her LIX birthday.
Hail! dearest wife and Grandmama.
That title, henceforth, thine to bear,
"Happy returns" from Old papa,
God bless and keep thee, is his prayer.

Last year hath brought thee interests new,
May they be blest to thee and thine,
On herb as falls the fresh'ning dew,
May they be felt as gift Divine.

As Ivy clings to stately tree,
And twines around the serried bark;
May bonnie Herbert cling to thee
As Dove that knows its safety Ark.
In him, may Grandma live again,
And see her early days renew'd,
Her Autumn life tho' on the wane,
With flowers of kindred offshoots strew'd.
May "Fairy Land of Science" bright,
(The Science of God-fearing love)
To failing age be shining Light,
The foretaste of Home joys above.
M.M.H. Jan'ry 3, 1879

Of Michael and Maria's nine children, three are notable.

The eldest, William was to become Bertie's father.

The fourth child, Maughan, became a clergyman and was the Vicar at Studley Roger, Ripon.

Bernard Maynard Humble was the ninth and final child, and the fourth son. He was born in Bath in 1864. Like his eldest brother, William, who became the founder of the Humble-Crofts dynasty, Bernard also changed his name to secure a bequest by founding the Humble-Burkitt family.

The story told to me by the family was that he went off to Canada in his youth and worked for the man who built the Canadian Pacific Railway, supposedly a Mr Burkitt, between 1881 and 1885.

Burkitt was said to be a single man who had taken Bernard under his wing, and then offered his estate upon death to Bernard for a change of name.

The story is true to a certain extent as Bernard had several spells in Canada, certainly between 1883 and 1885, and later 1896 to 1920.

The shipping lists show that he travelled back and forth to and from Canada on many occasions.

Bernard became a career soldier and eventually a Colonel in the Canadian Forces. He was a private during the North West Rebellion, in Saskatchewan in 1885, when aged 21. The 'rebellion' was by the indigenous Cree peoples against the building of the Canadian Pacific Railway, and was rapidly squashed. The rebel leader, Louis Riel was caught and later hung. Yet another glorious colonial triumph over the native population!

In 1891 he was back in England with his brother, Mansfield, working as a Tutor, but he went back to Canada before 1901.

In World War I, with his previous army experience, he became a Staff Captain with the Canadian Infantry Brigade and served with The British Columbian Regiment. He was awarded the D.S.O. in 1917, the C.M.G. in 1919, and was mentioned in dispatches twice. He would have been aged 54 by the time the war ended. He had falsely reduced his age at the start of the war by two years in order to be able to serve, giving it as 48 rather than 50.

The details from his war records showed that he had a tattoo of a 'Japanese Girl' on his right forearm! Where did that come from?

After the end of the war, in late 1919, in British Columbia, Bernard married Vera, a local girl 22 years his junior.

So the family story goes on, when Mr Burkitt died, leaving no heirs, he left his money to Bernard Humble on the basis that he took the Burkitt name. The problem is that when I researched the story, there were no Canadian Pacific records to support the story. There was no Mr Burkitt involved in the railway, and no evidence that Bernard Humble had worked for them.

The mystery was solved closer to home. The U.K. records show that he assumed the surname Burkitt by Royal Licence in England in 1921, becoming the first, and the last, Humble-Burkitt on earth.

I found the real story by pure chance in an on-line article in 'Wings', a magazine sponsored by the Wingerworth Garden Centre of all places! Wingerworth is a village close to Chesterfield, in Derbyshire. The article was the last in a series entitled, *Historical Fragments*, by Dr David Edwards, No: 52. The title was *Col. Humble-Burkitt*. It said:

'Colonel Bernard Maynard Humble-Burkitt owned Stubbing Court and its 600-acre estate from 1920 until 1935. He was born at Bath on 21 April 1864, the fourth and youngest son of the Rev. Michael Maughan Humble, rector of Sutton Scarsdale. He emigrated to Canada when young and enlisted in the army... At some time he obviously formed a very close friendship (if indeed there was not already a family relationship, though that remains to be discovered) with the Burkitts of Chesterfield, Maltsters, who had owned Stubbing Court since 1890.

When William Burkitt died unmarried in 1920, as the result of an accident at work, he left the Colonel the whole of the Stubbing property, plus a fortune of a quarter of a million (it was said) and the Burkitt share in Chesterfield Brewery Company (of which the Colonel later became Chairman). A condition of this inheritance was evidently that he should take the additional surname of Burkitt, which he did by Royal Licence in 1921. At the same time he was granted a coat of arms, featuring those of Burkitt quartering those of Humble.

Whilst in Canada, Col. Humble-Burkitt married Vera Mason of Victoria, BC. They had no children, and perhaps because of this they took a great interest in the school at Wingerworth, among their various local activities. In 1935, at the age of 71, the Humble-Burkitts decided to sell the Stubbing estate and leave Wingerworth for the possibly balmier climate of Sussex, where the Colonel bought Cowden Hall, near Horam. Just before they left the village, they were presented at the school with an inscribed silver fruit-basket, in thanks for the 'many kindnesses' that the two of them had paid to the children. On this occasion there were fulsome tributes to the pair, as recorded, with a group photograph, in the Derbyshire Times of 13 March 1936, p.27. Col. Humble-Burkitt died at Cowden Hall on 12 February 1945 in his eighty-first year. He was survived by his wife Vera. An obituary appeared in the Derbyshire Times of 16 March, p.4, though with a number of factual errors.'

So ended the Humble-Burkitts, not quite 24 years after they had started.

When Bernard took over the Chesterfield Brewery Company, it is apparent that he did not do very well, a fact glossed over by the article. 'The History of The Chesterfield Brewery', published in 1997, gives a different reason though it gets some other facts wrong. To quote, '...*control therefore passed to a distant relative of one of the original Directors, Col. Humble Burkitt. He was not interested in the brewery, leaving the running to the joint managing Directors... Without dedicated management, the company slipped into decline, the quality of the ales began to deteriorate, eventually to the extent where only 100 barrels of beer were being sold in the 100 tied houses. The company assets were also drained by the lavish spending on pubs, now with little revenue to recoup the investment. Seeing the company struggling, the Mansfield Brewery made a bid of £500,000 for the business, which was accepted at Christmas 1934.'*

So Bernard sold up and moved to Cowden Hall to be near his brother William at Waldron, and possibly to distance himself from the Brewery. The sale price would be the equivalent of about £18 million in today's money so he was not going to go short. Bernard and Vera had no children.

He died in 1945 aged 80, leaving the equivalent of in excess of £4 million. Most of his estate was left in a Trust Deed made in 1936. His wife Vera, then aged 59, got a healthy personal bequest equivalent to £1.5 million in today's money and an annual income free of income tax equivalent to £50,000. There were a large number of personal bequests to a large number of servants and employees, and his nieces and nephews, this totalling an equivalent of £2 million. None of his siblings were still alive at the time of his death.

His house and lands, and the residue were left to his niece, Una Humble-Crofts. The Cowden Hall Farm alone was 41,642 acres.

Vera died in Cirencester in 1959, leaving a relatively paltry sum, the equivalent of about £1 million. When Una died, she left £40,000 or so to Michael and his sister Bridget. Where all the £18 million pounds went is a mystery. Bernard or Vera must have spent or given away a lot of the money as none of it seems to have surfaced later.

The Reverend William John Humble, later Canon, was Bernard's brother and the eldest son of Rev. Michael Maughan Humble. He was to continue my direct family line. He was born in his father's Parish of Sutton Scarsdale in 1846, and went to school at Newark. He went on to Exeter College, Oxford gaining an M.A. in 1872.

Both he and his brother Bernard do seem to have had an uncommonly good nose for money. William married Bridget White.

Bridget White was born in 1853, at Cuckney Rectory, just inside Nottinghamshire, in the triangle formed by Worksop, Chesterfield and Mansfield. She was the second daughter of The Reverend Taylor White's second marriage, to Charlotte Bates Crofts.

Her father died the day before his 50th birthday, when she was just five months old. Her mother remarried four years later, and had six further children. With the children from her father's first marriage and her mother's second marriage, Bridget would have had 13 siblings, ranging in years of birth from 1829 to 1868.

Of the 13, she and her sister Charlotte Crofts White, known as Tootie, were the only children of that particular marriage. According to Bridget's daughter, Bridget Maud Innes, *'She was never very happy in her girlhood. Neither she nor her sister Tootie went to school, but were educated at home by governesses. She rode very well and hunted, but was well known for avoiding the kill and for helping the fox in every possible way.'* A rebellious streak!

William and Bridget were married in 1876, at Worksop. At about this time, William took up the post of Vicar at Clayton with Frickley, in South Yorkshire, about 15 miles north-west of Worksop.

During his short tenure in Clayton, in 1878, William and Bridget had their first child, my grandfather, John Herbert (Bertie) Humble, and two further children.

Just eight months after Bertie's birth, and before the birth of the next child in 1880, his parents changed the surnames of all three of them by Deed Poll to Humble-Crofts. To explain the reasoning for this, it is necessary to side-track for some time into Bridget White's splendid family history. Following the family will be helped by a tree.

Ancestors of Bridget White

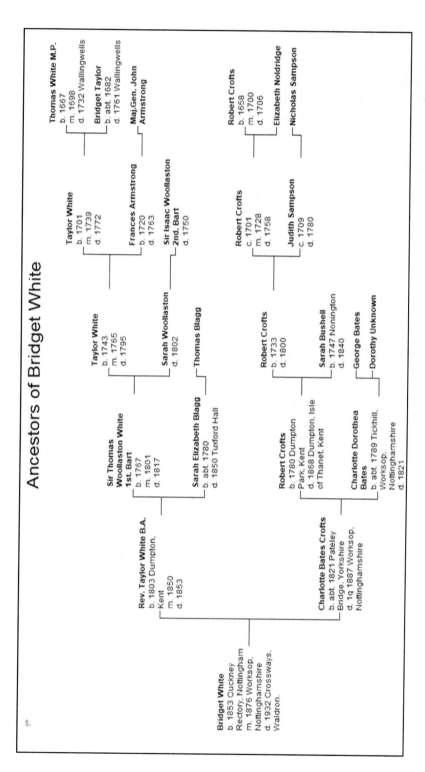

Bridget White
b. 1853 Cuckney
Rectory, Nottingham
m. 1876 Worksop,
Nottinghamshire
d. 1932 Crossways,
Waldron.

Rev. Taylor White B.A.
b. 1803 Dumpton,
Kent
m. 1850
d. 1853

**Sir Thomas
Woollaston White
1st. Bart**
b. 1767
m. 1801
d. 1817

Taylor White
b. 1743
m. 1765
d. 1795

Taylor White
b. 1701
m. 1739
d. 1772

Thomas White M.P.
b. 1667
m. 1698
d. 1732 Wallingwells

Bridget Taylor
b. abt. 1682
d. 1761 Wallingwells

Frances Armstrong
b. 1720
d. 1763

**Maj.Gen. John
Armstrong**

Sarah Woollaston
d. 1802

**Sir Isaac Woollaston
2nd. Bart**
d. 1750

Sarah Elizabeth Blagg
b. abt. 1780
d. 1850 Tuxford Hall

Thomas Blagg

Charlotte Bates Crofts
b. abt. 1821 Pateley
Bridge, Yorkshire
d. 1q 1887 Worksop,
Nottinghamshire

Robert Crofts
b. 1780 Dumpton
Park, Kent
d. 1868 Dumpton, Isle
of Thanet, Kent

Robert Crofts
b. 1733
d. 1800

Robert Crofts
c. 1701
m. 1728
d. 1758

Robert Crofts
b. 1658
m. 1700
d. 1706

Elizabeth Noldridge

Judith Sampson
c. 1709
d. 1780

Nicholas Sampson

Sarah Bushell
b. 1747 Nonington
d. 1840

**Charlotte Dorothea
Bates**
b. abt 1789 Tickhill,
Worksop,
Nottinghamshire
d. 1821

George Bates

Dorothy Unknown

Chart 14: Ancestors of Bridget White

The Whites, Taylors and Crofts

The house of the 'Whites of Wallingwells' starts, as far as has been found, in 1428, with the birth of John White, who lived at North Collingham, in Nottinghamshire, just north of Newark. It would be 400 years later that the Crofts joined the family.

The family is well documented in Burke's Peerage and in British History on Line. Two other documents have been invaluable in sorting out the family:

– A photocopy of the *'White Book'*. This was published for private circulation in 1886, entitled *'Memoirs of the House of White of Wallingwells and of its Collateral Branches'*. The author is unknown. It states that it was *'Compiled from the letters, journals, and legal documents in the Charter Chests of Wallingwells and Castor, and from the notices of contemporary annalists.'*

It consists of 105 pages packed with information. The original was given by the Reverend William Humble-Crofts to his wife Bridget, in 1898, with an inscription, *'Stemmata quid'.*

Roughly translated, this means 'What of Pedigrees?'

– Notes about the 'White Book', were compiled by Bridget Maud Innes, the youngest daughter of the Canon and mother of Maughan Innes, during the summer of 1965, whilst living at her house, Corners, in Waldron. Both items came to me from Maughan Innes.

The documents show that the family is awash with Knights and Peers of the Realm. The White Book states that: *'In 1428, the twelfth year of King Henry the Sixth, the King's Commissioners drew a list of the landed gentry of Notts, and therein stands the name of Johannes White of Colyngham, who owned land in North Collingham parish.'*

A grandson of John White, Thomas White, was married to Agnetis Cecil, the eldest sister of William Cecil, Lord Burleigh, Queen Elizabeth's first minister and Lord High Treasurer. Thomas White died in 1580 at Tuxford. By this time, he owned five Manors, and lands in Nottinghamshire, Lincolnshire, Huntingdonshire and Rutland.

White descendants witnessed the execution of Queen Mary of Scots, the dispersal of the Spanish Armada, the Gunpowder Plot, the discoveries of Galileo, the assassination of King Henry IV of France, the Puritan colonisation of New England and the English Civil War. They were Royalists through and through.

A great, great grandson of that Thomas White, also called Thomas White, was born at Tuxford in 1667, and married Bridget Taylor in 1698. The White Book tells the story of their first meeting, when Thomas would have been 30 years old. *'He was returning from a journey, and was on horseback, followed by his servant and baggage. He came to Sheffield, and intended to reach Tuxford the same evening; but all the country between them was then unenclosed, and the roads that traversed the common were only packhorse tracks. In the darkness, he lost his way, but found shelter and hospitable entertainment for the night at a moated house, an ancient hall which had once been a nunnery. The place was owned by Richard Taylor, a Captain in the Notts. Militia, M.P. for Retford, and lately High Sheriff of the county. He had married Bridget, daughter of Sir Ralph Knight of Langold and Warsop, and Bridget was their only child, then aged sixteen.'* The moated house was called 'Wallingwells'.

After further visits, Thomas married the heiress of Wallingwells. Her marriage 'portion' was £5,000, equal to something like £2.5 million pounds in today's value. The Taylors were from old stock, holding lands in the area since the time of Edward I. Apart from Wallingwells, Bridget brought with her the estate of Pateley, in Yorkshire, with its valuable lead mines, and a huge amount of household goods. It was a splendid marital alliance. Thomas was another man with an eye for the main chance.

Thomas and Bridget lived at Wallingwells, and Tuxford, the previous White family seat was used as a power house, and eventually fell into decay.

Thomas White became the M.P. for Retford, most of which belonged to him, and was appointed Clerk of Ordnance of the Tower, a very ancient, honourable, and indeed lucrative office. Thomas was described as a 'jovial country gentleman.' He died suddenly in an apoplectic fit at Wallingwells, in 1732, aged 65. He and Bridget had five children, and most of them proved to be either very successful as barristers or made extremely good marriages within the nobility.

The family went on accumulating more and more wealth. Thomas's grandson, Taylor White, born in 1743, was educated at Charterhouse, Harrow and Queen's College, Cambridge and became Deputy Lieutenant of Nottinghamshire. He married Sarah Woollaston, another heiress, so introducing the name Woollaston into the family. They had seven children. Five of them either joined the military or married into it, serving during the several French wars of the late 18th and early 19th century.

The eldest son was Sir Thomas Woollaston White, 1st Bart., He became notorious for marrying in 1801, Sarah Elizabeth Blagg, his gamekeeper's daughter. Despite the difference in background, it was a very successful marriage. It is said that Sarah gave the family the legacy of large hands and feet! Maughan Innes told me, I suspect during a discussion as to whether my father and Michael Humble-Crofts were really full brothers, that *'any member of the family should have Sarah Blaggs' hands, which were broad and signified domestic competence'.*

Bringing us nearer to the main point of interest in this lengthy diversion is the Reverend Taylor White, B.A., the second son of Thomas and Sarah, who was born in 1803. He was educated at Rugby and Sandhurst, and then gained a B.A. at Emmanuel College, Cambridge in 1827. He served initially in the army, and married his first wife, Dorothea Kirke in 1828, producing six children.

Soon after Dorothea's early death in 1840, he left the army and took Holy Orders, and was appointed to the Vicarage of Norton Cuckney in 1843.

Seven years later in 1850 he was married again, to Charlotte Bates Crofts, and so began the process which would end with a change of name for Bertie and his family.

Charlotte was 20 years younger than Taylor and was the only child of Robert Crofts, of Dumpton, on the Isle of Thanet, in Kent.

Now Robert Crofts was an extremely wealthy man, even by the standards of the Whites. It is suggested by the family that Robert Crofts owned most of the Isle of Thanet at one time. The Isle of Thanet is that portion of land on the most north-easterly point in Kent, bordered by Margate to the north, and Broadstairs and Ramsgate to the east. He was born at Dumpton Park, the family home near Broadstairs. Dumpton Hall, as it was later called, was a Regency House with more than 50 acres of parkland and two lodges, one at each end of the drive which ran through the Park. It was demolished around 1980 and is now the site of many houses.

As we heard earlier, Taylor White and his second wife Charlotte had two daughters, Charlotte Crofts and Bridget, and his wife Charlotte took on the six children of his earlier marriage. Taylor died in 1853, aged 49.

Four years later, in 1857, Charlotte Bates married again, to Henry Sweet Hodding, a Solicitor from Worksop, who was ten years younger than her. Henry and Charlotte Hodding had a further six children, her last child being born when she was aged 47. She ended up mother and step mother to 14 children from all these marriages, the children spanning almost 40 years.

However convoluted this may all seem, there is a point to this detail.

The Hoddings were a family of medical and legal men. Henry Sweet Hodding was well respected in the Workshop area, active in the public, political and social life of the district.

Henry and Charlotte's second son, John Edward Hodding, known as Jack, became a solicitor in Leicester. Like his father, Jack was an expert in liquidations and wills. Jack became good friends with his step-nephew, Bertie Humble-Crofts. Jack and Bertie turned out to be soul mates, perhaps even partners in crime, as we saw earlier.

Going back to Robert Crofts, the man who owned a large part of the Isle of Thanet.

Having had only a single child, a daughter, the family story is he was so furious that his first grandchild Charlotte was also a girl that he vowed he would leave his money to the next male child with the Crofts name, instead of her. Disappointingly for Robert, his second grandchild was also a girl, Bridget White.

Hence the Dumpton money and the Crofts name finally followed our line. Bridget White was obliged by the will to take the name of Crofts if she wanted to inherit, and after the birth of her and William's son Bertie, this suffix was added to the Humble name by Deed Poll.

A look at the very extensive Will of Robert Crofts tells a slightly different story. His will is very complex, with many pages of obscure legal language. It was not drawn up after the birth of his first grandchild as suggested by the family story, but four years before Robert's death in 1864, after the birth not only of the two granddaughters fathered by his son-in-law Taylor White, but after the birth of four of the children fathered by Henry Sweet Hodding. Of great significance, Henry Hodding and Charlotte called their first-born, a son born in 1858, Henry Robert Crofts Hodding.

Not only did they get the 'Crofts' in first, but buttered up grandfather by including Robert in the name. 1864 was also a year prior to the marriage of either of his grand-daughters, Charlotte and Bridget, who had not therefore had the chance to name a son with the correct name.

The last twist in this story was that Henry Robert Crofts Hodding, the first male holder of the coveted Crofts name, died of scarlet fever in 1868, when aged ten.

So, in 1868, the only other male descendant of Robert Crofts was Henry Hodding and Charlotte's second child, John Edward (Jack) Hodding. But he had no Crofts in the name.

The problem was solved when Bridget married William Humble, and their names were changed in 1878 after the birth of Bertie.

Robert Crofts' will is really quite difficult to interpret. It appoints as Trustees, Edward Thompson and James Debenham, both from London; both appeared in Chapter 17 when the Chancery case was detailed.

The will seems to state that his grand-daughter Bridget would stand to inherit a life interest in the Trust, at the age of 25, or within 18 months of that age or date of her marriage, if that is earlier, if she takes the surname of Crofts as the last and main name. There were multiple caveats, in the event of her death, or no children, etc. There is nothing to explain why she was given preference over her elder sister, nor why it seems she was the 'chosen one' whilst Henry Robert Crofts Hodding was still alive.

The name change in September 1878 was just before the specified 18-month deadline was reached. So Bertie was born a Humble, but grew up as a Humble-Crofts.

Having seen the convolutions of the family marriages and children, and the sums involved, it was almost inevitable that a case before Chancery began in 1871. This was some time before Bertie's birth, but not long after the death of Henry Robert Crofts Hodding, which at that time left the inheritance question open. The family were squabbling over the estate.

The Chancery case went on and on, at least for 30 years, as they often did. There were numerous changes in those involved as they died and others took over, and all the later documents, and the final conclusion, have not yet been found. The assumption is that Bertie was due to inherit at least a major part of the estate. That is until he and Jack Hodding got to work.

Reverend William and Bridget Humble (Humble-Crofts) and family

Of the eight children of William and Bridget, three were born in Clayton cum Frickley.

They were:

– John Herbert Humble (Humble-Crofts), or Bertie, born in 1878.

-Woollaston Gonville Bromhead Humble-Crofts, known as Gunn, or Gunny, born in 1880.

-Cyril Mitford Humble-Crofts, born in 1881.

Photograph 16: Beatrice Martha age 38, with Humble-Crofts family, about 1915
Front row L to R, Beatrice, Rev. William, Bridget, Winfred Podd; back row L to R,
Bertie, Maud, Arthur, Una, Cyril, Gunny

The following year, the Humble-Crofts family moved to Waldron, in East Sussex, when William was appointed Rector, a living which was in the gift of Exeter College, Oxford, William's alma mater. William was also appointed Prebendary of Chichester.

Waldron remains today much as it was a hundred years ago, a small and relatively unspoilt village.

William Humble-Crofts' start at Waldron was not as successful as he might have hoped for. His grandson, Maughan Innes, told of a petition from about 50 villagers which was presented to William the year after he had arrived, asking him to leave! As soon as he announced that he had agreed, they drew up another petition asking him to stay! He ended up staying for 42 years. The names of the petitioners are from many of the same families who continue to live in the village.

The other five children of William and Bridget were born in The Waldron Rectory:

-Arthur Maughan Humble-Crofts, born in 1883.

-Gerald Humble-Crofts, born in 1886. He died when aged seven with diphtheria.

-William Humble-Crofts, born in 1887. He died within a few hours of birth.

-Edith Una Humble-Crofts, born in 1889.

-Bridget Maud Humble-Crofts, born in 1892.

By the end of 1893, after Gerald died, William and Bridget had their four sons, the eldest siblings, and two daughters with them in Waldron.

The living was comfortable, presumably assisted by income from the Crofts inheritance and various other inherited Humble money, though it appears that Bridget tried hard to give away to charity as much as she could. The family had several servants, including a nanny and a governess.

One Governess, Gertrude Ackermann, was described by Maughan Innes: She was *an exquisite little person. In the course of World War I she found it prudent to drop the second "N" from the end of her family name – and anyone less Prussian I can't imagine.'* (To forestall any anti-German feeling.) *'Perfect English, perfect German and French; needlework to make your eyes water. Devoted to the family, and I'm happy to remember that after she retired to Cornwall, Polperro I think, Una and my mother were able to help her financially – in quite small measure – so that she could keep her own cottage there.'* The records show her to be Gertrude Georgette Ackermann, born in St. Pancras in London in 1862. I think she had left the Humble-Crofts before the war, as she was living in Troutbeck, Westmorland in 1911, and later moved to Cornwall. By 1914, the Humble-Crofts would not have needed a governess as the youngest 'child' was then 22. Having said that, the family nanny was still living with the family according to the 1911 census.

William was a well-built man with a full beard and Bridget a strikingly handsome woman.

As can be imagined, any family spending 42 years at the centre of the local community was bound to get heavily involved and be the source of many stories. William and his family were dearly loved. William was interested in archaeology and local history and wrote about it. He was a keen cricketer and became President of the Cross in Hand Working Men's Cricket Club and Waldron Cricket Club, playing for the latter until at least 1906, when he was 60 years old.

The Canon travelled round the Parish on his bicycle, using a horse for longer distances, and both William and Bridget enjoyed bicycling as a pastime. They once organised a Parish cycling tour to Rouen in France!

Bridget was generous, selfless and devoted both to her family and the parishioners.

John Herbert Humble-Crofts

Bertie, the first child of the family was covered in part in earlier chapters.

After failing to get into the Royal Navy, he became a Merchant Sea Officer, and rose to 1st Officer with the British India Steamship Company, a career which lasted 13 years and filled a large part of his early adult life. He served with them from 1898 to 1911, between the ages of 20 and 32 years, sailing almost exclusively around the Indian sub-continent.

By 1910, he was sailing regularly as 1st Officer and could soon expect to be given a full command.

At this point in his life, Beatrice Martha reappeared and put a spoke in the wheel as we saw.

Bertie' siblings were an interesting lot, and a short account of each follows.

Woollaston Gonville Bromhead Humble-Crofts was the second child of Reverend William and Bridget, and was born in 1880. He was known as Gun or Gunny. I was quite excited when I found out his middle names, 'Gonville Bromhead', for the first time. I knew these were the names of the Officer at the Battle of Rorke's Drift who was played by Michael Caine in the film, 'Zulu', and it seemed likely he was related to the family. A bit of research soon squashed this theory, but I did find that he had been named after Major Bromhead, who in fact was his godfather!

As Lieutenant Gonville Bromhead, of B Company the $2^{nd}/24^{th}$ Foot, he had won the V.C. at Rorke's Drift in 1879, one of 11 V.C.s won in that action. William Humble (Crofts) and he knew each other as they were at school together at Thomas Magnus Grammar School in Newark, Nottinghamshire, where one of the School Houses, 'Bromhead', is named after him.

Sadly, recent historical accounts of the Rorke's Drift action praise the other officers and N.C.O.s. and have called into question the part played by Bromhead.

Nevertheless, at that time in Victorian England he was a major hero.

Incidentally, contrary to what was portrayed in 'Zulu', where there was the stirring singing of 'Men of Harlech' featured, the majority of soldiers involved were English, not Welsh. The $2^{nd}/24^{th}$. Foot had amalgamated two years later with the South Wales Borderers.

Gunny was educated at Winchester House and Stubbington House like his brothers. According to his nephew, Maughan Innes, he was a *'morose fellow'* whose marriage was not successful.

Before World War I, Gunny worked as a Jobber with the firm of Huggins and Clarke in the Stock Exchange and lived in London. In 1914 he joined the Honorary Artillery Company, and later the 12th Battalion, Royal Sussex Regiment.

In 1915, he married Winifred Mary Podd, the eighth child of an Essex Farmer.

He served in France as a Lieutenant in the Royal Sussex, and was invalided out from the front in 1916. In 1919, he was an Assistant Provost Marshal, later becoming a temporary Major.

Gunny and Winifred had two children; his son Cyril emigrated to South Africa and died in Cape Town, aged 80, still a single man, whilst daughter Betty also remained single throughout her life; so no further Humble-Crofts resulted from this branch of the family.

Cyril Mitford Humble-Crofts, the third son, was born in 1881. I have always wondered, but do not know, if there was a similar relationship between the Humble family and the Mitford family as there had been with Bromhead. The Mitfords were originally in Northumberland but the infamous sisters did not hit the headlines until the following century.

Cyril was also educated at Winchester House and was a fine athlete. He was Captain of Waldron Cricket Club in 1906, and he also helped the football club.

In 1905 he became a Solicitor in Uckfield, Sussex, and just prior to World War I he worked for The National Cash Register Company.

At the start of the War in October 1914 he enlisted, firstly with the Honourable Artillery Company like his brother, and then transferred into C Company, the 13th Battalion, Royal Sussex Regiment. He was commissioned in December, 1914 and appointed Captain in May 1915.

The 13th Battalion crossed to France with the Expeditionary Force in March 1916 and they served in France and Flanders. The family hold a poignant letter from Cyril to his brother, Bertie sent in May 1916, in which he talks like a veteran, yet the letter's poignancy lies in its boyish hope and naivety.

Cyril Mitford died in action five weeks later at Boar's Head, Richebourg l'Avoué, in an action attempting to divert attention from an attack on the Somme the next day. He was 34 years old and unmarried.

The De Ruvigny's Roll of Honour states: *'he was killed in action...just as he had reached the barbed wire entanglements, while leading his company. His Colonel wrote, "He was one of the best types of English officer, keen and courageous, and his men were as devoted to him as he was to them. Everyone liked him, and I personally feel his loss very much indeed. He died at the head of his men, fighting like a gallant English gentleman in what is surely a righteous cause." He was an excellent cricket and football player, and won many prizes in athletic contests at his school.'*

His death is commemorated on the Loos Memorial, near Lens, France, and he is buried there.

Arthur Maughan Humble-Crofts was the fourth son and was born in 1883. Educated at Eastbourne College, he went on to gain his B.A. at Keble College, Oxford in 1905. He played cricket at Waldron like his father and brothers, and he was a good singer.

He became a Schoolmaster, firstly in Fermoy, Ireland, then at a pre-prep school, Cottesmore School, in Brighton.

In 1910, he married Margaret Gernon Cooper at Waldron Church. His father officiated. She was a famous Music Hall singer, pianist and entertainer. Margaret was slightly older than Arthur; she was born in 1877, and was the eldest daughter of a baker in Paddington.

A reference to Margaret is contained in Walter Macqueen-Pope's "The Melody Lingers On". He writes about a programme in 1911 at the Palace Theatre.

'There was Margaret Cooper, one of the greatest favourites the Palace ever knew and probably the best of all women entertainers at the piano. How she could put over a song and how she could play the piano! She was a regular in the Palace bill and they could not have enough of her. Beautifully dressed, she would sail on to the stage and acknowledge the welcoming applause with a short, sharp, spasmodic smile. There was no warmth in it, it was just a contraction of the muscles of the mouth; she was barely aware of her audience and gave them no recognition but this. Then she would seat herself, take off her elbow length

gloves with great care and in the most leisurely manner, and then proceed to remove her numerous rings and bracelets, which she placed one at a time and with considerable exactitude of touch on the top of the piano. It was a routine which the audience watched spell bound with apparent enjoyment. And then, she would begin. She was the perfect mistress of her art and of the art of songs at the piano; her touch, her diction and her inflections were beyond compare. Although her voice was neither strong nor powerful (quite the reverse indeed) she had the knack of making every syllable heard, every word tell, even in the largest building; and that without a microphone, which she would have scorned.'

After their wedding in 1910, Arthur and Margaret lived in Brondesbury, north-west London, and Arthur acted as her 'Private Secretary and Agent'.

During the War, Arthur became a Sub. Lieutenant in the R.N.V.R. attached to the Royal Naval Air Service. In 1914, like many in the R.N.V.R., he was to be found on shore with the R.N.A.S., serving with the guns defending the London area against air attacks. His brother, Cyril was scathing about his role in the War, because he worked most of the time at a desk in Whitehall. He later became Captain in the 5th Group, Headquarters, R.A.F., at Dover.

Having survived his rather quiet war, Arthur died in Dover in November, 1918, eight days after the armistice, and the day after his 35th birthday. He was a victim of the major world-wide influenza epidemic that lasted through into 1919 and eventually killed more worldwide than the war.

Arthur and Margaret had no children.

Margaret, after singing at her sister-in-law Maud's wedding in early 1922, died in December of that same year, aged 44.

'Whilst checking Arthur and Margaret's date of marriage when proof reading the book, I came across another marriage in 1905 for a Margaret G. Cooper, daughter of James, a baker in Paddington. I checked her intended, William Fisher Atkins, and could find no evidence of a divorce and he died much later, so I thought I had found evidence of bigamy. Always read the small print, they say. In the panel next to the wedding entry, was a small scribbled note. It said, 'Cancelled. Void. Parties did not come to be married.' Another story there.'

Gerald Humble-Crofts was the fifth consecutive son, born in Waldron in 1886. He died of diphtheria in 1893, aged seven.

William Humble-Crofts, the sixth boy, was born in 1887, and died when a few hours old.

Edith Una Humble-Crofts was the first girl of the family and was born in 1889. She was known as Una. She remained single throughout her life and lived for many years with her parents. After her father's death, she lived with her widowed mother at Little Dumpton near Broadstairs, and later at Crossways in Waldron.

Una was a singular character, and with five brothers during her early childhood, was not surprisingly a bit of a tomboy.

According to Pat Pallister, a servant in the household, she was universally liked by her family, the servants and the residents of Waldron. She thought Una was the nicest of all the Humble-Crofts.

Not a lot is known about Una's personal life, but there has been a lot of speculation. She was usually to be seen dressed like a man. There is a photograph of her in military uniform during World War I.

The uniform is that of an Officer, and the style was very much her own. The cap badge and lapel insignia are not clear enough to recognise and there are no traceable military records.

A niece recalled: *'I remember visiting Aunt Una, who always wore a tie and looked like a man, and had a cockatoo on a perch which was extremely noisy.'*

Soon after her mother's death in early 1932, Una used her new found freedom to take a holiday.

In 1933, aged 44, she sailed to Barbados for a trip of 15 weeks.

A photograph of the Waldron W.I. Choir in 1937 shows Una with her short hair and dressed in her usual masculine garb, and also shows her married sister, Maud Innes.

After her mother's death, Una's great friend, Florence Oakshott, a widow, moved in with Una at Crossways. Their exact relationship is shrouded in mystery. Relationships between women in those days were certainly not acknowledged, though unlike male homosexuality there was no legislation against such arrangements. Una and Florence eventually fell out, and Florence moved out to live with some of her family.

'WALDRON AT WAR – World War II seen through the eyes of the inhabitants of an East Sussex Village' was a book written by Valerie Chidson, a local historian. It was published in 2004, the 60th anniversary of the D-Day landings. It contains several references to Una and her father.

Valerie tells us that in 1939 pre-war Waldron, *'Miss Una Humble-Crofts and Mrs Maud Innes, daughters of the late Rector Canon Humble-Crofts had a finger in most village pies...*

The Reverend Stephenson was the Rector at All Saints, although his cerebral sermons were not universally popular with those who had grown up with and preferred the fire and brimstone of old Canon Humble-Crofts, who was still remembered, despite having died in 1924.'

Una died in 1957, at the age of 68. A plaque in Waldron Church in memory of Una commemorates the restoration of The Lady Chapel in her name. Her estate was surprisingly modest, considering she had inherited a large amount from her rich Uncle Bernard Humble-Burkitt.

Bridget Maud Humble-Crofts, known as Maud, was the eighth and last child of the Rector and his wife. She was born in 1892. Like her siblings, she took a full part in village life. She was a bell ringer at Waldron Church, and was said in

1906, at the age of 14, to have been the only lady ringer in the country. No doubt I will hear if this is not true.

She married Leslie Innes in 1922, in Waldron. She was aged 29, eight years older than Leslie. A wedding photograph suggests Bertie, her brother, may have given her away as her father officiated at the marriage. It was to prove to be the last photograph of Bertie, who died 18 months later.

Bertie was dressed to kill, much as might be expected, in top hat, morning suit and spats, Bertie was described by Maughan, Leslie and Maud's son, as *'very rakish in appearance... possibly already well-oiled and swaying gently'.*

According to Maughan Innes, the Innes family first moved into the Sussex area when his grandfather William George started farming. The family had originated in Kelso, Scotland with a metal fabricating business near the Armoury, and had migrated to Waldron via generations in Newcastle and London.

Reputedly, and rather fancifully, the Innes family were said to be descended from the infamous Berowald, who was Flemish. The history is well documented by Roland Dunbrack, writing about *'The origin of the Innes' in 2001*, but it is very difficult to follow.

The Maughan Innes version is much more amusing:

'There are an awful lot of Inneses around, in Scotland and elsewhere, but they're fairly easy to sort out because they all derive from one starting point – and he was Flemish, not Scottish; with a name like Beowald, he needed to be Flemish. But he got given a good chunk of Morayshire around 1168 and founded a dynasty. He may have lived just long enough to regret it.

Anyway, the family lurched through the next five centuries, collecting sundry baronetcies, various knighthoods, a bishop's mitre and a strong line in insolvency. A significant number of them were murdered, for the most part by one another; we like to keep things in the family. Around 1675, they achieved some stability by marrying into the Ker family who were Earls, later Dukes, of Roxburghe. A century later the title passed to James Innes-Ker and the family centre moved away from Moray to Floors Castle at Kelso.

Which brings me to George Innes, my great grandfather – a shadowy figure.' (In fact his great, great, great grandfather), *'I think I know who his mother was, but I don't know which of two brothers was his father. (His mother may have been in the same quandary, there are long dark nights in Scotland.) At Floors there are some letters from him to the duchess of the day; these explain little, certainly not the reasons for his presence at various places up and down the Thames Valley. It would be quite unfair to suppose that unserved writs issuing from the Edinburgh courts had anything to do with it.*

Anyway, George begat James, and set him up in a metal-fabricating business near the Armories in the City. James begat William James, who, against all genetic odds, became a very successful journalist. Perhaps too successful, because he in turn begat William George who became a very successful doer of nothing at all – and did most of it in Waldron. But, with some cooperation from my grandmother, he did beget Nita, Violet and Leslie.'

I was told that Maud Innes was a hypochondriac and spent much of her time in nursing homes and seeing doctors. Somehow, despite this, she seems to have played a full part in the village life. Maughan recalls that if his grandmother Bridget was unable to play the organ at Waldron Church, his mother would be called upon to perform. *'...in the direst of emergencies, my mother would try to follow suit – leading to some anxious moments for the curate, choir and congregation. She and All Saint's organ must have been born under different signs; she could tame any piano.'*

Leslie and Maud initially lived at Billingshurst, about 25 miles from Waldron. Nine months after their wedding in 1922 Maud gave birth to twin boys. Maughan was one; the other, Anthony died at birth. Maughan believes this event may have brought about the end of his parents' relationship.

However, when I visited Waldron in 1989, I met Violet Hogben, a long-standing resident, then aged 94 and blind. She told me that Leslie Innes left Maud soon after the marriage and went off with a 'Lucas girl'.

Maughan remained their only child. He was an invaluable source of gossip and stories about the family, told with his wicked sense of humour.

In 1950, Maughan married Helen Mary (Molly) Spyers. She was the daughter of Thomas Roper Spyers, who was another character and a man of many talents.

At various times in his life, Roper Spyers M.A. ran a hotel, was a barrister, a schoolmaster, took holy orders and was a professional actor.

Born in 1868, in Faversham, North Kent, the son of a local doctor, Roper was educated at Radley College, where he was a Scholar and a Prizeman. He went on to Keble College, Oxford, where he was a Racquets Blue, and gained an M.A. in 1892.

He became a Barrister at Inner Temple. In 1895 he studied music in Paris. By 1896, he was an actor, with Herbert Beerbohm Tree who had run the Theatre Royal, Haymarket since 1887.

Between 1901 and 1903, he was Assistant Master at his old school, Radley College, where he produced Aristophenes' 'Frogs' in Greek, and he was Honorary Secretary of the Radlein Society.

He was ordained a Deacon in 1901.

Later, he returned to the stage, re-joined Benson in 'Taming of the Shrew' and 'Prayer of the Sword'. He went on to be the Headmaster of the Prepatory School, Weybridge, between 1906 and 1918.

In 1919 he opened and managed the Willow Hayne Hotel, Angmering on Sea, near Littlehampton, Sussex, staying there until 1929.

He became a Barrister at Inner Temple at about this time.

Between 1930 and 1939 he was the proprietor of the Newlands Corner Hotel.

During this hectic life, or perhaps because of it, he managed to get married twice and had three children.

After an amazingly varied and full life, Roper died in 1961 in Chelsea, London, at the ripe age of 93.

So, despite William and Bridget Humble-Crofts having eight children and seven grandchildren, as the consequence of childhood deaths, deaths in early adult life, unmarried children and grandchildren, there remains today only one small family of Humble-Crofts in the world. This family live in Australia, the father being the son of Michael, grandson of Bertie and great grandson of William and Bridget. No wonder they proved so hard to locate!

During my research into the Humble-Crofts, I came across many stories about the Canon and his wife. It is not surprising that after 42 years' service to the community, they were held in such high regard many years after his death.

Violet Hogben, quoted earlier, told me: *'I remember Canon Humble-Crofts very well. Such a handsome man – he often used to visit us wearing a long black coat with cape, and a tall hat, arriving in a barouche. He would stay and chat with my parents and grandmother – they always enjoyed his visits. This would be between 1911 until he died in 1924.'*

Mrs V. Taylor, a local historian, wrote: *'When I was writing on Waldron, I got nothing I could write on him, but was touched that those who did remember him, remembered with so much love.'*

The Canon seemed to have kept himself quite busy during his time at Waldron. He wrote a lot of letters. The Public Records at Kew and the Bodleian Library at Oxford contain a number of references to correspondence from him regarding the history of the church and other more academic topics including Latin poetry.

The Canon and Bridget in old age were a very handsome couple.

Canon Humble-Crofts died in 1924, aged 77 years, whilst still in harness as the incumbent at Waldron. Ten months earlier he had lost his eldest son, Bertie, which must have hurt him greatly. By that time, only one of his six sons, Gunny, was still alive.

Bridget died in 1932 at Crossways, aged 79 years, with her daughter Maud, in attendance.

Bridget was the last of the Humble-Crofts to be buried in a grave at Waldron. The cortege arriving at the Church was on a horse and cart which belonged to a local farmer. Upon hearing of her death, the farmer had asked when he should bring round his horse and cart. He was told that motorised transport had been arranged. He asked again when he should bring round the horse and cart.

She was taken to her funeral by his horse and cart!

She wrote her own touching Valediction which says so much about her.

'My very dear love and blessing to all those, belonging to me, those who are very dear to me – I thank them for all their goodness, and for my many shortcomings, I ask their pardon – for when this is read, I shall have gone to the Land, where all is forgiven and forgotten – to which place, may God in His great mercy and love, bring us all, never to be parted again – Bridget Humble-Crofts.'

I will leave the end of this chapter to Canon William Humble-Crofts himself, who wrote in the July, 1893 issue of the Waldron Parish magazine, soon after the death of his son, Gerald from diphtheria.

'Dear Friends and Parishioners,

Although this Magazine is not intended for the publication of personal matters, I cannot refrain on the present occasion from trying to express to you our heartfelt gratitude for the sympathy and kindness unspeakable, shewn to us in time of distress and anxiety. We have had so many happy years amongst you, that we must expect as a matter of course to share in the sorrows common to all; and so many healthful years that we must not be surprised if sickness, even fatal sickness, occasionally remind us how frail and uncertain our tenure on this life is, and that in the midst of it we are in death. Meanwhile there is not a little comfort in the thought that your prayers have been with us, that he who has gone from us for a while, has been taken in the first freshness of life, from the evil to come and that during his brief and happy stay here we cannot recall an act or a word that ever caused a moment's pain. Gratefully and sincerely yours,

W.J. Humble-Crofts.'

No wonder they were so well liked.

Epilogue

It may sound rather obvious, but everyone has a family history.

Though my family seem to have left behind a story with more than their fair share of exciting and unexpected aspects, programmes like 'Who Do You Think You Are' have shown that almost everybody has parts of their family story that are interesting and intriguing.

My years of family research have taught me many lessons:

If it is possible, talk to other members of the family about the past whenever you can. It is never too early to start. Verbal history is richer in content, less time consuming and probably cheaper to collect than searching written and on-line records. So, pester your relatives as soon as possible.

Follow your hunches and instincts. Some of them will be correct. Coincidences seem to happen all the time. Chance findings are frequent.

When you hit what seems like a dead end, keep on nibbling away at it. It is amazing how often you can find a way to extract some more information.

There is no end point. There is always something else to chase. There will never be a right time to put your work down on paper, so just do it and worry about further research information later.

CPSIA information can be obtained
at www.ICGtesting.com
Printed in the USA
LVHW050922190221
679454LV00045B/1023